Thomas Donohue

The Iroquois and the Jesuits

The Story of the Labors of Catholic Missionaries among these Indians

Thomas Donohue

The Iroquois and the Jesuits
The Story of the Labors of Catholic Missionaries among these Indians

ISBN/EAN: 9783337060466

Printed in Europe, USA, Canada, Australia, Japan

Cover: Foto ©Lupo / pixelio.de

More available books at **www.hansebooks.com**

THE IROQUOIS

AND

THE JESUITS

The Story of the Labors of Catholic
Missionaries Among these Indians

By Rev. THOMAS DONOHOE, D. D.

BUFFALO, N. Y.:
BUFFALO CATHOLIC PUBLICATION CO.,
1895.

TO THE

RT. REV. S. V. RYAN,

BISHOP OF BUFFALO,

THIS VOLUME

IS RESPECTFULLY INSCRIBED.

PREFACE.

THE Indian race is slowly, but surely disappearing before the advancing hordes of their pale-faced brothers. The lives of these red men have formed the theme of many a story of love, and war, and hate. They knew not peace, for their chief glory was war. Though the race is fast fading, like the mists of the morning, the still hovering sun-tinted vapors suggest fanciful visions of mysterious life, and allure us to peer into the gloom to view their forest homes, for we are all children of nature. Indian story furnishes much of the romance for childhood, and the religious theory and progress of the race should constitute an interesting reality for mature years, as they are an integral part of the human race.

Many Indian nations dwelt along the shores of the lakes and streams now dotted with populous cities and towns, and their life for us must reflect a romantic hue, because so different from our own; and as the religious element is an important factor in the history of nations, races, and tribes, it is interesting to know what they believed and how they were led to the knowledge of God. Catholic missionaries bore the light of the Gospel to the

Iroquois, whilst these still dwelt in their forest homes, where the only memorials of their former habitation still linger in the names they had given to the rivers and lakes.

It was not necessary to delve into the dust bins of history, or hidden archives, for much of the material of this volume, as many of the events here narratated have been minutely described in the "Relations de la Nouvelle France;" but as these only exist in an obsolete form of a foreign language they are practically inaccessible to the general public.

These "Relations" were letters written by the Jesuits from their mission fields to their superiors at Quebec, giving an account of their labors, their success or failure, and the peculiarities of Indian life; and as these missionaries knew the language of the nations among whom they dwelt, and had the best opportunity of studying their customs, their writings form the most authentic sources of information upon the domestic and religious life of the Indians of America.

This subject was first undertaken as a matter of curiosity; but as it grew in interest it became a labor of love, until it seemed a duty to let the public view the distant past as it appeared to a student of many a musty tome and learned volume. The work might be made more comprehensive; but then it would exceed the limits of a small volume, and even in its present form it may serve to pass a profitable hour or to shed some light upon the glorious labors of those who first penetrated the forests of Central and Western New York to bear the Gospel to the powerful Iroquois.

It is with pleasure I acknowledge the aid I received in this work from General Clark, of Auburn. He has been very successful in establishing the locations of towns mentioned in celebrated documents, and he generously communicates the results of his labors to mere tyros in the field. To Dean Harris, to Father Jones, S. J., of St. Mary's College, Montreal, and to the Rev. J. V. Burtin, O. M. I., I also acknowledge my indebtedness for valuable information and advice.

THOMAS DONOHOE.

BUFFALO, N. Y., May 21, 1895.

CONTENTS.

PAGE.

CHAPTER I. THE IROQUOIS. 1

Their habits; their homes; their origin; the Kahquahs or Neuters; the Iroquois country; population; Kahquahs; food; social amusements of the Iroquois; festivals; marriage; league of the Iroquois; government; trade.

CHAPTER II. LOCATIONS OF THE IROQUOIS TOWNS. 13

Indian towns not permanent; Mohawk towns; destroyed by the French; Greenhalgh's description; Oneida towns; Onondaga the capital; St. Mary's of Ganentaa; Cayuga villages; many Cayugas remove to Canada; Seneca towns according to a Seneca chief; Jesuit names of Seneca villages; locations.

CHAPTER III. RELIGIOUS BELIEF. 21

Religious belief preserved by tradition; their idea of God; creation of the world; origin of evil; inferior spirits or manitous; dream theory; festival of dreams; the soul; the Indian's heaven; the soul can act independently of the body; veneration for the dead; festival of the dead; vices of savages.

CHAPTER IV. ADVENT OF EUROPEANS. . . . 27

Indians kindly disposed towards whites; Cartier explores the St. Lawrence; first meeting of French and Iroquois was hostile; Champlain fought with the Montagnais against the Mohawks; Iroquois fled at sound of guns; Champlain's expedition against the Iroquois; French made friends of the Hurons; missioners; the Recollects; the Huron mission; journey to the Huron country.

CHAPTER V. FIRST ATTEMPTS. 32

Capture of Father Paulain; Father D'Aillon, Recollect, visits the

x   CONTENTS.

Neuters; visited many villages; Brebeuf and Chaumonot, Jesuits, visit the Neuters; reach the Niagara; Huron Christians come as missioners; Jogues, first missioner to the Iroquois; taken prisoner; tortured; death of René Goupil; captivity; escape; first mission work.

CHAPTER VI.   WAR.   40

Montmagny builds Fort Richelieu; Iroquois, the scourge of Catholic missions and French colony; wealthy Catholics of France come to rescue; capture of Bressani; tortures; peace councils; Jogues, French ambassador to the Mohawks; consoles Christian captives; the mysterious box.

CHAPTER VII.   THE FIRST MISSIONER TO THE IROQUOIS.   46

Father Jogues goes as missioner to the Mohawks; predicts his death; the corn crop fails; the mysterious box; war party captures Jogues; clans do not agree on his fate; treacherously slain; the murderer takes Jogues' name in baptism.

CHAPTER VIII.   WAR OF EXTERMINATION.   .   .   49

Missioners among the Hurons; their manner of living; to arms, the Iroquois come; attack on St. Joseph's mission; Hurons fly to the chapel; Christian Hurons led captive to Iroquois country; St. Ignace destroyed; savage slaughter; Jesuit martyrs; the Huron nation dispersed; Iroquois exterminate the Kahquahs; fidelity of Huron captives.

CHAPTER IX.   EPISODES OF WAR.   55

Iroquois plunder French; Algonquins attacked; slaughter of Petuns; Father Garnier killed; capture of Father Poncet; tortured by Mohawks; restored to Quebec; Mohawks propose peace; Algonquin traders; new mission field; Father Garreau slain; Iroquois reason for peace; bright prospects.

CHAPTER X.   PEACE.   63

Onondagas and Oneidas propose peace; Senecas and Cayugas follow; Mohawks send deputies; preliminaries; French and Fathers rejoice; doubtful sincerity; Iroquois renounce cannibalism; LeMoyne visits the Iroquois country; hears confession of Hurons; many Christians; the council; Onondagas ask for missioners.

CONTENTS. xi

CHAPTER XI. MISSIONS BEGUN. 70
Chaumonot and Doblon, missioners to the Iroquois; fantastic faith in dreams; Chaumonot meets old friends; warm welcome; public meeting; Chaumonot's eloquence; Fathers begin to teach; first church in New York State; French colony at Onondaga; site for new chapel; progress; Gospel announced to the Cayugas; chapel built; opposition; Mesnard withdraws; Chaumonot bears the Gospel to the Senecas; many Huron Christians in Seneca country; Chaumonot and Mesnard visit the Oneidas; council held; the Mohawks attack Christian Hurons; LeMoyne visits Mohawks; success at Onondaga; danger; were the Iroquois sincere; treachery; secret council resolved to massacre French; preparing for flight; banqueting the enemy; flight of the French; result of the first mission.

CHAPTER XII. WAR AND PEACE. 93
Indian warfare; missioners blockaded; Onondagas propose peace; LeMoyne goes to Onondaga; council; French too weak to refuse peace; LaMoyne labors among Iroquois; faith of Christian Indians; troops arrive from France; expedition against Mohawks; peace.

CHAPTER XIII. NEW MISSIONS. 102
Blessings of peace; mission journey to the Iroquois; Indian offering to invisible people; visit to the Mohawks; council; chapel built; Huron fidelity; chapel built at Oneida; Garnier visits Onondaga; Garakontie assists; Carheil visits Cayuga; chapel built; few converts; Fremin visits the Senecas; chapel built; Christian Huron captives; daily routine; instructing captives at the stake; difficulties.

CHAPTER XIV. THE MISSION IN 1669. . . . 114
Pierron among the Mohawks; piety of Christians; excessive liquor drinking; Pierron pleads for temperance; Mohawk-Mohigan war; instructing captives; Bruyas at Oneida; Oneidas opposed to Christianity; reviving faith at Onondaga; dream worship; labors of Fathers; death at the stake; Carheil at Cayuga; Indian medical science; Cayugas dread baptism; building a grand chapel; Fathers among the Senecas; first church council; danger; new mission; progress of Christianity.

CHAPTER XV. THE MISSIONS IN THE YEAR 1670. . 127
Bright prospects; peace council at Quebec; baptism of Garakontie; opposition of the Dutch; Indians defend their faith; Pierron assails Mohawk customs; Mohawks reply; renounce worship of Agreskoue;

xii   CONTENTS.

drunken revelry at Oneida; zeal of Millet at Onondaga; Garakontie's counsel; good effects; Huron Christians; Pagan prejudices at Cayuga; dream theory; Huron Christians of Gandougarae; examples of piety; Indian idea of heaven; dreams.

CHAPTER XVI. THE IROQUOIS MISSIONS IN 1671.   .   147

Many baptisms; examples of piety; Garakontie's faith; condemns dream folly; hatred of sin; Gandougarae destroyed; liquor drinking; obstacles to faith; delayed conversions; baptism of Saonchiogwa; council at Quebec; Iroquois exiles.

CHAPTER XVII. MISSIONS IN THE IROQUOIS COUNTRY— 158
(CONTINUED).

Few converts; Catholic Iroquois emigrate; fervor among the Mohawks; Bruyas at Tionnontoguen; drunkenness; conferences at Oneida; influence of sorcerers; Pagan belief; Garakontie's example; obstacles to conversion; practice of medicine; Raffeix charmed with Cayuga; piety at Cayuga; chapels among the Senecas; false notions; omens of evil.

CHAPTER XVIII. THE MISSIONS IN THE IROQUOIS COUNTRY— 169
(CONTINUED).

Father Boniface retires; chief Assendasé; statue of Blessed Virgin; Bruyas goes to Onondaga; Pagans dominant at Oneida; Christian family life; converts become apostles; healing the sick; death of Garakontie; Carheil's patience; interest in sorcery; Pagan preaches Christianity; slaves willing converts; Iroquois invited to meet Governor Frontenac; Fort Cataroquoi; the liquor evil; rumblings of war.

CHAPTER XIX. CONCLUSION OF THE MISSIONS IN THE
IROQUOIS COUNTRY.   180

Dutch indifferent to Indian advancement; England and France rival powers for dominion; the fur trade; French missionaries divert trade from the English; efforts to counteract the missioners' influence; Dongan promises English priests if Iroquois will banish French; Iroquois valuable allies; both English and French claim territory of the Iroquois; Iroquois divided in fealty; Christian Iroquois leave their homes; missioners leave the Mohawks; close of the mission; Senecas' interests promoted by alliance with English; deceived by LaSalle; Governor De la Barre invites Iroquois to a council; Governor Dongan invites them to English council; threatened war forces Fathers to

CONTENTS.

leave; DeLamberville the innocent instrument of deceit; Denonville invades Seneca country; Senecas retaliate; Iroquois unite with English in war against France; Millet prisoner at Oneida; peace; Iroquois request missioners to return; Catholic priests banished from New York State by English law; Fathers return; close of missions.

CHAPTER XX. RESULT OF THE MISSIONS. . . 197

Cannibalism abandoned; hatred supplanted by love; Christian truths adopted by Iroquois; religious strife of Europeans obstacle to faith; sacrifices of Christian Indians; Indian martyrs; pious examples; kind and pious ladies of France help to educate Indians; Jesuits start seminary at Quebec; Ursulines open convent for Indians; Indians prefer forest freedom to convent walls; Iroquois girls most tractable; Christian Indians prized Catholic books; schools in the forests; schools at the Catholic settlements.

CHAPTER XXI. LASALLE AND FATHER HENNEPIN. . 207

LaSalle learns topography of country from Iroquois; water route to East Indies; expedition for faith and fame; visit Senecas; visitors regaled with roast dog; visit Niagara River; Dollier and Galinee build first chapel on Lake Erie; winter sojourn in the forest; lake storm ends missionary enterprise; second expedition; building of the Griffon; Te Deum at Niagara; first record of mass at Niagara; Hennepin's midwinter journey to Senecas; where the Griffon was built; Griffon anchored at Squaw Island; first religious service in Buffalo; loss of the Griffon.

CHAPTER XXII. GARACONTIE. 214

Great orator; hears the eloquent Chaumonot; encourages Christians; friend of the French; gives his cabin for a chapel; temperance advocate; eulogy of LeMoyne; Garacontie at the great council; his baptism; his piety and zeal; publicly professes Christianity; farewell banquets; preparing for the end; happy death.

CHAPTER XXIII. CATHERINE TEGAKOUITA. . . 222

Pagan Indians immoral; hidden virtues of converts; Catherine's birth place; her parents; small pox ravages; change of home; first meeting with missioners; desires to become a Christian; her baptism; persecution; flight; life at the Sault; vows virginity; failing health; honored as a saint; her relics.

CHAPTER XXIV.   FATHER JOGUES.   230

At college; on the Huron mission; journey to Quebec; capture; torture; captivity; escape; ambassador to Mohawks; the mysterious box; first missioner to Mohawks; danger; death; chapel erected to his memory; pilgrim shrine.

CHAPTER XXV.   MISSION OF THE PRESENTATION.   .   236

Father Piquet founds a mission for Iroquois; English opposition; mission house burned by Mohawks; Piquet's missionary cruise; French fort at Ogdensburg an encroachment upon English rights; war incidents; French forts fall; Piquet retires; returns to France.

CHAPTER XXVI.   THE REDUCTIONS.   .   .   .   242

Huron settlement at Lorette; Prairie de La Madeleine; new home for Iroquois Catholics; first settlers; chapel built; school started; visit of Bishop Laval; changes of location; model Christian community; famous pastors; bell for the church; bell captured by British; Indians lament the loss; to the rescue; recaptured; rejoicing; the saintly Mohawk; Cayuga settlement; Sulpitian missions; Recollects; St. Regis colony; church and schools; Mohawks fight with the British in the Revolution; Oneidas friendly to Americans; Oneidas in the west; recent converts; expedition against Onondagas; Sullivan's expedition; remnant of the race.

CHAPTER XXVII.   THE MISSIONERS.   .   .   .   261

The missionary spirit; religious orders; missionary life; travel to the mission fields; life on the Indian missions; missioners scientific explorers and discoverers; missioners first historians; Jesuit Relations most authentic source of early history; Jesuits pioneers among the Iroquois; martyrdom; missioner's reward; blood of martyrs the seed of Christians; virtues of the missioner.

APPENDIX.   270

CHAPTER I.

THE IROQUOIS.

THEIR HABITS—THEIR HOMES—THEIR ORIGIN—THE KAHQUAHS OR NEUTERS—THE IROQUOIS COUNTRY—POPULATION—KAHQUAHS —FOOD—SOCIAL AMUSEMENTS OF THE IROQUOIS—FESTIVALS— MARRIAGE—LEAGUE OF THE IROQUOIS—GOVERNMENT—TRADE.

WHEN the white man first placed foot on the soil of the present State of New York various Indian tribes inhabited different sections of the State. These tribes[1] were of a nomadic nature, for, although they had stable and populous villages and well-appointed towns, yet victory or defeat in war, the infertility of the soil, the insalubrity of climate, or malarial conditions arising from the absence of any sanitary system, often necessitated a change of locality, which was the more readily undertaken, as it was very easily accomplished. Their homes were made of the fresh chestnut or walnut saplings driven into the ground and lapped over at the top to form an arched roof, which was covered with bark, and when the intervening spaces were filled in with clay or rushes the Indian house was complete.

The interior decorations and furniture were of the most simple nature: a few bear, deer or buffalo skins, which served as a couch at night or an outer garment in the day; a few rude stone implements of agriculture or

[1] The mound builders were these same Indians, and their mounds were either forts built before the Iroquois Confederacy, or mausoleums of the dead.

instruments of war; a few dismal trophies of victory, formed the riches of the Indian's home, and, with some dried meat and corn, constituted the aggregate of his wealth.

When circumstances, therefore, required removal, in a few hours he could gather his riches, destroy his cabin, and be ready to migrate to another location, where a few hours' labor, with the materials that Nature everywhere abundantly supplied, would suffice for the formation of a new village and the establishment of a new home.[1] Split saplings were run transversely along the roof and sides of their cabins, and were firmly bound with linden cords to keep the back covering in position. These huts were sometimes made long enough to accommodate many families ranged on either side, with the fire places in the centre, and an aperture in the top, which served the double purpose of a window and a chimney. Often the towns were fortified; and in such cases they were built on an eminence, and were completely surrounded with strong palisades, twenty or thirty feet high, which were driven into the ground in close triple row around the town.

Where the Iroquois originally came from may be a matter of conjecture; but their own traditions relate that they came direct to New York State from the region of the Algonquins, near the present site of Montreal. Their traditions also indicate that they were not hunters and warriors, but captives and slaves of the Algonquins, who used them as menials in war and in the hunt; but so successful were they in these affairs that they awakened the jealousy and aroused the anger of their masters, and

[1] It is a difficult matter to give the exact location of their villages; and historian disagree on this point, because they treat of different periods of time.

THEIR ORIGIN.

several of the Iroquois braves were murdered by their envious Algonquins lords. This fact incited the entire tribe to rebel, and encouraged them to strive for liberty and the possession of a country of their own. They succeeded in escaping to the present State of New York; and, as five distinct nations, they settled in the valleys and along the lakes that now bear their names.

It is pretty well established that all the Indians of North America primitively came from Asia and Tartary across Behrings Strait to the American Continent. A fact corroborative of this theory shows, at least, the possibility and probability of such emigration.

Father Grelon was one of the first Jesuits on the Huron missions around Georgian Bay, and some years afterwards he was in Asia, where he met a female slave whom he had known in the Huron country. This slave had been sold from tribe to tribe until she finally, in her wanderings, reached the plains of Asia.

When white men first entered the present State of New York, and approached the homes of its Indian dwellers, the central and western sections of the State were inhabited principally by the tribes known to us as the Iroquois. There were five distinct nations of the Iroquois: The Mohawks, who dwelt in the Mohawk Valley; the Oneidas, near Lake Oneida; the Onondagas, near Lake Onondaga; the Cayugas, near Lake Cayuga; and the Senecas, who dwelt in the valley of the Genesee. West of the Senecas and between Lake Erie and Lake Ontario, near the Niagara River, were four villages of the Kahquahs, or Neuter Nation. Before 1639, however, another nation, called the Eurohronons,[1] dwelt west of the Genesee River, and between the Neuters and the Senecas,

[1] Relations, 1639.

and they were protected by the Neuters from the powerful Iroquois; but for some reason this alliance was dissolved, and for their own safety the Eurohronons migrated to the Huron country. East of the Mohawks, along the Hudson River, were various tribes of the Loup Indians. South of the Cayugas, in the present State of Pennsylvania, the Andastes dwelt. The populous Kahquahs, or Neuters, had their principal villages west of the Niagara River and Lake Erie, extending one hundred miles north into Canada. About one hundred miles northwest of the Kahquah territory, near Georgian Bay, were located the Hurons, the irreconcilable enemies of the Iroquois.

All these nations were powerful and populous, numbering from twelve thousand to thirty thousand souls in each nation. They were all warlike in disposition, and were continually at strife with some neighboring tribe or nation. Their young men considered their sublimest virtue, their greatest glory, and their highest title to fame to consist in the number of scalps, or trophies of enemies slain by their own hand; and although they had but rude stone tomahawks, warclubs, and stone or shell-pointed arrows, yet their savage natures made them quite formidable foes. Cruelty to an enemy was with them a virtue as great as love is to the Christian; and bravery in war and success in the hunt brought them honor from their fellow-beings during life, and happiness from the Great Spirit after death.

The country of the Iroquois was one of the most attractive and delightful in America, and its lakes and rivers furnished fish, while its forests and plains supplied game in abundance for the support of Indian life.

The land of the Mohawks was not so fertile as the land of the more western nations, yet it sufficed for their needs; for their wants were few, and their skill in hunting and fishing made amends for the defective soil. The country was picturesque and pleasant, and with its charming variety of hill and river, of vast forest and enchanting vale, made a fitting abode for this warrior race.

The Oneidas dwelt in a region of lofty forests, diversified with small fertile plains, which served to grow their corn and the vegetables of Indian husbandry. The lakes and rivers furnished fish, and the forests supplied game to support their easy life.

The capital of the league was situated on an eminence in a fertile valley, which grew an abundance of corn, which, with the many fishing stations along the rivers and lakes, furnished food for the Onondagas.

Father Raffeix says:[1] "The country of the Cayugas is the most beautiful I have seen in America. It is a continuous plain situated between two lakes,[2] whose borders are covered with noble trees without underbush, and so far apart that they admit of easy passage. The lakes supply fish, and the forests and plains great quantity of game. More than one thousand deer are killed here every year, and Lake Tiehero,[3] which adjoins our village, is covered in the winter and spring with geese, swan and other fowl. About ten miles from our village are four salt water fountains, where the Indians spread nets and capture great numbers of pigeons."

The country of the Senecas was a vast open plain extending from the borders of Lake Ontario to the hills and forests of the present Schuyler and Steuben Counties; and this plain was very fertile and was covered in the early summer season with grass nearly as tall as a man,[4] but

[1] Relations, 1672. [2] Lakes Cayuga and Owasco. [3] Lake Cayuga.
[4] Journal of Galince and Dolier.

studded along the borders of the lakes and banks of the streams with fine chestnut and walnut groves. .West of the Genesee River to the Niagara the country was an unbroken forest of beech, maple, oak, elm, basswood and hemlock on the high lands; of ash and cedar in the low lands; and pine along the rivers and streams. The wilderness was overrun with bear, deer, and smaller game, and was crossed in different directions by Indian trails which passed principally through swamps and low lands, except the great one along the ridge, near Lake Ontario, which extended from the Genesee, near Rochester, to the present site of Lewiston. The other great trail between the Genesee and Niagara Rivers ran from the Genesee near Avon, through Leroy and Batavia, where it divided into two branches, one running to Buffalo Creek and the other to Tonawanda.

The early missioners thought the climate was mild and salubrious, with about the same changes in temperature as the climate of France. The Seneca country at this period, the most western of the Iroquois cantons, was all east of the Genesee River.

The population of the Five Nations, when the missionaries first went amongst them, was between 25,000 and 30,000.[1] The Iroquois received from the French the name by which they have been known to the civilized world. In listening to speeches they express satisfaction or approval at the termination by the syllable "Iio," or "Eoh," which signified Amen; and the orator ended his speech by a syllable which sounded to French ears like "quois"—"I have spoken;" hence the word Iroquois.[2] They were known, however, among themselves and to other Indians as the Konoshioni, or Otin-

[1] Relations, 1660. [2] Schoolcraft, "Iroquois."

nonsionni, which signified a complete cabin, a name derived from the league which existed among the Five Nations.[1]

The French named these different nations: Agniers, Oneiouts, Onontagues, Goiogoens, and Tsonnontouans; but the English colonists gave them the names by which they are known to us: the Mohawks, the Oneidas, the Onondagas, the Cayugas, and the Senecas.

The Kahquahs were called the Neuter Nation from their neutrality in the Iroquois-Huron war. They were also called Attiwanderons, which signifies a people speaking a little different language. In the map of Decreux the country east of Niagara River, between Lake Ontario and Lake Erie, is called "Pagus Ondieronii," the country of the Ondieronons, and as the spelling is very bad this is evidently intended to express the country of the Kahquahs or Neuter Nation. Bressani says that this map is correct, but that the spelling is abominable.

Their territory was about one hundred and fifty miles in extent[2] and lay between the Hurons and the Iroquois on both sides of the Niagara River, but their principal villages were west of the Niagara. Before 1650 they had four villages east of Niagara, one at West[3] Seneca, one at Lewiston, or near Ontario Lake, and the others perhaps near Buffalo; but in that year those villages, as well as those of the entire nation, were destroyed by the Iroquois and their inhabitants slain or led captives to the Iroquois country.

[1] This name may have originated from the custom, existing among the Iroquois, of building long cabins to accommodate four, six, eight or ten families. These cabins, or houses, were fifty or sixty feet long, and the families dwelt on each side of the house with a fire in the center to accommodate every four families.

[2] The fishing was good; and there was a great abundance of game: deer, bear, buffalo, wild turkey, wolves, and wild cats.   [3] Champlain's map of 1612.

THE IROQUOIS AND THE JESUITS.

These Indians lived in cabins or huts of a single apartment, built in the shape of a camping tent, with an aperture in the top, which served as a chimney; and these cabins, in their villages, were arranged into well-ordered and comparatively clean streets.

Their food consisted of rudely ground corn, boiled in water without salt, but sometimes with fish, or beans, or squash; and when game was plenty and the hunt successful they mixed the fresh or dried meat of the bear, or deer, in the kettle with the cor... A highly prized dish was the flesh of a dog,[1] a dish not very palatable to modern tastes, yet considered a great luxury at an Indian banquet.

The women attended to the planting and the reaping, and all the drudgery around their homes; while the young men went on the war path, on hunting or fishing expeditions, and the old men held councils or gave advice for the guidance of the tribes.

These people had their social amusements and pastimes much the same as their more civilized white brethren. The men [2] engaged in games of chance or skill, and often became very much excited over the result, sometimes entire villages or representatives of different tribes entering the lists for important prizes. One game played by them was similar to the modern intellectual college game of football, though the ball used was very much smaller, and was carried by hand to the goal. They played the game of cross or la crosse with a leather covered ball filled with deer's hair, and they also indulged in several smaller games of chance, one of which consisted in tossing into the air six small cubes made of deer hoof, with the faces painted in different colors, and the winner

[1] Journal of Galince and Dolier   [2] Lafitau

was the one who had chosen the color which was uppermost on the greatest number of cubes as they reached the ground. They had banquets and festivities, at which they sang and danced to the sound of the kettledrum, accompanied by the monotonous "ho, hi, evohe," but as their voices were musical the sounds were not displeasing.[1]

They celebrate six regular festivals during the year, beginning with the festival of the New Year when the February new moon is five days old, and ending with the harvest festival in autumn. Some of these festivals are celebrated for several days, and are observed as a semi-religious, semi-social duty, in which all the people take part; and they are solemnized with banquets, speeches, dances, and song. Invitations to the banquets are given by placing grains of corn on pieces of wood upon the mat in the cabins of those to be invited, and at the same time telling them to come, whilst a crier proclaims through the village the place and the hour. The guests are seated on mats or skins around the cabin, according to their rank and age. These Indians are called copper colored; yet, Lafitau[2] says they are born white as Europeans, but the habit of going about almost naked and of greasing their bodies, together with the action of the sun and air, gives them this peculiar copper hue. They surpass[3] white men in physical qualities, being tall, well formed, well proportioned, active and strong. They are endowed with good animal spirit, and are gifted with

[1] Lafitau, "Moeurs des Suavages."

[2] Lafitau was a learned Jesuit who spent seven years among the Iroquois at Sault St. Louis, but he obtained most of his knowledge of the customs and life of the Indians from Garnier, who spent nearly sixty years among the Indians. Parkman says he is the best authority on Indian customs and life, because he knew the Indians when their manners and life were purely Indian, and before they had been changed by associating with Europeans.   [3] Lafitau.

lively imagination, fair intelligence and admirable memory.

Parents, after consulting the wishes and preference of the young people, make the matches for their children, and the marriages are prosperous and happy, both parties, generally, remaining faithful to the end. After parents of each party agree to the union the young man sends gifts of beads and furs to the girl as a pledge of their engagement; and shortly after, with his family, proceeds to the home of the bride elect, and seats himself on the mat before the fire, whilst the girl prepares a dish of soup or mush, which he devours in silence, with the girl sitting beside him. If there is a wedding feast, it is held at the cabin of the young man, but the girl must furnish the banquet; and she also, with her friends, brings food and a quantity of wood to the young man's home, in token of her willingness to perform the domestic duties.

Each village was composed of members of at least three different clans: the wolf, the bear, and the turtle.

The Iroquois were divided into different clans, or families, each clan having some animal as its distinctive totem or symbol. There were four principal clans: the wolf, the bear, the turtle, and the beaver; though there were several others of less importance named after other animals or birds, as the deer, the eagle, and the crane. The four principal clans were found in every village of each of the Five Nations, and although they were originally distinct tribes, yet they blended so admirably with each other by intermarriage that they preserved their identity only by having a distinct chief and warriors.

At the period of the advent of Europeans the Five Nations, with their different clans, were banded together in

---

1 La Moyne says they surpass in intelligence the peasantry of France.

the closest and most admirable form of political and civil union.¹

Each village as well as each nation had its chiefs and its ancients to decide upon local matters, but when any affair which affected the entire league was to be considered each village and nation sent its chiefs, its ancients, and orators, to the central council house at Onondaga to deliberate upon questions of state. According to the testimony of many different intelligent Europeans, who enjoyed the privilege of witnessing their proceedings, their assemblages would have done honor to any senate in the civilized world.

Their orators were selected for their ability to place the subject matter clearly and strongly before the council; and as they were endowed with good voices, and had lively and poetic imaginations, they often displayed a beauty of thought in their language, and a noble eloquence in their speech that placed them on a level with their more civilized white brethren, who strive to attain these qualities by artificial cultivation. Colden even declares that their speeches read better than those of educated English or French.²

Each village had its supreme chief whose office was hereditary, but succession to this office was made by selection from the ablest and most prominent of the former chief's immediate relatives; and generally this civil chief was the leader also in war, unless some younger chief was better qualified for this important task.

[1] Many claim that the Iroquois proposed their confederation to the colonies as a model form of government long before the revolution. Schoolcraft.
Perhaps the framers of our Constitution are indebted to the wisdom which inspired the formation of the Iroquois League. The admission of new states with equal rights is a doctrine of the Iroquois Grand Council.

[2] Colden's "History of Five Nations."

The young men, and the women also, held councils, and each had representatives at the Grand Council. All councils are subordinate to the Ancients, whose office is that of an upper house, or senate, and in their sessions they display all the dignity and wisdom of the Roman Senate. It was principally through their political sagacity that the Iroquois obtained supremacy over neighboring nations.

There was very little trade or traffic among the Indians, and their business transactions were limited to the simplest elements of exchange. They had wampum belts, which passed for money, and were the pledges of ambassadors and treaties of peace. These were made by Virginia Indians from shells gathered along the sea shore, and formed the public treasury of the country.

IROQUOIS HOUSE.

CHAPTER II.

LOCATIONS OF THE IROQUOIS TOWNS.

INDIAN TOWNS NOT PERMANENT—MOHAWK TOWNS—DESTROYED BY THE FRENCH—GREENHALGH'S DESCRIPTION—ONEIDA TOWNS—ONONDAGA THE CAPITAL—ST. MARY'S OF GENENTAA—CAYUGA VILLAGES—MANY CAYUGAS REMOVE TO CANADA—SENECA TOWNS ACCORDING TO A SENECA CHIEF—JESUIT NAMES OF SENECA VILLAGES—LOCATIONS.

THE Iroquois did not haul their fire-wood to the towns, like their more civilized white brethren, but moved their towns close to the wood; so there was no permanency to their homes. The names, too, of their villages changed as they were removed to different sites, because it was a peculiarity of Indian nomenclature to name places after topographical features; and they sometimes gave their towns the name of a prominent chief. The Indians, moreover, had no written language; and their names must sound in various forms to ears unaccustomed to their speech, as a word in any strange tongue is difficult to pronounce or comprehend.

The Mohawks, the first and the most easternly situated of the Five Nations, at the time of Father Jogues' visit,[1] had three large villages located in the beautiful valley of the Mohawk, on the south bank of the Mohawk River, and west of the Schoharie River. Ossernenon[2] was situated on an eminence a little west of the junction of the Schoharie with the Mohawk, near the present

---
[1] 1642.
[2] This is the place where René Goupil was slain, and the people of the same town afterwards put the saintly Jogues to death.

Auriesville. Andagaron was about ten miles west of Ossernenon. Tionnontoguen, the capital, was about twelve miles west of Andagaron, directly east of Flat Creek, near the site of the present town of Sprakers. There was also a fourth village located some miles west of Tionnontoguen, at the time of the captivity of Father Jogues.[1]

Small pox wrought great havoc in these towns about the years 1660-61, and the inhabitants moved westward from the plague spots.

In October, 1666, De Tracy came through the forests with his army of Indians and French to humble the fierce Mohawks, and to destroy their towns. The Mohawks fled at the approach of the French; the torch was applied to their towns, and the charred embers and burnt corn alone indicated the location of their former dwellings. They rebuilt their towns on the north side of the river; and they erected a strong stockade around the easternmost town, as a protection against the French and their old enemies from the region of Manhatta. The towns remained in their new positions during the years of the missions, and although time has effaced nearly all traces of the eastern door of the Long Cabin, yet General Clark has succeeded in pretty certainly locating their sites.

Wentworth Greenhalgh, who made a journey through the Iroquois country in May and June, 1677, reports the following names and locations of the Mohawk villages: "Cahaniaga is double stockadoed, ... and is situate upon the edge of an hill, about a bow shott from the river side. Canagora is situated upon a flatt, a stone's throw from ye water side. Canajorha, the like situacion,

---

[1] Martin, "Life of Father Jogues," p. 92.

only about two miles distant from the water. Tionondogue is situated on an hill, a bow shott from ye river. The small village lyes close by the river side, on the north side, as do all the former."

The Oneidas were originally members of the Onondaga nation, but they separated from the parent community before the advent of Europeans. They first dwelt on the southern shore of the lake that bears their name, near the mouth of Oneida Creek. They moved farther up the valley before the period of the missions, and located near the present site of Oneida Castle. They evidently moved again in 1676, as Greenhalgh found them in a newly settled town the next year; and this town was later stockaded, and was called Kunawaloa.[1]

Greenhalgh says: "The Oneidas have but one town, which lyes about 130 miles westward of the Maques (Mohawks). It is situate about twenty miles from a small river which comes out of the hills to the southward, and runs into Lake Teshirogue (Oneida), and about thirty miles distant from the Maques River, which lyes to the northward. The town is newly settled, double stockadoed, but little cleared ground so that they are forced to send to the Onondagoes to buy corn; the towne consists of about one hundred houses. Their corne grows round about the towne."

Onondaga was the central nation of the Iroquois, and the capital of the league; and here was the great council house to which the delegates of the Five Nations came to discuss affairs of state. The capital had a regular order of streets, which were comparatively clean, for an Indian town. It was situated on an elevation, now called Indian Hill, between the ravines formed by the

[1] Schoolcraft. This was probably at Stockbridge, Madison County.

west and middle branches of Limestone Creek, in the town of Pompey, two miles south of Manlius.

It was to this place that Fathers Chanmonot and Dablon came in the fall of 1655, as the first missionaries to the Iroquois. It was here, also, that the first chapel was built in the State of New York. It was built in one day, November 18, 1655; and was immediately sanctified by the baptism of three Indian children.[1]

There was a little hamlet on the eastern shore of Onondaga Lake, at Liverpool, where the French colony was located, and where the beautiful little chapel of our Lady of Ganentaa was built, near the salt springs, which were afterwards known as the "Jesuits' Well."

There were three villages in the Cayuga country pleasantly situated on the borders of Lake Cayuga, or on the banks of the Seneca River. Cayuga (St. Joseph's), the principal village, was situated about three and one-half miles south of Union Springs, near Great Gully Brook.[2] Tiehero was ten miles distant, on the east side of Seneca River, at the northern extremity of Seneca Lake. A smaller village, Onontare (St. René), was situated at a place known as Fort Hill, in the town of Savannah, Wayne County.

The Cayugas were at continual war with the powerful Andastes, from the region of the Susquehanna; and many of them left their pleasant homes near Lake Tiehero,[3] in 1665, and removed to the northern shores of Ontario Lake, where they would be free from the attacks of their enemies. These emigrants were probably from the smaller villages of Tiehero and Onontare, as these were weaker and more liable to attack. They gradually came

---

[1] Relations, 1656, p. 20.

[2] Hawley, "Cayuga." It was here the first chapel was built.   [3] Lake Cayuga.

back to their old homes; and in 1676 they had built new towns near Tiehero Lake, about a mile eastward of Cayuga. Here Greenhalgh found them in 1677. "The Cayugas," he says, "have three townes about a mile distant from each other; they are not stockadoed. They intend the next spring to build all their houses together and stockade them; they have abundance of corne; they lye within two or three miles of the Lake Tiehero."

The Senecas occupied the valley of the Genesee, and their territory extended to the lands of the Onondagas in the east, and to the Cayugas in the south; whilst the Genesee River at this time formed the western limit of their domain. They had four large villages, which formed the angles of a square, and they also had several hamlets, which were located in different places, for convenience in hunting and fishing. Their villages were situated about twenty miles from Lake Ontario, which was reached by trails to the head of Irondoquoit Bay; and great trails led from their towns to the neighboring nations.

Blacksmith, an old Seneca chief, gave the names, and described the location of the villages for Mr. Marshall[1] as he had learned them from the traditions of his race. The villages were: Ga-o-sa-eh-ga-aah, at Boughton Hill, south of Victor; De-yu-di-haah-do, about ten miles south of Rochester; Chi-nos-hah-geh, four miles southeast of Victor; Deodonset, five miles southeast of Avon Springs. The names, however, which the missionaries used to designate these villages were probably derived from the Mohawk tongue, and were: Gannagaro, or Gandagaro (St. James'); Gandachioragou (Immaculate Conception); Gannougarae, or Gandougarae (St. Michael's); Gannounata (St. John's).

[1] Marshall, "First Visit of LaSalle."

Gannagaro was a very large village of about 150 houses; and had a population of 2,000 or 3,000, as each long house was the home of from two to six families. It was situated on a large hill, called Boughton Hill,[1] which rises immediately south of the little station at Victor on the Auburn branch of the New York Central Railroad.

About one mile and a quarter westerly, on an eminence, called by the early settlers "Fort Hill," was a fortified enclosure, which could be used as a place of protection for women and children in case of an attack on Gannagaro.

Gannagaro was called St. James' by the Jesuits; and it was Ga-o-sa-eh-ga-aah in the Seneca tongue. The Rev. James Pierron came here in 1672, as the first resident missionary.

Gannougarae, or Gandougarae, was about four miles southward of Gannagaro, on the banks of a stream called Mud Creek, in the northeast part of the present town of East Bloomfield. It was called St. Michael's by the Jesuits, and was composed almost entirely of Huron, Neuter, and Onnontioga captives. A large number of these Hurons were Christians;[2] and it was here that Father Fremin established his residence in the fall of 1669. A chapel was soon built, and Father Fremin said his first mass here November 3, 1669.

In the language of the Senecas it was called "Chinos-hah-geh," which means "on the slope of the valley." The town was destroyed by fire in the spring of 1671; but was soon rebuilt, probably on another site, two miles nearer the village of Gannagaro.

Another large town, which has been called by various

[1] It was most probably located farther southward, at the time of the missions.
[2] Many beads and crosses have been found in the vicinity.

names, was situated about ten miles west of Gannagaro, in a large bend of the Honeoye Creek, north of the present village of West Mendon.[1] Although there seems to be some confusion of names among authorities on the subject, yet this apparently was the Gandachioragou of the Jesuits, the Tagarondies of Hennepin, the Totiakton of Denonville, and the Deyudihaakdah of the Senecas. It was at one time the most populous of the Seneca towns; the houses were very large, being fifty or sixty feet in length, with room for ten or twelve families in each house.

Many vestiges of former Indian towns have been found at Lima, and also on the main road between Lima and Honeoye Falls. These places were known to the early settlers as Indian burial grounds, and many relics have been found to show that they were formerly the sites of Seneca towns.[2]

Gandachioragou was very probably the Seneca capital; and it was situated on a hill at, or a little north of, Lima. It was here that Father Garnier located, and spent nearly twenty years of missionary life. The town was sometimes called Tagorondies, because this was the name of the chief. It was also called Totiakton; but as this is the Iroquois word for trout,[3] this name may have been given to the town when it was moved to the banks of Honeoye Creek, which is noted still as the place of the trout.

There was a fourth village, called Ganuaunata by Denonville and Dyudoosot by the Senecas, which was

[1] Marshall, "Expedition of Denonville." This was the site in 1688.

[2] The Rev. Dr. Quigley, of St. Joseph's Cathedral, Buffalo, whose boyhood home was at Lima, often visited these places; and he says that the lower part of Academy Hill, at Lima, was an Indian burial ground, and there was another a mile north of the town on the road to Honeoye Falls.

[3] Some authorities claim this word means "bending," but in either case it would indicate the same place. The town was also called Sonnontouan.

located[1] a few miles south of Gandachioragou, but the furrows of the ploughman, and the dwellings of the pale-faces have covered up the vestiges of the Sonnontouan towns. There was no chapel at this village, but the Fathers often came here on their ministrations of mercy and grace.

When La Salle and Galinee came to Gandagaro, in 1669, the town was enclosed by a palisade, but when Greenhalgh came, in 1677, not one of the Seneca towns was thus fortified; so the location of the town was changed during this period.[2]

After the country was devastated by Denonville, the eastern Seneca towns moved eastward toward Canandaigua and Geneva, and the western group moved south and west towards the Genesee.[3] There was a small village of Senecas near the mouth of Niagara River, on the Canadian side, although they probably dwelt on the New York State side at an earlier period.

There was a town of an independent tribe, called the "Oniasonts," at Bemus Point, on Lake Chautauqua; but these were most likely an offshoot of the Eries.

[1] Doty locates it on the Douglas farm, two miles north of Livonia Station. "History of Livingston County."

[2] There is some evidence that this town was located just north of Victor at the time of La Salle's visit, and that it was sometime later removed to Boughton Hill.

[3] General Clark.

DEA OF GOD
IL—INFERIOR
. OF DREAMS
AN ACT IN-
THE DEAD—

ritten lan-
petuate the
ligious be-
ere recited
f the faith,
g: and al-
 admirable
faith must
se accord-
d the cir-

lief is the
ires of the
reece, and
und work

 indistinct
d Ruler of

located¹ a
furrows o
faces have
towns.
Fathers of
and grace
　Whe
1669, the
Greenhalg
was thus
changed (
　After
eastern S(
gua and
and west
lage of Se
Canadian
York Stat
　Ther
the "Oni;
but these

¹ Doty lo(
of Livingston
² There is
of La Salle's vi:
3. General

CHAPTER III.

RELIGIOUS BELIEF.

RELIGIOUS BELIEF PRESERVED BY TRADITION—THEIR IDEA OF GOD—CREATION OF THE WORLD—ORIGIN OF EVIL—INFERIOR SPIRITS OR MANITOUS—DREAM THEORY—FESTIVAL OF DREAMS—THE SOUL—THE INDIAN'S HEAVEN—THE SOUL CAN ACT INDEPENDENTLY OF THE BODY—VENERATION FOR THE DEAD—FESTIVAL OF THE DEAD—VICES OF SAVAGES.

THE Indians of North America had no written language, no hieroglyphics, no symbols to perpetuate the events or theories of the past; so their religious belief, as well as historical lore, were traditional, were recited in their councils by their old men, preservers of the faith, for the instruction and edification of the young: and although they were endowed with tenacious and admirable memories, yet it is evident that their religious faith must necessarily change and assume a different phase according to the characteristics of the individuals and the circumstances of life.

The first foundation of their religious belief is the same as that which formed the principal features of the religion of the Barbarians who first occupied Greece, and spread through Asia, and which forms the ground work of all Pagan Mythology.[1]

They had only a general, confused, and indistinct knowledge of the Supreme Being, Creator, and Ruler of

[1] Lafitau.

the universe. Thohoroniawagon was their nearest approach to God; and he was to their mind one who embraced the heavens, who was happy in himself, and indifferent to the affairs of this world.

The Indian God had nothing to do with morality or justice among men, and they believed that their race was under the direct control of subordinate spirits; and these were good or evil as they brought good or bad luck, health and plenty, or disease, famine, and death.[1] Many of the tribes confound Thohoroniawagon with the sun; and although they believe that he once dwelt on the earth, yet they have no apotheosis of men, nor do they worship any star or planet but the sun, which they call the god of day.

They have but a very confused notion of Creation, and they give many fantastic and ridiculous explanations of the beginning of life and the formation of the world.

The Senecas say that in the far distant past waters covered the entire earth; and thousands of ducks of every plumage swam upon the surface of the water. One morning, when the sun was bright, a beautiful woman appeared in the sky; as she was falling towards the waters the ducks held a council and resolved to spread out their wings and break the force of the fall. The ducks also called a turtle from the deep so the woman might have a place to alight, and they spread over the back of the turtle a slime from which a green spot soon appeared, which grew larger and larger until the earth was formed. This woman had two sons: one the author of everything good; the other, author of everything noxious or evil.[2]

Like most of the Oriental nations, the Iroquois wor-

[1] Parkman.   [2] Sanborn.

THE IROQUOIS BELIEF.

shipped the sun, Agreskoue, which was also the god of war, and to which they made offerings of porcelain beads, ears of corn, and animals taken in the hunt. Although they did not worship fire, yet it was for them a sacred emblem, and was continually burning in their council houses to the end, how warm soever the weather might be.

They believed also in the existence of multitudes of inferior spirits which they called manitous—a kind of subtle, quasi-spiritual species of genii—which inhabited the forests and streams, the rivers and lakes, the mountains and caves, the meadows and the moorlands, and every place of unusual strangeness or beauty. These manitous presided over the destinies of men; and the Indians often invoked their aid for success in fishing, in hunting, and in war, often making a direct appeal to the presiding genius of the woods or the waters to crown their efforts. They believed that these manitous resided in birds and in animals; and that they controlled the elements, and when in an angry mood gave fury to the storm, or when in a happier mood gave the pleasant, delightful weather.

Every Indian had a particular manitou, which each one selected by fasting for eight days, and at the end of this fast whatever first came to mind was a symbol of his manitou, or Okki. The manitous manifested their will and pleasure in dreams, and the Indians believed that they were under a most solemn and sacred duty to do whatever was revealed to them in this manner, being ready to sacrifice their own lives or the lives of others to fulfill the commands of their manitou.

They celebrate a festival of dreams, which is called "Onnon-hon-a-rori", the folly or the turning of the brain.

During the festivities they dress in a fantastic manner; cover their faces with bark masks, and go about at night from cabin to cabin with torches, breaking whatever they can lay hands on and compelling people to give them objects they may fancy, or to do what they command to fulfill their dreams. They act like veritable demons, and many take advantage of this occasion to gratify their passions of hatred, lust, or revenge.

The Iroquois believe in the existence of the soul as a spiritual entity, but they cannot exactly define its nature. They call it "Ganno-gonr-ha", and "Erienta"; but these appelations do not signify being, but action, as the former expresses the operations of spirit and mind, and the latter, the operations of heart and will.[1] They do not understand that the soul is purely spiritual, but a kind of Egyptian double, or shadow of one's self. They believe that the soul is immortal, and that after death it will begin its long and weary journey to the happy hunting ground, or eternal home, far to the westward over rocky paths, through briars and thorns until it comes to a deep river where the only passageway, a fallen tree, is disputed by an immense dog or beast that threatens to devour the soul, or cast it into the flood where it is whirled by the waters over precipices and rocks. After passing this river, the souls are judged and sent to a place of torments or delights, according as the individual was good or bad in this life. The delights of their heaven consist in good hunting, good fishing, in singing and dancing at eternal feasts in the presence of their gods. The virtues which merit such reward are bravery in war, skill in hunting, and excessive cruelty to enemies and captives. The old and feeble, and little children who are

[1] Lafitau.

unable to walk to the happy hunting ground, are heard sighing around the cabins in the moaning of the wind, in the soughing of the forest, and the rustling of the leaves.

They believe also that the soul acts independently of the body, and makes long journeys at will, through the air, and to most hidden places; and, as it is a spirit, nothing can arrest its progress; yet it does not cease to animate the body, but makes these journeys when the body is asleep. This explains why they are so infatuated with dreams, as they believe their dreams are actual occurrences, and are the doings of the soul while the body sleeps.

They had the greatest veneration for their dead, and when a member of a family died all the relatives and friends assembled to mourn over the departed, whilst some chief made a funeral oration, in which he related the noble deeds of the dead, and all silently and sadly followed the remains to the grave, or to its resting place in the trees where it might receive sunshine and air. Every ten years they held the festival of the dead,[1] or the festival of souls, at some place selected by the council; and here at the appointed time assembled all the different clans and tribes and nations from hundreds of miles, bearing on their shoulders the remains of their dead. These Indians presented a weird sight as they wended their way through the forest, conveying the skeletons of their dead on their backs, and singing a low lamentation as they proceeded to the place of celebration. At this place banquets were given to noted guests, and games were played by the young people until the day appointed; and then all the dead were placed in a large pit lined with

[1] Lafitau.

rich furs, and covered with earth so that a mound was formed.

These people, however, were savages with all the cruel instincts of their race; for cruelty with them was a virtue as great as charity is among Christians; and they were cannibals, often devouring the flesh of their still living victims; nor had they ideas of moral relations or religious duty, except such as interest or self-preservation dictated.

Such was the social, political, and religious life of the Iroquois and their Indian neighbors when the Recollect and Jesuit Missionaries came to them with the light of faith and the Gospel of Jesus Christ.

CHAPTER IV.

ADVENT OF EUROPEANS.

INDIANS KINDLY DISPOSED TOWARDS WHITES—CARTIER EXPLORES THE ST. LAWRENCE—FIRST MEETING OF FRENCH AND IROQUOIS WAS HOSTILE—CHAMPLAIN FOUGHT WITH THE MONTAGNAIS AGAINST THE MOHAWKS—IROQUOIS FLED AT SOUND OF GUNS—CHAMPLAIN'S EXPEDITION AGAINST THE IROQUOIS—FRENCH MADE FRIENDS OF THE HURONS—MISSIONERS—THE RECOLLECTS—THE HURON MISSION—JOURNEY TO THE HURON COUNTRY.

THE first vision of the white men may have awakened thoughts of wonder and astonishment in the minds of the Indians, but it does not seem to have aroused any feeling of hatred or resentment. Turner[1] says: "Savage in many respects yet kindest hospitality from purest motives always extended to foreign guests; and perhaps the golden chord of friendship would forever have remained unbroken had the red man been the first to begin hostilities. 'Welcome English,'[2] are words intimately associated with early American History."

When Jacques Cartier was exploring the gulf and river of St. Lawrence[3] in 1535 he learned from the Indians, along the shore, of a great lake (Ontario) which emptied

---

[1] History of the Holy Pilgrims.

[2] Indians could not pronounce English, but in their mouth it became "Yengeish." Hence, Yankee.

[3] Which he named in honor of the saint whose name it bears because discovered on his feast day, August 10, 1535.

into the St. Lawrence; and of another river, in which there was a great cataract; and of a vast sea beyond all these. This was the first historical notice of this region; but Cartier did not ascend this river any further than the present site of Montreal.

Unfortunately for the influence and the labors of the future missionaries, the first coming of the French to the Iroquois territory was on a hostile mission; and as the Indians never forgive an injury, this first unfriendly act had a baneful effect upon the subsequent relations of the Iroquois and French. The French and Dutch entered New York State about the same time, but from different directions; and while the Dutch made a treaty with the Iroquois which lasted till the English took possession of their country, the French came practically declaring war.

The country immediately north and south of Lake Ontario was Neutral territory and the mutual battle ground of different Indian nations.[1]

In 1609 the Montagnais induced Champlain to explore north of Lake Ontario and give battle to their old enemies, the Mohawks. Champlain left Quebec June 18th, with fifty Indians and two soldiers, and July 30th he attacked two hundred Mohawks near the present site of Ticonderaga, at the northern extremity of Lake George. Champlain fired his arquebus, killing two chiefs; the other soldiers also fired, and as this was the first exhibition of fire arms the Iroquois had witnessed they fled in confusion. This was the first greeting from the French.

When Champlain reached Quebec after his third voyage to France he found Hurons, Algonquins, and Montagnais waiting for him to go on a grand expedition of war into the heart of the Iroquois country. Cham-

[1] "Narrative and Critical History of America."

plain, with his Indian allies, started in canoes up the River St. Lawrence in September, 1615. When they reached Lake Ontario they crossed over to the south shore of the lake, concealed their canoes in the weeds and underbrush along the beach, and started overland to a fortified town[1] of the Iroquois. On October 10, they attacked the town, which was so strongly fortified with interlaced pallisades, thirty feet high, that they were unable to capture it, and were forced to retreat with considerable loss.

The French at Quebec, and later at Montreal and Three Rivers, formed alliances with the Montagnais, the Algonquins, and the Hurons; and established among them trading posts for furs, and the French Fathers established missions for their enlightenment and conversion.

Missionaries accompanied the early explorers on all their important expeditions, as anxious and zealous for the salvation of souls as these lay explorers were to discover a northwest passage[2] to the wealth of the Indies.

The Recollects, or Franciscans, were the first to enter the field; but they were soon followed by the Jesuits, whose sacrifices and labors on these Indian missions have gained the admiration, and merited the encomiums of writers professedly inimical to their Order. The Huron Missions were especially prosperous and successful; and although far removed from the scene of our story, yet they exercised a great influence upon the subsequent missions among the Iroquois.

Missionaries[3] first went to the Huron Country in

[1] Marshall maintains that this town was on Onondaga Lake. Clark and Shea contend that it was a few miles south of the east end of Lake Oneida.

[2] The French believed that such a passage existed, and it was for the purpose of discovering this water route to China and the Indies that the expeditions of La Salle and other explorers were fitted out, and with the further hope of thus acquiring wealth and fame.

[3] Father Le Caron, Recollect. Recollects invited Jesuits to help them and Fathers Brebeuf, Lallemont, and Masse came in 1625.

1615, and labored there with but slight intermissions until 1649 and 1650, when the principal Huron villages were destroyed by the Iroquois, the missionaries were killed, and hundreds of the Hurons were led captives to the Iroquois cantons.[1]

Many of these were well instructed converts; and they brought to the land of the Iroquois the Christian truths they had learned from the Fathers.

The journey from Quebec to the Huron Country was very long and tedious, and the travelers were exposed to many dangers and hardships. They were obliged to follow the route of the Ottawa River through fear of the Iroquois, who lurked in every dangerous place to waylay their enemies. The distance from Quebec to the Huron Country was about seven hundred miles, and many miles of the way they were obliged to carry their boats, with baggage and supplies for the missions, upon their shoulders, as in many places they were unable to follow the water course in their canoes. The missionaries could not make this journey more than once a year, and sometimes two or three years might pass before they could descend to Quebec; so they planted wheat to make bread, and pressed the juice from the wild grapes of the country to make wine for the altar. These missionaries, however, willingly sacrificed the social intercourse and pleasures of civilized life for the love of God and the salvation of men. They had many prosperous and populous mission churches in the Huron villages before the fatal onslaught of the Iroquois, who burned the churches, killed or led captive hundreds of Christians, and practically destroyed the Huron Nation. Many of the Hurons who escaped sought refuge under the protection of the French

[1] About 700 captives were brought to the Iroquois country.

at Quebec, where they might live and practice their religion in peace.

As the French were in league with the enemies of the Iroquois, they did not come in friendly contact with the latter for nearly fifty years after Champlain landed at Quebec; yet there was no open act of hostility on either side till 1641

CHAPTER V.

FIRST ATTEMPTS.

CAPTURE OF FATHER PAULAIN–FATHER D'AILLON, RECOLLECT, VISITS THE NEUTERS–VISITED MANY VILLAGES–BREBEUF AND CHAUMONOT, JESUITS, VISIT THE NEUTERS–REACH THE NIAGARA–HURON CHRISTIANS COME AS MISSIONERS–JOGUES, FIRST MISSIONER TO THE IROQUOIS–TAKEN PRISONER–TORTURED–DEATH OF RENE GOUPIL–CAPTIVITY–ESCAPE–FIRST MISSION WORK.

IN 1621, while Father Paulain was on an errand of mercy,[1] following a trading party up the river to the rapids of St. Louis, he was captured by a roving band of Iroquois warriors, who shortly after exchanged him for some of their own people, prisoners near Quebec; but two of the Iroquois prisoners remained with the French, and were instructed in Christianity. This was, perhaps, the first knowledge any of the Iroquois obtained of the Christian religion.

Some Historians[2] maintain that Father de la Roche D'Aillon, a Recollect, entered Western New York in the fall or winter of 1626, on a visit to the villages of the Neuter Nation situated east of Niagara River, but they offer no positive proof that he entered this region.

It is true that he visited many villages of the Neuter Nation, and that he mentions the last village of the Neuters nearest to the Iroquois; but in the letter[3] in which

---

[1] Le Clerq. "Establishment of the faith."
[2] Bp. Timon. Shea, p. 225.
[3] This letter was written to a friend but is preserved in the archives of the order Le Clerq. Vol. 1, p. 263.

he gives an account of his visit he does not mention any journey to the Iroquois, neither does he state that he crossed Niagara River or passed over either lake. He also wished to discover the river leading to the Iroquois country, but the Hurons and Neuters would not guide or direct him, as they did not wish the Iroquois to trade with the French.

D'Aillon left the Huron country October 18, 1626, in company with Grenole and Lavallee, Frenchmen by birth, and, entering the territory of the Petun nation, he obtained a guide and Indians to carry his baggage and provisions. After five days' travel, sleeping at night under the protection of some tall tree of the forest, they entered the first village of the Neuters and passed on through four other villages, where the people vied with one another in their attentions to the strange visitors. They remained at the sixth village, where a council was held, and D'Aillon was adopted by the tribe, and was given in charge of Souharrisen, chief of the entire nation.

There were twenty-eight villages of this nation, and seven or eight hamlets, located for convenience in hunting or fishing. One village called Onaroronon[1] was only one day's journey from the Senecas. The country was the most beautiful he had seen, and was overrun with deer, bear, and all kinds of wild game. The people were tall and well formed, and had no cripples or deformed among them. The village in which D'Aillon and his companions remained was called Onnontisaston,[2] and was very likely the capitol of the nation. He remained with the Neuters only three months, as the French then sent for him, fearing that his presence might provoke

[1] This was not only the name of a village but of an entire tribe or nation. See p. 4
[2] This was in center of nation.

some hostile act on the part of those Indians, who did not understand his language or his mission. He did very little missionary work among them, as they were not disposed to accept his teaching in the absence of the chiefs who were then on the war-path; so he spent the greater portion of his time in learning their language and in visiting their villages.

Another attempt at evangelizing the Kahquahs, or Neuters,[1] was made in 1640 and 1641, when the celebrated missionaries, Fathers Brebeuf and Chaumonot, S. J., visited their country, and remained several months among them, baptizing some of the sick and dying and instructing them in the truths of Christianity. The Relations of 1641, say: "We began this year a mission among one of the most powerful and important nations of this country. We had long since desired to establish this mission, but the difference of language and fewness of missionaries prevented us from undertaking this work." Fathers Brebeuf and Chaumonot left the Huron Mission of St. Mary's, on Georgian Bay, November 2, 1640, and on November 9th, they reached Kandacho, the first of the Neuter villages. From this place they proceeded to the central village, or capital of the nation, where they were kindly welcomed as guests and were given permission to teach; but their presents[2] were not accepted, as the chiefs were absent in war. These Fathers state that they visited eighteen[3] of the forty villages of this nation, doing

---

[1] The missionaries gave these people the name Neuter, on account of their neutrality in the Huron-Iroquois Wars. [2] The exchange of presents meant a treaty or alliance.

[3] They call the Niagara River "Onguiahra," from a village on its banks of same name. Samson, in his map of 1656, calls it Ongiara. Father Hennepin, in his map of 1682, was the first to write it Niagara. It is not probable that they entered the present State of New York (though nearly all historians claim they did), because the villages of this Nation east of the Niagara River were the farthest away, and because Brebeuf was accused of intending to visit the Senecas to bring them to destroy the Neuters, and the Fathers did not wish to give them any foundation for such an accusation.

what spiritual work they could; but their presence soon awakened the suspicion[1] and mistrust of these people, and in the month of March they returned to the Hurons.

Two years afterwards some of the zealous and enlightened Huron converts visited the Neuters to instruct and convert them. They were well received and attentively listened to, as the Indians had more confidence in them than they would have in Europeans, and their labors were not in vain as they prepared many of these people for admission into the Church, which took place some years later, when they were captives among the Iroquois. These zealous Huron Christians, no doubt, entered Western New York, as they went as far west as the Erie, or Cat Nation, whose territory extended along the southern shore of Lake Erie; yet, no permanent mission was ever established among the Kahquahs while they existed as a distinct nation.

In the fall of 1641 about 200 Iroquois warriors descended the St. Lawrence and divided into two parties.[2] One party intended to commit the first act of hostility against the French at Three Rivers, but as two of their chiefs died on the way, they considered this an evil omen and returned to their homes. The other party descended the river and attacked the Algonquins near Quebec, destroyed their homes, and carried off many of their prisoners to the Iroquois country. Some of the female[3] captives escaped in the early spring, and from them it was learned that the Iroquois were very anxious to know the

[1] Pagan Hurons had told the Neuters that the missionaries were sorcerers and would bring disease and misfortune to their Nation, and as the Jesuits' lives were so different from the Indians, these stories were readily believed; and hence their breveries, their ink and pen, and, more especially, their writings became a source not only of wonder but of alarm to the Indian mind. The Fathers could not say Mass in that country on account of this mistrust. [2] Parkman.
[3] Their children were roasted and eaten by these cannibals.

strength of the French, and also the duty, office, and life of the Black Gowns, or Jesuit missionaries. The Iroquois could easily have destoyed the French colonies in Canada had they known their weakness, as the entire army at this time at Quebec, Montreal, and Three Rivers, comprised but 115 men.[1]

The first priest to come to the Iroquois country was Rev. Isaac Jogues, and he did not come as an accredited minister of Christ, or ambassador of the French, but as a prisoner of war. On the second day of August, 1642, twelve canoes[2] paddled by Christian Hurons and carrying Father Jogues, and two other Frenchmen,[3] and Teresa, a young Huron girl who had been educated by the Sisters at Quebec, were moving rapidly over the waters of the St. Lawrence at one of its expansions called St. Peter's Lake, when they were suddenly fired upon from the shore by a roving band of Iroquois warriors. The suddeness of the attack confused the Huron party, and most of them were taken prisoners, while some escaped through the thick forests that lined the shore. One of the Hurons was killed, and his flesh was roasted and eaten by the Iroquois. Father Jogues might have escaped but he thought that duty called him to remain with his Huron neophytes, some of whom were not yet baptized, as he expected they would be tortured or put to death; and he wished to be near to share their fate, to console them, and prepare them in their last hour for a Christian death.

The Iroquois hurried across the St. Lawrence to the Richelieu, or Iroquois River, where they halted to divide the spoils. These captives were hurried off towards the

[1] Manuscript in the Louvre Library. [2] Martin, "Life of Father Jogues."
[3] René Goupil and William Couture.

Mohawk villages, and at the southern end of Lake Champlain[1] they met a war party of Iroquois encamped on an island, and the poor captives were obliged to run the gauntlet between two files of these warriors who were armed with clubs, sticks, or other weapons, and aimed vigorous and well-directed blows at the unfortunate prisoners as they ran along the line.

Father Jogues was not only beaten into insensibility by the blows, but his fingers were burned with live coals, and lacerated by the teeth of these savages; yet, this holy man seemed to grieve more over the tortures of his companions than he did over his own sufferings. After leaving the island other war parties were met, and on each occasion similar tortures were inflicted on these unfortunate victims, as the Iroquois considered cruelty to captives a happy omen of success in war.

The prisoners were brought to the Mohawk villages where the most cruel tortures that these savages could devise were inflicted on them until they were so exhausted, and in such agony, that even death would be a relief; yet, they were consoled by the example and the presence of the holy Jesuit, who was ready at a given signal to impart absolution and his last blessing to the dying Christian Hurons or French. René Goupil,[2] Father Jogues' companion, and a very holy young man, was killed shortly after their arrival, near one of the Mohawk villages, a martyr to his faith and zeal; as it was on account of his teaching the children the rudiments of Christianity, and instructing them to make the sign of the cross[3] that he was put to death.

[1] Champlain gave his name to the lake when he came with the Montagnais to give battle to the Mohawks [2] He had studied medicine but desired to become a Jesuit.
[3] The Dutch had told the Mohawks that the sign of the cross was evil, and brought misfortune. Martin, "Life of Jogues."

René Goupil's death was a severe loss to Father Jogues, who found one of the greatest comforts of his captivity in the hours of conversation and prayer in company with this young man, roaming through the vast forests, or kneeling at the base of some lofty tree, on which they had carved a rude symbol of the cross to remind them of the greater sufferings of their Lord and Master; but now the holy missioner's only conversation was with God in prayer, when he could steal away for a few hours from the drudgery of his slave life in the village. As the Mohawks began to treat him more kindly he gave much of his time to the acquisition of their language; as he hoped some day to be able to teach these people the truths of Christianity, and to lead them to God. He was obliged to accompany hunting and fishing parties, to prepare wood for their fires, and to carry loads of their fish and game; but he performed this labor the more willingly as it gave him greater liberty to spend many hours in prayer in some secluded spot, where he erected a diminutive bark or brush chapel, which concealed his presence from these savages, and left him free to commune with God. Whilst on one of these fishing expeditions, on the Hudson, near Rensselaerswyck,[1] he was advised by the Dutch to make his escape in a vessel which was soon to sail for Europe; and he was the more readily induced to take this step as he learned the Mohawks intended to put him to death when he returned to their village. His first attempt, however, at escape was frustrated by the Indians; but, after many weeks of hiding, and of negotiations between the Dutch and the Mohawks, he finally reached Manhattan,[2] whence he sailed for Europe.

[1] Albany.　　[2] New York.

Father Jogues visited different villages and baptized about seventy during the period of his captivity, so his fate was not so dismal, but had its rays of hope and joy; and although his hands were fearfully mutilated yet he rejoiced that he was able to use them in the work of his Divine Master. He was the first priest to administer the sacraments of the Church within the bounds of the present State of New York, as there were no Catholics then in the State, except two that he found at Manhattan when he arrived there in September, 1643, having escaped from the Mohawks through the assistance of the Dutch at Albany.

CHAPTER VI.

WAR.

MONTMAGNY BUILDS FORT RICHELIEU—IROQUOIS, THE SCOURGE OF CATHOLIC MISSIONS AND FRENCH COLONY—WEALTHY CATHOLICS OF FRANCE COME TO RESCUE—CAPTURE OF BRESSANI—TORTURES—PEACE COUNCILS—JOGUES, FRENCH AMBASSADOR TO THE MOHAWKS—CONSOLES CHRISTIAN CAPTIVES—THE MYSTERIOUS BOX.

SO bold and insidious had the Iroquois become, and so frequently did they attack stray parties of Hurons and French, that the latter did not dare go on a fishing or hunting expedition, or even till the soil, through fear of the roving bands of these warriors, who would often lie in ambush for days at a time in some deep ravine, dense forest, or tall grass, to surprise and slay their unsuspecting enemies. Gov. Montmagny resolved to remove some of this danger from the colonists, and put a check upon the depredations of these savages. He, therefore, sent one hundred men, with Father Vimont as chaplain, to build a fort on the Richelieu river, on the route between the St. Lawrence and the Mohawk country. They selected a site on August 13, 1642, only ten days after the capture of Father Jogues and his companions, near a spot which still bore sad evidence of the capture and of the cruelty of the Mohawks: for the heads of some of the Hurons were still dangling from poles driven in the ground, and rude pictures were found traced upon the bark of trees, delineating the victory of the Iroquois. Before beginning the fort all assisted at mass, which was said by Father Vimont.

The Iroquois were the scourge[1] of the infant church in the western world, as through their desultory warfare they practically cut off all communication between Quebec and the Huron missions. They were the scourge also of the French colony, destroying the trade in furs upon which the colonists expected to thrive; and agriculture was impossible in the presence of such savage and relentless foes. The colony[2] must fail, if its existence depended upon commercial or business success, but religion came to its aid, and what trade could not effect faith accomplished. The interest and zeal of the wealthy nobles and ladies of France were awakened in behalf of the missions of the New World, and as early as 1635 the liberality of these pious persons enabled the Jesuits to establish at Quebec an hospital for the sick, a seminary for Indian boys, and a convent for Indian girls, while the place was still a mere hamlet.[3] The "Society of Montreal" was composed of about forty zealous Catholics, and they were organized for the purpose of propagating the faith and founding a Catholic colony in New France. These institutions contributed greatly towards the conversion of the savages; for the charity displayed at the hospital was not soon forgotten, and the example and instruction given in the convents made a favorable and lasting impression upon the minds of the young Indians.

In April, 1644, as Father Bressani and some young Hurons, who had been at the seminary of Quebec, were on their way up the river to the Huron country, they were surprised by a band of Iroquois near the same place

[1] Relations, 1642. [2] Faillon, "Colonies Francaise." [3] Parkman, p. 178

where Father Jogues was captured two years before;[1] and they were hurried off to be tortured in the Iroquois country. At Saratoga Lake they met a large fishing party, and the prisoners were compelled to run the gauntlet between rows of these savages who beat them with clubs or stones, or hacked them with their rude knives. They were then placed on a platform, stripped of their clothing, and forced to sing and dance for the delectation of this savage throng; and whilst the blood flowed from their lacerated limbs the Iroquois applied new instruments of torture to make the dance of their captives more like their own wild orgies. The prisoners were taken through the different Mohawk villages, where they were subjected to many other indignities; but the life of Father Bressani was spared, and he was given to a family who sold him to the Dutch at Albany.

In the spring of 1645 the French released some of the Iroquois who had been prisoners at Quebec; and July 5, 1645, some of these former captives, with the celebrated chief Kiotsaeton as their leader, and bringing with them William Couture, who was captured with Father Jogues in 1642, arrived at Three Rivers to make a treaty of peace with the French and their Indian allies. The Governor came up from Quebec, and delegates were also sent to the proposed council by the Algonquins, the Montagnais, the Allikemegues, and the Hurons. These representatives of different nations and races assembled for the first time in their history to cement the bonds of friendship, and a most inspiring scene they presented. Sails were taken from the vessels in the river to make a tent; and poles were erected by the Iroquois, on which were hung the seventeen belts of wampum, representing the articles

---

[1] On the St. Lawrence near St Peter's Lake.

of their treaty and the wishes of their people. Father Lallemant, the Superior of the missions, was to represent the Church, but as he did not return from the Huron country, Father Vimont took his place.

The Governor and his suite, and the Jesuit Father, the representatives of European civilization, and the Church, took their places at one end of the awning-covered space, and the Indian allies of the French seated themselves in a circle; whilst the tall and graceful Iroquois chief most eloquently told the purport of his mission, and with song and dance manifested the joy of his people, and, with most appropriate gestures, portrayed their future friendly relations, or erased from their memory past hostile deeds, and sealed his sincerity with belts of wampum. The Governor afterwards spoke for the French and their Indian allies, and gave presents to the Iroquois as a sign of good will.

This council was only a preliminary step towards peace, as these proceedings should be sanctioned by larger representations from the different nations. They assembled, therefore, at Three Rivers, in September, to the number of 400, and watched the arrival of the Iroquois delegates, who were received with military honor; whilst their old enemies, the Hurons and Algonquins, looked on with feelings of hatred and distrust, yet, with admiration for their lithe and graceful forms and warlike bearing. The usual pledges were given at this council, and the missionaries rejoiced, perhaps more than any others, at the prospect of peace, as it meant for them greater security on their Huron missions, and the opening of a new and vast field for their zeal in spreading the Gospel. Father Lallemant says that it seemed to them more like a dream than reality; that after so many years of warfare they should not only have peace but a prospect of establishing a mission among these old enemies, which they intended to call the Mission of the Martyrs, on account of the many Christians already put to death by them, and because many more martyrs would probably be sent to heaven before this savage race could be converted to God.

The Governor resolved to send two representatives to the Mohawks[1] to manifest his good will towards his new friends; and as Father Jogues was present, and knew the Mohawk tongue, he very readily consented to go on this embassy, as he hoped to establish a mission there for the conversion of his former persecutors.

Father Jogues, with four Mohawks and two Algonquins, left Three Rivers, May 16, 1646, as an ambassador to the people who formerly held him as a slave. At Saratoga Lake they met a fishing party of Mohawks, and with them was Theresà, the Huron, who had been educated in the convent at Quebec, and who was captured by the Mohawks in 1642, while returning to her home with Father Jogues and his party. The holy missionary heard her confession and gave her his blessing; and the poor captive was overjoyed with this favor, as it was the only religious consolation she had received in this Pagan land.

Father Jogues went first to the Dutch settlement at Albany, and then proceeded to the first Mohawk village, Ossernonon, where a council was held and presents exchanged. The Father assembled the Christian captives, heard their confessions, and encouraged them to

[1] The route to the Mohawk country was along the St. Lawrence River to the Richelieu River, Lake Champlain and Lake George. On his second visit Father Jogues named Lake George, "Lake of the Blessed Sacrament," as he discovered it on the Feast of Corpus Christi; and this name it retained for a century.

fidelity to their faith. At this village he left a small box containing a few articles necessary for his proposed mission; and this box was the cause of much evil suspicion and distrust among these savages, who believed that it contained an evil spirit that would blight their corn and spread disease among the people.

CHAPTER VII.

THE FIRST MISSIONER TO THE IROQUOIS.

FATHER JOGUES GOES AS MISSIONER TO THE MOHAWKS—PREDICTS HIS DEATH—THE CORN CROP FAILS—THE MYSTERIOUS BOX—WAR PARTY CAPTURES JOGUES—CLANS DO NOT AGREE ON HIS FATE—TREACHEROUSLY SLAIN—THE MURDERER TAKES JOGUES' NAME IN BAPTISM.

FATHER Jogues was kindly treated on his mission to the Mohawks, and he believed that God had wrought a wonderful change in the hearts of these people. After having baptized some he returned to Three Rivers, where he remained until September 24, when he again, and for the last time, turned his steps towards the country of the Mohawks. In a letter to a friend in France he stated that his heart told him if he had the happiness of being selected for this mission he would never return; but he was pleased to think that the Lord would accept the sacrifice of his life where it had been nearly completed, in the days of his captivity.

He left Three Rivers in company with a young Frenchman, John De La Lande, and some Hurons, but all except one of the latter soon abandoned the missionary and returned to their homes. Nothing was heard at Three Rivers of Father Jogues or his mission until the following summer, when some Algonquin and Huron women, who had escaped from captivity among the Iroquois, circulated vague rumors of the death of the missionary and his companion. These rumors were verified by letters from the Governor of New Netherlands, which reached Montreal in June, 1647, giving many of the particulars of the death of this holy martyr.

The corn crop was a partial failure in the Mohawk country in the fall of 1646, and disease had ravaged the villages; and in the minds of those savages all those misfortunes arose from the presence of the mysterious box which Father Jogues had left in their land.[1] The box, therefore, was taken and cast into the river, as they hoped in this way to drown the evil spirit it contained. Of a treacherous nature themselves, they were easily induced to believe that the French were not sincere in their protestations of peace, and some of their young men were already on the war path when Father Jogues was on his way up the St. Lawrence to his new mission.

A party of Mohawks set out to attack the French at Fort Richelieu, but meeting Father Jogues and his companion within two days' journey of this place, they immediately seized them, stripped them of their clothing and valuables, and hurried them off to Ossernonon,[2] the first Mohawk village, where the missioner had already spent thirteen months in captivity.

In vain did Father Jogues plead that he and his companion came on a mission of mercy and love, as these savages only replied by blows; and whilst the chiefs were in council discussing their doom, some members of the Bear clan secretly resolved to put them to death.

On the evening of October 18, 1646, Father Jogues was called to sup in the cabin of one of the conspirators, and as he entered the door he was struck dead with a blow of a hatchet. His head was cut off and placed on a

[1] Martin, "Life of Jogues."
[2] At Auriesville, N. Y., where a shrine has been erected, and is visited every year by thousands of pilgrims.

pole outside the town with the face towards Three Rivers, whence he came; and thus passed away, says Parkman, "One of the purest examples of Roman Catholic virtue which the Western Continent has seen." The next evening Father Jogues' companion was slain, and both bodies were thrown into the river; and thus ended the first mission among the Iroquois, a mission appropriately callled, "The Mission of the Martyrs."

The Mohawk who killed Father Jogues was afterwards taken prisoner by the French, and was taken to Quebec where he was instructed and baptized, and the name of the holy martyr, Isaac Jogues, was given to him in baptism. He was given to some Algonquins, who put him to death, but he died not like a savage, but like his saintly namesake, with the holy name of Jesus on his lips.[1]

He was captured by a young Frenchman near Three Rivers, September 16, 1647, and was given by the Governor to the Algonquins of the mission of Sillery. Many of the friends of these Algonquins had been killed or made captives by Iroquois war parties, and as the Governor wished to make an example to terrify others, he handed the prisoner over to them, to be punished according to their custom. In the interval between his capture and death he related the circumstances attending the death of Father Jogues, and finally acknowledged that he was the murderer of the holy martyr.

Hostilities were renewed after the death of Father Jogues, and the roving bands of Iroquois warriors became the terror of every hunting, fishing, or trading party along the banks of the Ottawa and St. Lawrence rivers.

[1] Relations 1647, p. 74.

CHAPTER VIII.

WAR OF EXTERMINATION.

MISSIONERS AMONG THE HURONS—THEIR MANNER OF LIVING—TO ARMS, THE IROQUOIS COME—ATTACK ON ST. JOSEPH'S MISSION—HURONS FLY TO THE CHAPEL—CHRISTIAN HURONS LED CAPTIVE TO IROQUOIS COUNTRY—ST. IGNACE DESTROYED—SAVAGE SLAUGHTER—JESUIT MARTYRS—THE HURON NATION DISPERSED—IROQUOIS EXTERMINATE THE KAHQUAHS—FIDELITY OF HURON CAPTIVES.

MISSIONARIES had labored for nearly forty years among the Hurons, the Algonquins, and neighboring nations in the north of Canada, and along the shores of Georgian Bay, before the period of the Iroquois mission. In 1648 there were eighteen missionaries among the Hurons, four lay brothers, and some other Europeans who were interested in the fur trade. Deprived of all the comforts of civilized life, these missionaries devoted their lives to the enlightenment and evangelization of these poor, benighted barbarians; and their only regret seemed to be that they could not effect more good among them. "By night a bundle of faggots served them for a pillow, and their mantles formed their only covering. Their meals were taken on the ground, while reclining on mats of rushes or seated on billets of wood. The earth or their knees furnished a table, and leaves of Indian corn were their only napkins. Knives they had, but they were useless; for there was no bread to eat, and meat was so rare, that if by chance the Indians gave them a portion of their game, it was carefully laid aside and kept for Easter. Their ordinary food consisted of Indian sagamite or corn pounded between stones or in a wooden mortar, and boiled in water. Into this was thrown, to give it relish, some sweet majoram, purslain, or balm, and a kind of wild onion which they found in the woods. Their only drink was water from the brook, or the sap which they caught from the maple in their trough of bark. Wild grapes, bruised and pressed in a cloth over a bark vessel, furnished them wine for the mass or for medicinal purposes."[1] They rose at four o'clock in the morning and spent three hours in prayer, in meditation, and in celebrating mass. At eight o'clock they admitted the Indians to instruction, and afterwards they visited the cabins to instruct and baptize the sick. About five o'clock they closed the chapel and spent the evening in prayer and study, by the fitful light of pine or hemlock logs.[2]

On the morning of July 4, 1648, Father Anthony Daniel, who had charge of the Huron Mission of St. Joseph, had just finished mass, and his people were still engaged in their devotions when the alarm was given, and the cry "to arms" was heard.[3] The dreaded Iroquois had come. The greatest confusion followed, and the terror-stricken Hurons flocked around their spiritual Father for protection. The catechumens sought for baptism at the hands of the Jesuit, as a preparation for the certain death that awaited them. But the number was too large, and the danger too imminent to take them singly; so, dipping the handkerchief in water, he performed the rite upon the whole crowd by aspersion. Although the Hurons were brave warriors, yet they made no effort to

[1] Relations, translated by Marshall. [2] Parkman. [3] Relations.

defend their homes; the numbers of the enemy, the arguebuses with which they were armed, and the unexpected attack seeming to entirely dishearten them.

The Iroquois burned and pillaged the homes of the Hurons and killed indiscriminately men, women, and children, throwing many of them into the flames as a more convenient and cruel form of death.

Crowds hastened to the chapel where Father Daniels remained to console and encourage them. The enemy soon discovered this place of refuge, and with a wild whoop assembled to apply the torch to the chapel and the tomahawk to the defenseless Christians. Father Daniels was the first to fall, pierced with arrows, and his death made him the first Jesuit martyr of the Huron missions. Many escaped to neighboring villages; but about seven hundred were led captives to the Iroquois territory, and as many of these were well instructed converts, they constituted the first large body of Christians in the land of the Iroquois.

On the night of March 16, 1649, a well armed body of about two thousand Iroquois glided swiftly and noiselessly over the snow-covered ground to the Huron village of St. Ignace. Although the place was well situated for defense, and was fortified with palisades and a ditch, yet there were no sentinels or guards, and the Iroquois succeeded in effecting an entrance at the break of day, while the Hurons were wrapped in profound sleep.

Of the four hundred inhabitants of this village but three escaped. All the others fell victims to the tomahawk, the arrow or the flames, or were reserved for mere cruel tortures. The victorious Iroquois immediately hastened to the adjacent villages, where they continued their work of destruction, rapine, and slaughter.

Savage and cruel as they were by nature, yet they seemed to act more like demons than human beings in the tortures they inflicted upon the defenseless Hurons and the Jesuit missionaries. They would bind their victims to stakes driven in the earthen cabin floors, and applying any convenient combustible material to their feet and bodies would start the fire; and while the odor of burning flesh ascended with the flames they would dance in savage joy, and with the groans of the dying they would mingle their demoniac yells of fiendish glee. They plucked out the eyes of some and in the vacant sockets put living coals; they put necklaces of heated iron or stone hatchets around the necks of others, or cut off pieces of flesh, roasted and devoured them while the victims were still living. This diabolical frenzy continued for three days when the Iroquois became panic-stricken, and fled in confusion and disorder towards their homes, bearing with them much plunder and many captives.

Two of the celebrated Jesuit missionaries, Fathers Brebeuf and Lallemant, perished in this conflict, after enduring the most cruel torments. Shortly after, the Hurons, accompanied by the remaining Jesuits, abandoned their homes and bade farewell forever to their ancient domains. The lake which bears their name is the only remaining vestige of the once powerful and populous race that dwelt along its shores; and in its ceaseless ebb and flow, and storm-tossed waves is a fitting symbolic memorial of this turbulent tribe of Indians.

After the Iroquois' invasion they ceased to exist as a nation, and wandered away in different bands to seek a new home in the islands of the lake, or among some friendly nation. About 600 descended to Quebec with Father Ragueneau, and settled on the Island of Orleans, under the protection of the French.

The success of the Iroquois in their war with the Hurons emboldened them to attack their neighbors, the Kahquahs,[1] or Neuters; and so savage and persistent was the onslaught, that about the year 1651 they destroyed the entire nation, excepting some few who escaped, and some others whom they led in captivity to their own villages. They sent an army of 1,200 warriors to attack the frontier towns of the Neuters in the autumn of 1650, and they destroyed one of the large towns, where they massacred or mutilated the old, the infirm, and the infants, who would be of no use to them in their own land, and they led many captives across the border. The Neuters gathered all their warriors and transferred the scene of carnage to the land of the Iroquois. They succeeded in killing a large number of the Iroquois, probably near the Genesee River. The Iroquois patiently waited till spring, when their entire army of warriors crossed the border and made a savage attack upon the Neuter towns. They completely routed the Neuters, burned their town, and destroyed the entire nation. Many of the Neuters fled, like their Huron brethren, to the islands or bays of the west or south, to seek a new home among some friendly tribe, whilst many more meekly followed their captors to strengthen their army or replenish their numbers.

Some of the old Huron Christians had sought an asylum among the Neuters after the dispersion of their own people, and now that the arms of their friendly hosts

[1] Because they offered an asylum to the Hurons. General Clark maintains that the Kahquahs and the Neuters were not identical, and the former were an independent tribe, dwelling on the south shore of Lake Erie, westward of the Neuter towns. He has discovered the vestiges of the Neuter towns, east of the Niagara, and has located them in almost a direct line east of Lewiston. One was situated a little east of Lewiston, another in the center of the town of Cambria; the third, one mile west of Lockport; the fourth, two miles west of Shelby Centre, Orleans Co.

are bound as Iroquois captives, they, too, follow voluntarily, and beg to be admitted as members of some of the clans of their old enemies.

Some of the Fathers could see in this dispersion of the Christians the Providence of God, which thus paved the way for the propagation of the Gospel in the land of the Iroquois.

For many years the Hurons and other Christian captives were deprived of the sacraments and all spiritual ministrations of the missionaries; yet, the intelligent and zealous ones among them kept alive, by public prayers and exhortations, the spirit of faith and devotion. They assembled on Sundays in some friendly cabin, and listened to the rehearsal of the teachings of the Jesuits, from the lips of some able and eloquent chief.[1]

Many of the Iroquois were favorably disposed towards Christianity from what they had seen and experienced of the ceremonies and institutions of the Church at Quebec, and were not inclined to interfere with the devotions of their Huron slaves.

[1] Faillon, "Colonie Francaise."

CHAPTER IX.

EPISODES OF WAR.

IROQUOIS PLUNDER FRENCH—ALGONQUINS ATTACKED—SLAUGHTER OF PETUNS—FATHER GARNIER KILLED—CAPTURE OF FATHER PONCET—TORTURED BY MOHAWKS—RESTORED TO QUEBEC—MOHAWKS PROPOSE PEACE—ALGONQUIN TRADERS—NEW MISSION FIELD—FATHER GARREAU SLAIN—IROQUOIS REASON FOR PEACE—BRIGHT PROSPECTS.

ON the morning of March 16, 1647, all the French at Three Rivers went to the church, as it was Ash Wednesday, to begin, in a proper manner, the holy season of Lent. When they returned to their homes they discovered that the Iroquois had taken advantage of their absence, and carried off many of their fire-arms and furs.

This band of Iroquois learned that some Algonquins had left their homes to hunt for deer, and they immediately divided into two parties, and hastened to attack their old foes. One of these parties met the famous Algonquin Chief, Pieskaret, who had taken such a prominent part in the peace councils the preceding year, and as he was alone they found him an easy prey to their fury. They met other parties of Algonquin hunters, upon whom they wreaked their cruel vengeance, and they tortured, killed, or led them captives to their Mohawk homes. Some of the Algonquins escaped, and they brought news to the French of the death of Father Jogues.

Elated with the success which attended their slaughter of the Hurons, the Iroquois turned their conquering arms against other nations, and they had evidently resolved to subjugate all the Indians of America, or destroy their homes.

The Petun, or Tobacco Nation, was situated between the Hurons and the Neuters, and several large and prosperous missions were established among them by the Fathers from the Huron towns. After the destruction of their neighbors, the Hurons, the Petuns daily looked for a visitation from the dreaded Iroquois. There was one town of about 2,000 inhabitants, which the French called St. John's; and Father Charles Garnier had a little chapel here, and a goodly number of Christians, before their northern skies were lit by the flames of the fire-brands from the south.

Early in December, 1649, news came to St. John's that a band of about 300 Iroquois warriors was rapidly advancing to attack the town. The Petuns were brave warriors, and did not fear this small band of invaders, so instead of fortifying their town and waiting for the battle in a favorable location, they went boldly forth to meet the enemy.

Many years of warfare had taught the Iroquois to use all the strategies of successful generalship; and instead of following the direct path they circled round the town, and entered from the opposite direction, before the warriors of the place were aware of their presence.

The deeds of carnage and horror enacted in the Huron towns were repeated here. Taken at a disadvantage, the Petuns seemed to lose all courage; and they fell before the onslaught of the Iroquois like the ripened grain before the reaper's blows. Many hastened to the little chapel where Father Garnier gave them his blessing, and urged them to flee. They begged him to fly with them; but no, charity and the duties of his office compelled him to remain—to comfort the dying, to bury the dead. Whilst performing his deeds of mercy he was shot by an Iroquois, and his skull was afterwards crushed by the blow of a tomahawk.

Many of the inhabitants of St. John's escaped to the neighboring town where two Fathers were located, bringing the news of their loss. The Fathers hastened the next morning to St. John's, where they beheld a scene of sad desolation. The Iroquois had departed, leaving the charred embers of the cabins, and the burnt and mutilated bodies of their victims as evidence of their savage destruction.

The body of Father Garnier was found, and was buried beneath the ashes of the little chapel; and thus was added another holy Jesuit martyr to the number already slain by the Iroquois.

The Franch were obliged to carry to the harvest fields their fire-arms as well as their reapers and sickles, for the forests were infested with Iroquois, waiting to scalp the unwary; so the colonists went in well-armed bands to reap their grain.

Father Poncet, with Mathurin Franchetot, set out from Quebec to organize one of these little bands to assist a poor widow to gather her grain. Whilst they were looking for men to aid them in their work of charity, they were seized by the Iroquois, and were hurried off to the Mohawk towns, before the French could come to their rescue.

Father Poncet carried a little reliquary about his neck, in which was inclosed a slip of paper with the names of the Jesuits martyred by the Iroquois, with a note stating that he hoped his own name would soon be added to the list. He could easily believe that the martyr's crown was not far distant when he was compelled to run the gauntlet at the Mohawk town, whilst heavy blows fell upon his back and limbs. He was forced to sing for them; and he sang the Litany of the Blessed Virgin, and the *"Veni Creator."* He was stripped of most of his clothing, and was led to the cabin of his captor. Here a woman offered a belt of beads for one of his fingers. The price was accepted; and a knife was given to a little child, who cut off one of the fingers of his left hand. A red-hot ember was then applied to the stump, to sear the wound, and to stop the bleeding.

He was marched bare-headed and bare-footed to the next village where similar atrocities were perpetrated, as every one who met him struck him a blow, or applied a lighted ember or pipe to his flesh.

The ancients recommended that his life should be spared, as he was an important captive, so he was given to an old woman who had lost a brother in war. His companion, however, Mathurin, was taken to the third village, where he was burned at the stake.

Father Poncet was kindly treated after his first few days of torture, as orders evidently came from a Mohawk war party on the St. Lawrence to save his life, and to bring him back to Quebec. He was taken to Albany, where new clothes were purchased for him, and he was supplied with provisions[1] for his homeward journey.

About 500 Mohawk warriors lurked around Three Rivers for many days, hoping to surprise the inhabitants

---

[1] A kindly Scotch lady procured a surgeon to heal his wounds; and a Belgian Catholic merchant at Albany gave him a quantity of dried fish.

and destroy the town. Father Poncet was greatly beloved by the people of Quebec, and when the news of his capture spread through the town, a party of fifty or sixty well-armed and determined men was organized to rescue him from the hands of his captors. When the party reached Three Rivers the place was beseiged by the Mohawks; and, as these believed that the little army of French was a reinforcement for the town, they immediately sued for peace. The French replied that they would not listen to any terms of peace until the Mohawks had brought Father Poncet back to his home, so the Mohawks hastely sent a canoe load of their warriors for the Jesuit Father, and restored him to Quebec.

Although the Mohawks made overtures of peace, yet they continued to wage war upon the Indian allies of the French, and they did not scruple to scalp any unprotected Frenchman they met in the forest or on the river.

Many Indians came hundreds of miles to trade with the French; and often enterprising merchants, or daring explorers, returned with them to their own country, to promote the trade in furs, or to discover new lands. In the fall of 1655 two young Frenchmen returned with some Algonquins to their home in the far northwest, about 1,200 miles from Quebec, and they did not return till August of the following year, when about 250 Algonquins came with them, richly laden with furs. These young Frenchmen were zealous Christians, and they not only instructed and baptized some of the dying, but they also told the Indians about Christianity, and about the Jesuit missioners: so when they came again to Quebec they gave presents to invite the French to their country, and to request the Fathers to come to preach the Gospel.

The Revs. Leonard Garreau and Gabriel Dreuillettes

knew the Huron and Algonquin languages well, and with one lay brother, and three Frenchmen, they were selected for this distant mission.[1] Thirty Frenchmen also prepared to go, to promote the fur trade; and all departed amid great rejoicing, and the booming of cannon. Some distance up the river they met two soldiers in a canoe, who were sent from Three Rivers to warn them that the Mohawks were on the warpath. The thirty French merchants and explorers had no taste for Mohawk warfare, so they returned to Quebec.

Some of these Algonquins had never before handled fire-arms, and they were as pleased with their new weapon as a child would be with a toy pistol; and they kept firing their guns in the air to listen to the sound, although warned that they would attract the Mohawks by the noise. About 120 Mohawks were lying in ambush, and discovered the voyagers; but as the Algonquin party was so large they did not deem it prudent to openly attack them, so they hastened through the forest to a favorable position on the river, where they constructed a little breastwork, and awaited the enemy. Six canoes were a short distance in advance of the main body; and upon these the Monawks fired, mortally wounding Father Garreau. The Algonquins landed and pursued the enemy to their vantage ground, from which they could not dislodge them; so, after some parleying and strategy,[2] they hastened away, under the cover of night, leaving the French to their fate.

The Mohawks dragged Father Garreau to their little fort, stripped him of his clothing, and left him upon the ground for three days without food or drink. They then

[1] Relations, 1656.
[2] As night was near they agreed with the Mohawks upon a truce till morning.

FATHER GARREAU'S DEATH.

brought him to Montreal, where he died the day of his arrival, September 2, 1656.

Father Garreau was greatly beloved by the French, and his death was mourned as a public loss. He died with no feelings of resentment towards the Iroquois for their ill treatment, but rejoiced that he could die like his Master, stripped of his garments. His death added another bead to the rosary string of Jesuit martyrs.

The French fasted, and prayed, and made novenas, that they might be delivered from the Iroquois scourge. Bands of warriors from the different nations would come to sue for peace; but soon after would commit some hostile act, which showed that in these negotiations they were not sincere, or that they wished to secure immunity of attack from the French, or their neutrality in their wars with other Indians.

When the Mohawks restored Father Poncet they made the customary proposition of peace; but at midnight they aroused some of the Huron chiefs, offered them presents, and tried to induce them to leave the French and come to dwell in the land of the Mohawks. The Hurons did not dare refuse the presents offered, so they fearfully accepted them, as they believed that the Mohawks intended by this plan to weaken the French, or take the Hurons away from their protection, when they could more easily slaughter them.

The Onondagas also came early in 1654 to hold a parley of peace, but their chief object was to induce the Hurons, living near Quebec, to abandon the French, and to come to dwell at Onondaga. To conceal their design from the French, they advised the Hurons to say they wished to move to Montreal; and, when they reached this point, 400 or 500 Onondagas would be ready to cover their flight. The Onondagas advised the Hurons not to reveal these plans to the women or children, to more effectually hide them from the French. This scheme was proposed to a few Huron chiefs at midnight, and presents were exchanged, as had been done with the Mohawks on a similar occasion.

As the Hurons had killed a large number of Onondagas, and had burned a great Mohawk chief, they firmly believed that these people wished to lead them away to captivity, to torture, or to death. They placed the matter before the French, who advised them to temporize with the Iroquois, as they did not like to see the bright visions of peace so suddenly vanish. Another meeting was held, at which the Governor was present, and the Hurons gave two presents: First, to delay their going to the following year; second, to ask the Onondagas to build a Catholic chapel, and they would willingly go wherever the Fathers went.

Bright prospects of peace began to dawn on the French colony in the spring of 1654. The colonists could till their fields without fear of molestation, and the forest contained a great abundance of game. The great Erie-Iroquois war had already begun, and the French felt secure, because the arms of their old enemies would be employed in exterminating their powerful neighbors.

Another band of Onondagas came to Montreal in May, and they gave a large number of presents in the names of the Onondagas, the Oneidas, the Cayugas, and the Senecas. They gave one present as a pledge that they would burn the scaffolds upon which they tortured their prisoners; secondly, they asked for a priest; thirdly, they promised to respect him; finally, they wished to have their people taught the truths of the Master of Life[1]

Peace, at last, seemed to smile through the grim visage of war.

[1] Relations, 1654.

CHAPTER X.

PEACE.

ONONDAGAS AND ONEIDAS PROPOSE PEACE—SENECAS AND CAYUGAS FOLLOW—MOHAWKS SEND DEPUTIES—PRELIMINARIES—FRENCH AND FATHERS REJOICE—DOUBTFUL SINCERITY—IROQUOIS RENOUNCE CANNIBALISM—LE MOYNE VISITS THE IROQUOIS COUNTRY—HEARS CONFESSION OF HURONS—MANY CHRISTIANS—THE COUNCIL—ONONDAGAS ASK FOR MISSIONERS.

DIFFERENT parties of Iroquois made proposals of peace to the French, but, as they would not include the Indian allies of the latter in their treaty, friendly relations could not be established. The Onondagas and Oneidas, near neighbors, were the first to come with proposals of peace, and with presents as pledges of their sincerity.[1] They made speeches invoking the sun to dissipate the clouds that obscured the light of mutual understanding and friendship, and they offered their belts of wampum to wipe away the tears shed over those slain in war; to cheer the heart after past sorrows; to cover the slain, so that thoughts of their loss might not be an obstacle to peace; and to cleanse the waters of the river soiled with the blood of their victims.

The Senecas and the Cayugas also came pleading for peace, but the French would not conclude any treaty which did not include every one of the Five Nations, and also their own Indian allies. The Mohawks were still

[1] Relations, 1653.

hostile, but finally sent a deputation to Quebec; and as these warriors witnessed the procession in honor of the Nativity of the Blessed Virgin, in which 400 well armed, and well drilled, French soldiers took part, they realized that these soldiers would make formidable foes, and that it would be to their own interests to join in the proposals of peace which the other four nations were making. The French, however, as a preliminary step towards peace insisted on the restoration of Father Poncet, S. J., whom the Mohawks had captured in August, 1652. The Mohawks complied, and brought the missioner back to Quebec, in November, 1652. The entire French colony then rejoiced at the prospective peace and consequent prosperity which would ensue from the removal of the great shadow of death which hung over the colony from the beginning, blighting every hope of religious advancement or commercial success. The hostile Iroquois had destroyed or dispersed the infant churches among the Hurons and the Algonquins, and had prevented the Missionaries from carrying the light of the Gospel to the populous nations of the south and west; but through the prospective peace these zealous Fathers could see vast fields of abundant harvests awaiting the laborers of the Lord. The French authorities were willing to make sacrifices and take great risks in order to secure peace, but they had very grave reasons to doubt the sincerity of the Iroquois.

Father Poncet,[1] who had just returned from the Mohawk country, was fully convinced that these people were sincere; but the Hurons at the Island of Orleans firmly believed[2] that the Iroquois intended, under the cloak of peace, to induce themselves and some French to

---

[1] Relations, 1653.   [2] Relations, 1654.

THE IROQUOIS AND THE JESUITS. 65

emigrate to their country so they could more easily disarm and torture them, make them slaves, or put them to death. They asked for missionaries,[1] but they well knew that the Hurons were Catholics and would not leave their own homes unless priests accompanied them. One good effect produced by these preliminaries of peace was the offering by the Onondagas of a belt to the French in February, 1654, by which they pledged themselves to bury forever the caldron of war, in which they boiled human flesh[2] which they afterwards devoured. It was judged necessary to send an envoy or embassador, to the Iroquois country, and Father LeMoyne was selected for this delicate mission. He started, therefore, from Montreal July 17, 1654, in company with some Iroquois, the first messenger of peace to these savage people. The journey up the river was long and toilsome, wading at times waist deep in the water, and dragging their boats through the rapids and between the rocks, sleeping at night under trees or under their light canoes as a shelter from the rain, or carrying their boats and baggage over the portages on their shoulders. They had, however, the charming view of the virgin forest, and the enchanting scene of the Thousand Islands, inhabited by deer,[3] and other game, to relieve the monotony of their toil. They reached Lake Ontario the last day of July, and the next day they arrived at a fishing village where Le Moyne heard the confessions of some Hurons whose firm faith, preserved intact in their years of captivity, drew tears of joy from his eyes.

[1] Faillon.
[2] Relations, 1654. The Iroquois were cannibals only in war, or torturing an enemy; as then they devoured the flesh of their victims as a greater mark of cruelty, or to acquire their spirit of bravery.
[3] LeMoyne calls these wild cows, and they may have been buffaloes.

They proceeded overland towards Onondaga, and in every village[1] through which they passed the Christian Hurons gathered around the missioner to receive from him the blessing and the sacrament of which they had been deprived for years. On August 7 he baptized a young Neuter who had been instructed by Teresa, the Huron. LeMoyne rejoiced that he found himself in an already formed Christian community.[1] Some of the Iroquois had become Catholics, or at least, had learned from their Huron captives to practice Christian works of piety and devotion; as the latter told Father LeMoyne that many of them died with prayers on their lips, and invoking the name of Jesus.

On August 10, a council was held at the chief village,[2] about ten miles southeast of Lake Onondaga, on Indian Hill, two miles south of the village of Manlius,[3] at which all the Iroquois nations except the Mohawks were represented. Father Le Moyne opened the proceedings[4] by invoking God's blessing on their deliberations, beseeching Him to give wisdom to their councils, and understanding to the hearts of his hearers. He addressed them in the Huron language, which they understood, and in Indian style, giving a present with each proposition. First he offered a belt of green glass beads, the diamonds of the country, and a valuable robe as a pledge of the good will of the Governor. He gave them pledges of the release of eight Senecas, captives at Quebec, and also of the release of some Loup Indian prisoners, who were allies of the Iroquois. He assured them that the gates of the French cities were open to the

---

[1] These were little fishing hamlets.   [2] Relations, 1654.
[3] Gen. John S. Clark. Gen. Clark was the first to locate the Onondaga sites.
[4] Relations, 1654.

THE IROQUOIS AND THE JESUITS. 67

Iroquois, and that the missionaries desired to come and instruct them in the faith.

A celebrated Onondaga chief replied for all. In the first place, he desired to express his belief in the existence of the Master of Life, whom the French called God; and secondly, he insisted on the missionaries coming among them, to instruct them and be fathers to them, and they would be obedient children. They, moreover, agreed to send young girls as hostages to the sisters at Quebec, if a missionary would return in autumn and spend the winter with the Iroquois. LeMoyne believed that there were, at least, one thousand[1] Huron Christians in the Iroquois country who had not lost the faith, and this fact alone inspired the missionaries with the determination of going to that region and laboring for these souls, even at the risk of their lives. As a proof of his acceptance of the proposition of the Onondaga orator, LeMoyne selected a site,[2] and drove a stake in the ground as a corner stone for the future chapel.

Father LeMoyne started on his return to Quebec, August 15, satisfied that he had made some progress towards peace, and rejoicing at the prospect of the establishment of a new and promising mission. At this time all the Iroquois, except the Mohawks, were at war with the Eries; and, as the French could not rely on the specious promises of their newly-made friends, nothing more was done until the following year towards carrying out the provisions of peace, or the formation of the mission.

Whilst the Mohawks were negotiating for peace with the French, they continued their savage warfare upon all the Indians who came to trade at the French

[1] Relations, 1654.   [2] It was not on this site that St. Mary's was built.

towns. The French, however, were not in a position to resent these affronts, and they gladly fostered the friendly feeling manifested by these savage foes. Indian diplomatic etiquette required mutual visits from representatives of the nations negotiating peace; so the French felt obliged to observe this law, and to send a delegate to the Mohawks' towns. Father LeMoyne was selected for this important office, as he knew the language and was highly esteemed by the Iroquois.

Father LeMoyne, twelve Iroquois, and two French, left Montreal, August 17, 1655, on a friendly visit to the Mohawks. On the voyage they enjoyed pleasant weather, and suffered the inconvenience of storms; they paddled peacefully over smooth waters, and encountered rocks and falls; they met with abundance of game, and again were destitute of food, but nothing serious befell them, and they arrived safely at the first Mohawk village the middle of September. The priest was kindly received, and presents were exchanged, protesting sincerity and peace. Instead of beginning his address with a song, in Indian style, Father LeMoyne called upon God to witness the truth of his words, and to punish either party which would violate their solemn pledge. A Mohawk chief gave a beautiful belt of 6,000 beads of porcelain, arranged to represent the sun, and he called upon this heavenly orb to shed its light upon their deeds, and to reveal their inmost thoughts to the French, because there was no guile in their hearts. LeMoyne believed they were treacherous, yet he placed his life in their hands, in the hope of promoting peace and propagating the Gospel.

After the council the Father started for the Dutch settlement at Albany; and on the way he met an old

Huron Christian, who was very much delighted with his visit, as she had a child to be baptized. LeMoyne returned again to the Mohawks after his visit to the Dutch; and this time he had a slight taste of the poisonous fruits of peace they might expect from the Mohawks. A crazy Mohawk ran about the cabins, shouting that he must kill Ondesonk;[1] and he would undoubtedly have brained the Father with his tomahawk had not a woman offered her dog as a substitute victim to his fury.

The home journey was made with great difficulty, as the winter season had begun, and the danger of encountering war parties on the water routes forced them to follow unbeaten paths through the woods. To add to their discomfort they lost the trail in the forest; and they wandered about for many days, cold and hungry, before they found the path to Montreal.

[1] Indian name of the Father.

CHAPTER XI.

MISSIONS BEGUN.

CHAUMONOT AND DOBLON, MISSIONERS TO THE IROQUOIS—FANTASTIC FAITH IN DREAMS—CHAUMONOT MEETS OLD FRIENDS—WARM WELCOME—PUBLIC MEETING—CHAUMONOT'S ELOQUENCE—FATHERS BEGIN TO TEACH—FIRST CHURCH IN NEW YORK STATE—FRENCH COLONY AT ONONDAGA—SITE FOR NEW CHAPEL—PROGRESS—GOSPEL ANNOUNCED TO THE CAYUGAS — CHAPEL BUILT — OPPOSITION — MESNARD WITHDRAWS—CHAUMONOT BEARS THE GOSPEL TO THE SENECAS—MANY HURON CHRISTIANS IN SENECA COUNTRY—CHAUMONOT AND MESNARD VISIT THE ONEIDAS—COUNCIL HELD—THE MOHAWKS ATTACK CHRISTIAN HURONS—LE MOYNE VISITS MOHAWKS—SUCCESS AT ONONDAGA—DANGER—WERE THE IROQUOIS SINCERE?—TREACHERY—SECRET COUNCIL RESOLVED TO MASSACRE FRENCH—PREPARING FOR FLIGHT—BANQUETING THE ENEMY—FLIGHT OF THE FRENCH—RESULT OF THE FIRST MISSION.

IN September, 1655, a delegation o. Onondagas, representing also the Oneidas, the Cayugas, and the Senecas came to Quebec to induce the French to put in operation the proposals agreed on the preceding year. They offered, in the first place, presents to the Algonquins and Hurons to allay any suspicions which these ancient enemies might entertain of their sincerity, or of their evil designs. Then they requested the French to establish a colony among them, so they might learn the customs of the French and become one people. They wanted the Fathers to come to instruct them, so they might become a Christian people; and they also wished to have a chapel erected at Onondaga, which would be a central mission for the entire country. The French agreed to send two missionaries to begin the work, and Fathers Joseph Chaumonot and Claude Dablon were selected; the former on account of his experience and knowledge of the language, and the latter for his zeal, as he had just arrived from France and this would be his first work on these wild and hazardous missions. They prepared immediately for their mission, and left Quebec on September 19, 1655; but waited at Montreal until October 7, when they set out in company with some Iroquois and Hurons. They made slow progress up the river, as their provisions gave out, and they were obliged to wait for the hunting and fishing parties to supply them with food. They met a party of Seneca hunters, who told them that their nation would soon send an embassy to Quebec to ask for missionaries.[1]

The missionaries had a very strange experience[2] of Indian life and belief on the night of October 18. They were awakened at midnight by the screams and wild yells of an Iroquois of their party who was in great agony, and was suffering from violent convulsions. They ran to his assistance, but he escaped and threw himself into the river. They dragged him out, and placed him near the fire; but he again broke away, and said he must climb a tree to get warm. He told them to give the medicine they had prepared for him to a bear skin, and they were obliged to do as he ordered them. Then he told them he dreamed that a certain animal which plunges in the

[1] A party of ten Senecas came in January, 1656, and the richest present they gave was a request for the Fathers to preach the Gospel in their land. The chief of this party was killed by the Mohawks.
[2] Relations 1655.

water got into his stomach, and he imitated the animal to get rid of it. Then commenced a most curious scene. Every one of the score of Indians began to shout and jump about, beating his stomach to kill the animal, imitating its cry, or yelling to frighten it away; but all acted as seriously as if the whole affair were a reality and not a fantastic dream. The solemn hour of midnight, and the wild forest surroundings added a sombre hue to the ludicrous scene; and these Indians looked and acted like demons revelling in their midnight orgies. The cause of all this commotion fortunately soon felt relieved of the presence of the animal through the efforts of his companions, and allowed the others to rest after their successful yet exhausting labors.

The party suffered some from the insufficient supply of food; but the hunters were successful in killing a great number of bears, and at the Thousand Islands they encountered a number of deer and wild cows[1] which furnished abundance of provisions. They met a fishing party at Oswego River, who received them with great manifestations of joy; and the Huron Christians flung themselves on the neck of Father Chaumonot, whom they had known in their own land, and profited by the presence of the Fathers to receive the sacrament of penance. They[2] were kindly welcomed by all parties, and especially by the Christian Hurons, some of them coming many leagues to again behold their loved Black Robes, and receive from them the consolations of religion. On November 5, they met a chief who escorted them to a place a short distance from Onondaga where the Ancients awaited their arrival. A banquet was prepared, and an aged chief welcomed them in the name of the

[1] Buffalos, probably. [2] Clark, Onondaga.

four nations, the Mohawks still remaining obstinate; but he said they would resent. They then proceeded between files of Indians to Onondaga where the streets were very clean, and the roofs of the cabins were covered with women and children to receive the strange guests with shouts of welcome. In the evening a council was held, at which presents were exchanged, and the missionaries were formally welcomed. Teatonharason, an eminent Indian woman of the nation, who had dwelt some time at Quebec, offered her cabin as a chapel until the Onondagas could fulfill their promise of erecting a large mission house and chapel for the Fathers. The Cayuga deputies came on Sunday,[1] November 14, and the next day a meeting was held in a public place where all could attend. Father Chaumonot opened the proceedings with prayer, and delivered a very impressive address in the Huron language, and in Indian style, walking back and forth as he spoke, and giving a present[2] with each proposition as a pledge of faith. The Father occupied over two hours in delivering the address, which was the first able presentation of Christianity to the Iroquois, and these Indians listened with attention, and were charmed with his eloquence. The Iroquois commenced their reply by singing songs of welcome to the French, whom they invited to remain and instruct the people in the faith, giving them full liberty to enter their villages and their homes, or wheresoever duty called them. A Cayuga chief also made a speech of welcome, and gave

[1] The Fathers said mass early in the morning, and this was probably the first time that mass was said in the State of New York.

[2] The wampum belt given that day by Chaumonot, as a pledge that he would preach the Gospel to them, was highly prized by the Iroquois, and is still preserved among the treasures of the League. Shea, p. 250. Gen. Clark gave Shea a photographic copy of the belt. See, also, Powell "Report of Bureau of Ethnology," p. 225.

a present signifying his desire to have the Gospel announced to his people.

Iroquois Song of Welcome.

I.

O blessed land, O blessed land,
In which the French will dwell.

II.

O joyful tidings, joyful tidings:
This is good, my brother;
'Tis well to hear the word of heaven.

III.

I salute thee, brother.
My brother, thou art welcome;
   Ai, ai, ai, hi:
O, sweet voice, thy voice is sweet;
   Ai, ai, ai, hi;
O, sweet voice, thy voice is sweet;
   Ai, ai, ai, hi.

IV.

My brother, I salute thee.
Once again I salute thee:
Heartily I receive the Heaven thou teachest;
Yes, I agree, I accept it.

V.

Adieu to war; adieu to hatchet;
Until now we were foolish.
Henceforth we will be brothers;
Yes, we will be brothers true.

VI.

Now great peace is made,
Adieu to war, adieu to arms;
Blessed is the whole transaction,
Thou adorn'st our cabins with thy presence.

On Sunday, November 24, the Fathers commenced giving regular catechetical instructions, which were very well attended by an attentive and orderly multitude of Indians, who were also very civil and polite in every day life, so much so that they no longer seemed to be the savages they really were. Although these Fathers did not formally come as missionaries, or preachers of the Gospel, but as ambassadors from the French to test the sincerity of the Iroquois in seeking peace, and to learn their disposition towards Christianity; yet they did a vast amount of good, baptizing[1] over four hundred in a short time, and they paved the way for the success of future missions.

The Fathers had constructed a little bark chapel,[2] with the assistance of the Indians, and this first house of worship erected in the State of New York,[3] and dedicated to the service of God, was named St. John the Baptist, and the whole country was placed under the protection of the same saint. In the following spring the Iroquois again insisted on the fulfillment on the part of the French of the agreement to establish a colony at Onondaga, so Father Dablon started for Quebec to induce the Governor to carry out this condition of peace.

The French feared to establish this colony, as they realized they would be placing their lives in the hands of the treacherous Iroquois; yet they knew also that these revengeful people would declare war against them if they did not fulfill their promise. The Jesuits[4] were very willing to go, as they were ready at any time to sacrifice their lives in the cause of their Divine Master; and they said they could baptize more Iroquois before the probable massacre than the number of French colonists, and this would only be exchanging perishable bodies for immortal souls.

The Revs. René Mesnard, Claude Dablon, James Fremin, and Francis LeMercier,[5] with two lay brothers,

---

[1] Clark, "Onondaga."
[2] Shea, "Church in Colonial Days."
[3] This was about twelve miles from the lake, two miles south of the present village of Manlius. Clark, in Hawley's "Early Chapters," p. 23.
[4] Relations, 1657.
[5] These early missionaries had faculties from the Archbishop of Rouen. Shea. LeMercier was superior, and not Dablon as Shea states.

prepared immediately for this perilous mission; while fifty Frenchmen under the lead of Depuis, commander at Quebec, volunteered to establish the new colony. The little flotilla started from Quebec May 16, 1656, bearing aloft a white banner on which was inscribed the word "Jesus"; and accompanied by Onondagas, Senecas, and some Hurons they sailed up the river, while the people lined the shore and cheered them on, amid many sobs and sighs of regret, as they looked upon them as certain victims of Iroquois treachery. They left Montreal June 8; and after much suffering they reached Lake Onondaga on July 11, and moved over the waters in naval array, firing their five cannon and their arquebuses, forming a most impressive sight in the midst of the Indian wilderness. The next day they sang mass[1] and Te Deum, and took possession of the country in the name of Jesus Christ. The site[2] selected by them was on the north shore of the lake,[3] about midway between either extremity, and near two springs,[4] one of salt and the other of fresh water. They afterwards proceeded to Onondaga, the capital, where they were received with such hearty welcome that Le Jeune says: "If the Iroquois should kill the French colonists I could not accuse them of treachery, but of inconstancy, so sincere seemed their manifestations of joy."

Delegates from the Five Nations assembled at Onondaga to hold an important council of war, and to discuss matters pertaining to the French colony. This gave the

[1] This was the first time mass was sung in the state.
[2] Clark, "Onondaga."
[3] The French evidently claimed title to the country by right of occupation, as Gov. DeLauzon, in 1656, made a grant to the Jesuits of a vast tract of land, ten square leagues, running eastward from the lake. See manuscript copy of grant in St. Mary's College, Montreal.
[4] Great numbers of pigeons came to the salt springs every year, and many rattlesnakes were seen on the hillsides and around the lake.

Fathers an excellent opportunity of announcing the Gospel. The council opened July 24, and the French knelt and sang the "Veni Creator." Father Chaumonot then began his celebrated address by expressions of grief for the loss of so many slain in war; then he gave presents to cement the bonds of peace between the Iroquois and the Hurons and Algonquins; and he gave presents to express the gratitude of the French for the kindly hospitality extended to them by their hosts. Then he eloquently proclaimed the object of their mission: they came not to seek wealth, or to barter for furs, but to enlighten the minds of the Iroquois, and to save their souls. The Fathers left their pleasant homes to dwell in bark cabins; they abandoned wholesome food for Indian fare, and they exposed their lives in frail canoes, on a perilous journey, to preach the Gospel. The Iroquois had promised to open their hearts to the influences of faith. Now is the time. Behold, he preaches it. Then he told them of the creation of the world, of the Incarnation, and of Heaven and Hell, as the reward or punishment for good or evil deeds. The Redeemer had commanded His apostles to bring His word to every nation and tribe in the world. This was their mission, and the Iroquois would be condemned unless they believed.

  The Iroquois were charmed with the Father's eloquence, and gave very enthusiastic expressions of approval.

  At dawn the next day the Iroquois again assembled, and an eminent chief repeated the principal points of the Father's discourse of the preceding day; and he gave a present to signify his desire to become a Christian.

  After many banquets and much rejoicing the French

returned to Ganentaa to build their mission house and chapel.

The work of evangelizing the Iroquois must necessarily encounter opposition from a people who had never learned to appreciate the beauty and importance of the spiritual and supernatural life. The chief enemies of the Gospel were the Pagan Hurons, who said that misfortunes came to their nation along with the French and the faith; but the courage and devotion of the Fathers, visiting the sick at all hours, instructing the ignorant, consoling the dying, without any hope of visible reward, soon gained the confidence and admiration of the Indians, and many chiefs and ancients were to be found among their disciples.

As the missionaries had adopted the Oneidas and Cayugas as their children, it was necessary to seal this union by personal visitation and presents, which would give them an opportunity of announcing the faith. At the request[1] of the nation Fathers Chaumonot and Mesnard started for the Cayuga[2] country, where they were the guests of Saonchiogwa, the chief who had replied to Chaumonot at the council the previous year. They were coldly received at first on account of the prejudices of the Pagan Hurons;[3] but as the chiefs concluded that their temporal interests were involved in the peace with the French, they resolved to allow the missionaries to announce the Gospel, at least, to their captives and slaves.

The Fathers, however, soon won the hearts of these people, and in four days they began to erect the chapel: and so many and such willing hands were employed in the work that in two days the building was completed, carpeted with pretty mats, and adorned with pictures of Our Lord and of the Blessed Virgin.

[1] Hawley, "Early Chapters.' [2] For location of village see page 16.
[3] Mesnard, "Relations," 1657.

FATHER MESNARD'S RETURN.

Father Mesnard did not understand the language of the country, which was a great obstacle to successful work, yet the Indians came in great crowds to behold the pictures; and they kept the good Father busy striving to explain their meaning, and the great mysteries of faith with which they are associated. Parents soon brought their children to have them baptized, and the larger children, who at first feared and shunned the missioner, soon learned to love him; and they told him the names, and conducted him to the cabins, of the sick. He encountered much opposition through misrepresentations of his office and his power, which were industriously circulated by the Pagan Hurons, and the Dutch at Albany, who were displeased at the ascendancy of French influence over the Iroquois.

After two months of labor and danger Father Mesnard was called to Onondaga, but the Cayugas immediately sent a delegation beseeching him to return. He complied with their request and was received with great joy, and the people manifested their gratitude by greater willingness to have the children and the sick receive baptism, and by a larger attendance at instructions.

When Father Chaumonot left[1] Mesnard at Cayuga, he proceeded with a young Frenchman[2] along the Indian trail to the Seneca towns. The Seneca country was more fertile than the territory of the other Iroquois nations, and the inhabitants were very numerous, comprising nearly half the population of the entire league. At this time there were two large villages and many smaller ones. One of these villages was composed entirely of Hurons, a majority of them being Christians, and was christened

[1] Relations, 1657.
[2] This was David LeMoyne, who died near Lake Cayuga on his return from the Senecas.

by Chaumonot, St. Michael's.[1] The missioner assembled the ancients of the principal village, Gannagaro,[2] and eloquently addressed them on the Christian religion, and proffered three beautiful presents as pledges of his sincerity and the truth of his words. He told them that neither he nor his companions would leave the comforts and luxuries of their own beautiful land, and would come so far, and endure the hardships of Indian life, to teach falsehood. According to their custom they held a council, at which they decided to accept his teaching, and requested him to remain and instruct them. He also visited the other villages where he instructed and baptized some; but it was at the Huron village of St. Michael that he met with a warm welcome, and found consolation in the lives of the Christians who remained faithful to the teachings of the missionaries during all the years of their captivity. Notwithstanding the bad example of the Pagans that surrounded them, they hastened to the missioner to get absolution for themselves and baptism for their children.

Although the field seemed inviting and the prospects bright of introducing Christianity among the Senecas, yet the Fathers were too few to supply permanent missioners to the different villages; and as each of the four nations had formally invited them, they could not postpone, at least, a first visit without offense, so Chaumonot was obliged to leave the Seneca country to hasten to the Oneidas.

He had labored about two months among the Senecas and the Huron Christians on this first visit, baptizing many children and some adults;[3] and on his return to

---

[1] In honor and memory of the Huron Mission of the same name.   [2] See page 18.
[3] The great chief, Annonkentitaoui, was afflicted with a cancer, but he was cured by Father Chaumonot, and was baptized and became a zealous Christian.

THE JOURNEY TO THE ONEIDAS.

Cayuga he took Father Mesnard from his little chapel on the banks of Lake Tiehero[1] to accompany him on his visit to the Oneida territory.

The journey to the Oneidas was not undertaken without some misgivings on the part of the Onondaga chiefs, who feared that these people might prove treacherous to their French guests, and they tried to dissuade the missioners from visiting these people at that time, as one of the Oneida warriors had killed a Huron at Three Rivers, and he threatened to treat the French ambassadors in the same manner. The Fathers, however, were not to be deterred by so slight a danger, and in company with two Frenchmen, and some Onondagas, they set out for their new mission.

The first night of the journey was spent in the forest, and an Onondaga chief complimented the missioners on their courage and patient suffering of the hardships of the journey, traveling over ice and snow, and through water; but he told them to be of good heart, as they could find abundant consolation in the importance of their mission. Then he called on the manitous of the place to protect them from harm, and he addressed the great and ancient trees of the forest; and besought them not to fall and envelope in their own ruins those who had come to prevent the ruin of the land.

The Feast of Dreams was being celebrated when the missioners arrived at the Oneida town, but the orgies soon ceased, and the visitors were kindly received. The old Huron Christian captives joyfully welcomed the Fathers; and the Oneidas, too, sang their songs of welcome, as they were not unmindful of the difficult journey the Fathers had undertaken to visit their children. On

[1] Lake Cayuga.

the second day a council was held, presents were exchanged, and the Oneidas were formally adopted as children of Onontio;[1] and belts were given by the Fathers as pledges that they would preach the Gospel to them. The Fathers also took this opportunity to explain the most important teachings of Christianity, and exhorted the Oneidas to receive the beautiful light of the Gospel which would enlighten their minds. They instructed two old men, and baptized them and some sick children; but the Onondagas urged the missioners to return, as they feared the Oneidas might prove treacherous and carry out the threat the young warrior had made.

The Mohawks were under the influence of the Dutch at Albany, and had strenuously opposed the proposals of peace made by the other four Iroquois nations to the French; and they continued their desultory warfare on the Hurons, even killing some Senecas who had come to Quebec with peace presents for the Governor.[2]

Early in May, 1656, three hundred Mohawk warriors descended the river St. Lawrence in their canoes, exchanged presents and friendly greetings with the French at Three Rivers; and, through the intervention of Father LeMoyne, they promised to return peacefully to their own country. They dispersed in small bands on seemingly peaceful pursuits, but in reality to reunite at Quebec to attack the Huron Christians at the Isle of Orleans. On the night of May 19, 1656, about forty canoes of Mohawk warriors glided noiselessly over the waters near the Huron settlement, and hiding their boats along the shore, and concealing themselves in the forest, they waited the coming of day to attack by surprise their unsuspecting

[1] Indian name for the Governor of New France.
[2] Relations, 1657.

Huron foes. The Hurons attended mass, as usual, on the morning of May 20th, and were returning to their homes, or to their different avocations, when suddenly the shrill war-whoop of the Mohawks was heard; and before the Hurons had time to prepare for defence many of them were slain, and a number of others were led captives to the homes of the Iroquois. Many of the prisoners were burned at the stake, and some of the better instructed Christians among them ended their lives in a manner worthy of the early Christian martyrs; as instead of the usual death song, recounting their great deeds of valor, they sang the praises of God, the instability of life, and the happiness of Heaven as the reward for fidelity in this world.

The Hurons sued for peace after this sudden attack by their old enemies; but the Mohawks would only accede to their request on condition that the Hurons would leave their homes at the Isle and migrate to the land of the Mohawks. The Onondagas had also urged the Hurons to dwell with them, and the latter feared to offend either nation; so at a council they decided to divide into three bands, or clans: one to go to the Mohawks, another to the Onondagas, and a third to remain with the French. LeMoyne, who acted as negotiator of this peace, asked for delay until the following year, as he hoped in the meantime to visit the Mohawk towns, and prepare the way for the coming of his Huron friends.

Father LeMoyne[1] had visited the Mohawks in 1655, and had promised to return the following year; but, after the slaughter of the Hurons at the Isle of Orleans, and the killing of one of his brother Jesuits by the Mo-

---

[1] Father LeMoyne visited the Dutch at Albany and told them of the salt springs at Onondaga; but these steady going burghers were not to be deceived by such strange stories, and they said this was a Jesuit lie.

hawks, he hesitated in undertaking the journey. As the Indians, however, consider the breaking of a promise a breach of peace, and a sufficient cause for hostility, he was willing to risk his life to gain the friendship of these people. He, therefore, visited their country, and was kindly received by them; and, after exchanging the usual presents, he visited the Huron Christains, heard their confessions, baptized their children, and admonished them to be firm in their faith.

The Mohawks had made efforts to bring the Hurons from the Isle of Orleans to the Mohawk country, and, in exchanging presents, Father LeMoyne gave a belt as a pledge of the willingness of the Governor to allow the Hurons to depart. As the Hurons had not received from the French the protection they expected, they readily consented to migrate to the Mohawk country, and become members of the Iroquois League. In the spring, therefore, of 1657, when another party of Mohawks came, a large party of Hurons returned with them, and some more followed shortly after with Father LeMoyne. As all of these Hurons were Christians, the Mohawks asked for a priest to accompany this emigrant band, and to teach the Mohawks also the faith which the Hurons loved so well. Father LeMoyne promised to follow as soon as his Superior would give his consent; but, as the Mohawks had been the most savage and unrelenting foes among the Five Nations of the French and Hurons, he did not think he could safely open a mission among these people.

The Onondagas had also made overtures to the Hurons to become members of their nation; and they were so incensed at the exodus of the small band for the Mohawk country that they immediately set out for Quebec to force the remnant at the Isle to join their nation.

As, at this time, there was a call for more laborers in the mission-fields among the Iroquois; and as the spirit of peace seemed to have settled in the land, two more Jesuits, Fathers Ragueneau, and Duperon, resolved to accompany the band of Hurons to Onondaga. The Onondagas were waiting at Montreal to escort the Hurons up the river, but they refused to admit the Fathers into their canoes. This boded ill for the Hurons; and it was the first intimation of any hostile feeling on the part of the Iroquois. The Fathers, however, followed in another canoe, and no further trouble arose until they reached the Thousand Islands, when the Onondagas made a sudden attack upon their new friends, and killed seven of them. News of this slaughter was brought to the French, and it was then they realized the danger of the little colony at Onondaga; as it was evident the Iroquois, under the cloak of peace, intended to wreak their wrath upon their old enemies.

There was a well-grounded belief that the Iroquois intended at this time to massacre the French colony at Onondaga; but all the Hurons had, fortunately, not left their home near Quebec, and these found a pretext to detain the large band of Onondagas near the forts of the French until the following spring. This ruse averted, for a time, the impending calamity.

In October, a party of Oneidas killed three Frenchmen near Montreal, and this would, probably, have been the signal for a general massacre had the Governor not promptly cast into prison all the Iroquois within reach, and held them as hostages for the safety of the colonists at Onondaga. This decisive action effectually checked further hostilities, and the Governor immediately dispatched messengers to Father LeMoyne and to Onondaga, to warn them of danger; but the Fathers were not prepared to leave, and they labored on, hoping that their missions might be saved.

The missionaries met with success in all the villages in which they labored; but, it was at Onondaga, where two of the Fathers were incessantly employed, that the best results of their work were visible as here: "The divine office is recited, the sacraments are administered, and Christian virtues are practised with as much modesty, care, and fervor, as they are in the most Catholic and devout provinces of Europe."[1] More than two hundred were baptized in a short time, and of this number five were the most prominent personages of the village. "Most of the children learn the catechism, most of the dying become Christians, and all receive us joyfully in their cabins."[2]

The frequent visits which the Iroquois made to Quebec, where they witnessed the beautiful ceremonies of the Church, or were made the recipients of the kindness and charity of the nuns at the hospital, when they were sick, favorably impressed these Indians, and kindly disposed them towards the French and their religion. The bright example of the Christian Hurons—coming seventy or eighty miles to renew their fervor by hearing the word of God and receiving the sacraments—had also its influence in turning the thoughts of the iroquois to the teachings of Christianity. They were also quick to perceive that the missioners did not seek any temporal gain in preaching the Gospel, but sacrificed the luxury of pleasant homes in France to expose themselves to hardship, to danger, and death on these Indian missions.

The mission to the Iroquois was considered the most

[1] Relations, 1657.   [2] Ibid.

dangerous, but also the most glorious and important of all the fields of labor of the Jesuits in New France. The Neros and the Diocletians never invented more cruel tortures for the early Christians than those which these savages inflicted upon some of the Jesuit Fathers; yet others were ever ready to take the places of the martyred missionaries, never doubting that God, who made most illustrious apostles out of the most bitter persecutors of his Church, would some day make docile deciples out of these barbarous foes.[1]

Many of the Fathers believed that the Iroquois had sinster designs in asking the French and Hurons to dwell among them, as these would materially aid them in their wars; and as soon as the Iroquois would be victorious over their enemies, and successful in their war with the Eries, they could destroy the Hurons and French.

Others[2] claim that the Iroquois were sincere at first, but that they changed their minds when they found that the French were a burden to them. They were obliged to support the colonists, as the French at Quebec were too poor to offer any assistance, and the colonists themselves, were unable to raise corn and provisions for their own support, but relied upon the charity of their Indian neighbors, who soon grew tired of the task and resolved to rid the country of these helpless guests.

There are many reasons for believing that the Iroquois had peaceful but selfish motives in bringing the French and Hurons to their country. For three years the four upper nations of the Iroquois had labored to bring the French and Hurons to dwell among them. It is true the Mohawks continually opposed their com-

[1] Letter of LeMercier to superior in France June 6, 1656.   [2] Charlevoix.

ing, yet they may have been actuated by jealousy, or were influenced by the Dutch[1] at Albany. The ancients and chiefs desired these colonists, because the Hurons increased the number of their warriors, and the French would furnish them with fire-arms and make iron implements of war, and the latter would also teach them how to build strong forts to protect them against the attack of their enemies, and which would be a place of refuge for the women and children when the warriors were away on the war-path or the hunt. The common people were also desirous of having the French dwell among them, as they hoped to reap some profit from their presence by the receipt of the little gifts which were so highly prized; and they could also learn some of the arts of European life. The Huron Christian captives stimulated, no doubt, this desire of seeing the French by their favorable report of the missioners, whom they loved, and of the Christian religion, to which they were so firmly attached.

The Fathers had noticed that many of the Iroquois acted in an unfriendly manner towards them, but thought that this might be the effect of individual hate until an event occurred which served to show them how insecure were their lives. One clan of the Hurons at the Isle of Orleans had resolved to cast their lot with the Onondagas, and in company with Fathers Ragueneau and DuPerron,[2] they left Quebec in July, 1658, for their new home, which many of them never reached except as slaves, for their Onondaga guides proved treacherous,

---

[1] The English took New York in 1664, but the Dutch recaptured it in 1673, and the next year it again fell into England's power.

[2] The Iroquois refused to take the Fathers in their canoes, and they were obliged to follow in another boat; and this objection to the presence of the Fathers boded ill for the Hurons.

A SECRET COUNCIL HELD BY THE IROQUOIS. 89

and on August 2d, killed some of the Huron emigrants on an island near the entrance to Lake Ontario, and led the others captives to their cantons. On hearing of this massacre the Governor caused all the Iroquois at Quebec, Montreal, and Three Rivers, to be arrested and held as hostages for the safety of the French colony at Onondaga. Shortly afterwards three French were killed by some Oneidas near Montreal; and the Iroquois were only restrained from further acts of hostility by the prompt action of the Governor, who held the Iroquois hostages responsible for the deeds of their countrymen.

Father Ragueneau,[1] however, thinks that the Iroquois induced the French and Hurons to leave Quebec and locate in their villages so they might put them to death when their victims would be helpless; for, although greatly superior in numbers, the Iroquois feared the military superiority and the cannon of the French.

A secret council was held by the Iroquois in February, 1658, at which they resolved to kill all the French in the country; but, fortunately for the colony, they decided to await the return of their young warriors[2] from Quebec, where they were detained as hostages by the Governor on account of the murder of the Huron party the preceding year. One Iroquois chief, who had been converted and baptized, told the French of the decision of the Council, and they made immediate preparations for flight. Their carpenters began secretly to build two large flat-bottom boats and four canoes in the loft of their houses; while the Fathers and the colonists were occupied in their daily avocations, as if they had no thought of impending evil. When all things were in readiness,

[1] Relations, 1657.
[2] They expected Father LeMoyne would secure the release of these warriors, on his return from the Mohawk country.

they adopted a novel and successful scheme to effect their escape without detection.

A young Frenchman who had been adopted by one of the Onondaga chiefs, told his host he dreamt he would soon die unless he gave a great banquet—one in which all the food must necessarily be eaten—to the warriors of the nation. As this chief firmly believed in the sacred obligation of fulfilling dreams he readily consented to the project; and the warriors were perfectly willing to gorge themselves with food to save a life. A great supply of provisions was gathered for the feast. The colonists gave their pigs and all they could spare from their slender store, as they hoped by treating their guests sumptuously, and by their happy mood, to allay any suspicion of comtemplated flight. When the guests were pretty well gorged with food they were induced to shout, sing, and dance, with all their might; and this gave some of the colonists, who had silently stolen away from the banquet hall, an opportunity to launch and load their boats, and prepare for flight. A few of the French kept up the riot until their guests became wearied or overpowered with sleep, when all hastened to their homes. The Indians, half stupified with the heavy banquet, slumbered in their cabins long into the succeeding day, whilst the missionaries and colonists sped on their adventurous and dangerous journey towards Quebec.

The Iroquois evidently never even suspected that their intended victims thought of leaving the country at that early season, while the lakes and rivers were still filled with ice, and rapid travel over land was impossible. The first intimation the Indians had of their departure came very late the next day—March 21, 1658—when some of them, not seeing any of the French, nor hearing any evidence of life, entered their homes only to find that not one of them remained.

It was a struggle between life and death with the French; and they put all their strength and energy into the work of forcing their boats through the floes of ice, or cutting a passageway with their hatchets, guided by the dim light of the stars or the flare of a pine torch, expecting every moment to hear the shrill war-hoop of their savage enemies in pursuit.

After they had proceeded about twenty-five miles in this manner they were compelled to carry on their shoulders their boats, their baggage, and provisions, for four hours through snow, and slush, and swampy lands, never delaying for rest until the following evening, when they reached Lake Ontario. With fifty miles between them and Onondaga, they began to feel that their lives were safe, and that they could take a few hours of needed rest and sleep. The lake was covered with ice, and they were again obliged to use their hatchets to cut a passageway for their boats; but they reached Montreal in safety, with the exception of three of the party who were drowned by the upsetting of a canoe in the rapids.

On this first mission the Fathers baptized more than five hundred children and many adults; they renewed the fervor and the faith of the Huron Christians, and preached the Gospel to all the Five Nations[1] of Iroquois. They also instructed and baptized more than four hundred prisoners, who were brought to the Iroquois villages, to be held as slaves, or to be put to death. A temporary termination, however, was put to the work of the missionaries among the Iroquois; yet their labors were not in vain, as many

---

[1] Father LeMoyne, who had gone to the Mohawk country in August, 1657, and had labored there among the Hurons and captives, was brought back to Quebec in June, 1658.

through their efforts were prepared for a Christian death, and many more were convinced at heart of the truth of their teaching.

CHAPTER XII.

WAR AND PEACE.

INDIAN WARFARE—MISSIONERS BLOCKADED—ONONDAGAS PROPOSE PEACE—LE MOYNE GOES TO ONONDAGA—COUNCIL—FRENCH TOO WEAK TO REFUSE PEACE—LE MOYNE LABORS AMONG IROQUOIS—FAITH OF CHRISTIAN INDIANS—TROOPS ARRIVE FROM FRANCE—EXPEDITION AGAINST MOHAWKS—PEACE.

PEACE between the Iroquois and French was broken by the killing of three Frenchmen by Oneidas near Montreal, in October, 1657; and the hostilities thus begun continued, with slight intermissions, for nearly ten years.

The Iroquois prowled around the French settlements ever ready to attack any individual or small party of the French, or their Indian allies, when found at a safe distance from the forts; and although they made no concerted attack on Three Rivers,[1] Montreal, or Quebec, yet they hung like a specter of death over the colony, obscuring the light of the Gospel, and impeding the commercial success of New France. Nature assisted the Iroquois in terrifying the hapless French colonists. A frightful earthquake shook the homes of the colonists at Montreal, and the din and glare of a remarkable electric storm added terrors to the unusual disturbance of the elements. The lowing of the cattle and the whistling of the winds

[1] The Five Nations intended to unite their forces in an attack on Three Rivers in the fall of 1661. They had already captured 13 French near Montreal and killed Rev. Le Maistre.

seemed to the distracted inhabitants like human voices floating in the air, and they imagined they were the voices of their captive friends among the Iroquois bemoaning their lot. In the flashes of lightning some thought they saw fiery canoes laden with Iroquois warriors hovering over their homes. A comet also appeared, having a tail shaped like a bundle of rods— an omen of impending calamity.[1]

The Rt. Rev. Francis de Laval, first Bishop of Canada, landed at Quebec, June 16, 1659, and the missioners were inspired with renewed zeal for the conversion and civilization of the Indians; but they found their field of labors bounded by a cordon of Iroquois warriors. The Huron Christians, who had fled to the regions around Lake Superior, asked the Fathers to come to them; but the rivers were infested by their ubiquitous enemies, and numerous and populous nations, who heard of the missioners, desired to see them, but the waterways were closed by war.

The Iroquois also prevented these nations from coming to Three Rivers and Quebec with their rich loads of furs to exchange them for the toys and the goods of the French, and, as these formed the chief commerce of the country, the colony suffered greatly from the stagnation of trade.

The Hurons and the Algonquins, who knew well the treacherous nature of the Iroquois, told the French that the colony would never prosper unless the Iroquois were destroyed. The French realized that their only hope of prosperity lay in the destruction or complete defeat of their old enemies; but as they were not sufficiently strong to attack these wiley savages in their own land,

[1] Charlevoix, "History of New France," Vol. III, p. 58.

they appealed to the king of France for aid, as the interests of the Church and of France required the defeat of these foes.

The Fathers, however, believed that more could be obtained by peace than by war, and they were ready to grasp any opportunity that promised the re-establishment of friendly relations between the Iroquois and the French.

In July,[1] 1661, two canoes of Indians came down the river to Montreal, bearing a white flag of truce. They were Iroquois representing the Onondagas and Cayugas, under the lead of the former host of Mesnard,[2] who came to sue for peace. They brought four French prisoners with them, and presents to bring back the light of the sun; to bring back the old love which existed between them, and to bring back the Fathers to the missions they had abandoned, but where the fires were still burning. They asked that one Father, at least, should return with them, as the lives of twenty French prisoners depended upon his presence.

They wanted the sisters also to come, to establish an hospital for the care of the sick, and a convent for the education of their daughters. They were no longer, they said, savages, but Christians; as there were more Christians than Pagans at Onondaga, where one of their principal chiefs rang the bell every morning to call the Christians to prayers. The French, however, were not willing to entertain any proposition of peace until they consulted the Governor at Quebec; but Father LeMoyne was prepared to risk his life in the interests of harmony and religion, and he returned to Onondaga with the Iroquois,

[1] Relations, 1661.
[2] Mesnard, first to bring the light of faith to the Cayugas, died in the forest on the Ottawa Mission, in August, 1662.

where he was received with great joy and hearty welcome. The people turned out in great numbers to greet him; they loaded him with presents, and formed an escort to conduct him to the town. Here the women and children had climbed to the roofs of their cabins, and into the trees, to gaze upon the fearless Black Robe, who did not hesitate to endanger his life to ransom his countrymen, and who now marched through their streets crying out his mission as embassador of the French. The celebrated chief, Garakontie,[1] came forth to receive him, offering him the hospitality of his own home, which he proposed to convert into a chapel for the celebration of divine service.

The Ancients invited the representatives of the Five Nations to meet Father LeMoyne at Onondaga, and listen to the message he brought from the Governor of the French. The delegates met in the cabin of Garakontie on August 12; and Father LeMoyne gave them presents to restore peace, to exchange prisoners, and to encourage the Senecas and Cayugas to visit Quebec on a friendly mission. He also spoke to them about the truths of Christianity, and they seemed pleased with his propositions and his address.

The presence of this holy missioner was very consoling to the French captives, as well as to the many Huron and Iroquois Christians; and many of them assembled in Garakontie's chapel before the break of day to

[1] Garakontie was the friend and protector of the French captives, and he had about twenty at his home at this time, whom he rescued from the fire through his pleadings and his presents, or purchased them from their masters with costly gifts. Although at this time he was not a Christian, yet he assembled the Christian captives at the sound of the bell in his cabin for morning and evening prayers; and on Sunday he prepared some little feast for them to keep them faithful to their duty and offset the bad example of the Pagans. He purchased a crucifix that had been stolen by the Mohawks, as he knew they would profane it, and placed it in the little chapel he had adorned for the Christians at Onondaga.

hear mass, and they came again at evening to listen to instructions and to recite the evening prayer.

About the middle of September Garakontie set out for Quebec with some Onondagas and Senecas, and nine French captives, with rich gifts for Onontio,[1] and with an earnest desire of procuring peace.[2] At the meeting with the Governor, Garakontie gave one present to represent the liberation of the French captives; he gave another, representing the keys of the towns of the Onondagas, the Cayugas, and the Senecas, giving the freedom of these towns to the Fathers so they might restore the churches that had fallen to ruins, and assemble the congregations that were scattered; and he gave another present, inviting the French to come and dwell among the Iroquois in large numbers, to establish Christianity among these three nations that they might be united with the French in the firm bonds of permanent peace.

Although the Onondagas had often allured the French into danger by their protestations of peace; and although they may have come with the Senecas on this occasion to obtain the aid of French arms against the powerful Andastes, yet the French were too weak to reject an alliance which offered even temporary peace with these powerful nations. The French had only about five hundred soldiers, whilst the Onondagas, Cayugas, and Senecas, could send out, at least, fifteen hundred warriors against their enemies; and the French colony was surrounded by other unfriendly Indian tribes, such as the Mohigans, and the Abnakis, who might unite with the Iroquois against the French in the event of war. The

[1] The Governor.
[2] On the way they met a band of Onondagas returning from Montreal where their chief, Orreowati, had killed Father LeMaistre. This murder discouraged many of the delegates, and they returned to their homes.

Mohawks[1] and the Oneidas would not join the other Iroquois nations in the proposals of peace, but they were not so much to be feared if peace could be established with the latter; and the French hoped to reduce them to subjection as soon as reïnforcements arrived from France.

The Fathers also hoped to establish extensive missions among the Onondagas, Cayugas, and Senecas, as soon as they could safely visit these nations; as there were already many Christians among them, and many others were well disposed towards the Faith.

LeMoyne came principally to save some French prisoners, but he found the Christian Indians so anxious to receive his ministrations that he prolonged his visit into the following summer.

The Christian Hurons and Iroquois came from Oneida, and Cayuga, under the pretext of trading, in order to receive the sacraments; and as the missionary had full liberty to mingle with the people, he was kept busy attending to their spiritual wants. He visited Cayuga[2] and remained four or five weeks among the Christian Hurons and Iroquois, who were delighted with his visit, and profited by his presence by receiving the sacraments. He baptized about two hundred during the year he remained in the country; and he found that the Christians were generally firm in their faith, even in the midst of persecution. Garakontie secured the release of eighteen French captives, and with these Father LeMoyne returned to Montreal in August, 1662, after an absence of more than a year. His visit to Onondaga averted war for the time,

[1] The Mohawks were then at war with the Mohigans, but peace was soon declared. The upper cantons were also successful in their war with the Andastes, and extended their conquests as far south as the Spanish Colony on the Gulf of Mexico. Charlevoix.

[2] He was invited to Cayuga, and very kindly received by some of the chiefs, on account of the insolent attack made on his person, and on the chapel, by some drunken Onondagas.

and it gave the French farmers an opportunity to till their fields.

During these years of warfare the Christians in the Iroquois country, though deprived of missionaries, enlivened their faith by prayers. There were French prisoners who raised their mutilated and fingerless hands to God in prayer; there were Huron captives who proclaimed the name and faith of Jesus Christ; and there were Iroquois preachers, as well as persecutors of the Faith. Garakontie at Onondaga, though not yet baptized, assembled the Christians by the sound of the bell every morning and evening for prayers; and he frequently invited them to some banquet or feast to encourage them in the practice of their religious duties. Some of the women often met at the cabin of some pious Christian to recite the rosary, or to listen to a rehearsal of the teaching of the Jesuit Fathers; and they brought their children to some prominent Catholic Indian to have them baptized. One of the Huron Christian captives among the Mohawks kept account of the Sundays, so that the Christians might observe the day by prayer.

Efforts were made at different times to establish friendly relations between the French and Iroquois, but nothing more was done than to merely exchange presents.

The great Garakontie gathered all the treasures he could command, and, with thirty Onondagas, started for Quebec in the fall of 1663 with this load of porcelain, or shell beads and belts, the gold of the country, to strive to appease the minds of the French, and bring back the light of Faith to his land. A party of Algonquins met these Iroquois on the way, and killed some, and led others away as captives. Garakontie, however, reached Quebec in safety, and was joyfully welcomed. A treaty of peace was concluded; which was the first formal treaty between the French and Indians.[1] The French were not averse to these negotiations; as they checked the hostility of the Iroquois, and gave them time to receive aid from France, when they would be in a position to enforce peace with the arms of war.

The long hoped for aid[2] from France came at last, and in June, 1665, the Marquis de Tracy reached Quebec with a regiment of French veterans.

The new Governor began at once to strengthen the position of the colony by erecting forts on the Iroquois River.[3] He believed there could be no permanent peace unless the Iroquois learned to fear the power of the colony; so he sought an early opportunity to send a powerful expedition against the Mohawks, the most inveterate enemies of the French. The Senecas and the Cayugas had never engaged in direct warfare against the colony; and the Onondagas, under the leadership of Garakontie, were well disposed towards the French.

In January, 1666, De Courcelles led five hundred French soldiers on snow shoes to the Mohawk villages; but all the warriors were absent on an expedition against some Virginia tribes, and the French soldiers were obliged to retrace their weary way to Quebec without striking any fear into the hearts of their Indian enemies.

In September of the same year DeTracy led twelve hundred men into the Mohawk country; burned their

---

[1] December 13, 1663, N. Y. Col. Doc. III. P. 121.

[2] Horses were also sent over on these vessels, and the sight of these animals excited the admiration of the Indians.

[3] This was the Richelieu River, on which three forts were erected; one at the mouth of the river, another about forty miles up the river, at the falls; the third, about ten miles nearer Lake Champlain. Fort St. Ann was erected the following year, on an island at the north end of Lake Champlain.

villages,[1] destroyed their provisions, sang Te Deum, and erected a cross on the site of the principal village, as a reminder of the power of the French and the importance of Christianity.

The warlike spirit of the Mohawks was thoroughly subdued, and they came the following summer to Quebec, humbly suing for peace, and asking for missionaries to teach them the truths of Christianity. The other nations, also, soon sent delegations with proposals of peace, and asked for missionaries to come to their homes and instruct them; but the Governor would not allow the Fathers to depart until the Iroquois gave hostages for each one, to secure their lives against the inconstancy, or treachery, of these unreliable Indians.

[1] The act of possession mentions five villages. The cabins were neat and well built, and were very long, some being 120 feet in length. All the cabins were burned.

CHAPTER XIII.
NEW MISSIONS.

BLESSINGS OF PEACE—MISSION JOURNEY TO THE IROQUOIS—INDIAN OFFERING TO INVISIBLE PEOPLE—VISIT TO THE MOHAWKS—COUNCIL—CHAPEL BUILT—HURON FIDELITY—CHAPEL BUILT AT ONEIDA—GARNIER VISITS ONONDAGA—GARAKONTIE ASSISTS—CARHEIL VISITS CAYUGA—CHAPEL BUILT—FEW CONVERTS—FREMIN VISITS THE SENECAS—CHAPEL BUILT—CHRISTIAN HURON CAPTIVES—DAILY ROUTINE—INSTRUCTING CAPTIVES AT THE STAKE—DIFFICULTIES.

PEACE and the presence of so many French soldiers brought a feeling of security to the colonists, and they began to settle on the banks of the St. Lawrence, to till the soil, to hunt, and fish; but one of the greatest blessings of peace was the renewal of the Iroquois missions, where six Fathers were soon employed among the different nations.

The Mohawks and the Oneidas had sent deputies to Quebec to cement the bonds of peace, and to ask priests to come to their homes to instruct their people. Father LeMoyne had prepared the minds of the Mohawks for the teachings of Christianity on his various visits to these people, and now three Fathers were ready to establish missions among them.

Fathers Pierron, Fremin, and Bruyas, left Quebec n July, 1667, for the Iroquois country with a party of Mohawk and Oneida warriors. They were delayed about one month at Fort St. Anne, on Lake Champlain, on account of a party of Mohigans, who were in ambush on the shore of the lake awaiting to attack the Mohawks on their return from the French.

After this delay the party proceeded without interruption along the west shore of the lake until they reached a point about two miles from the Falls, where the Fathers witnessed the observance of a superstitious custom peculiar to Indian life. At this place the Mohawks gathered a quantity of flint stone that was heaped up along the shore, and they threw great quantities of tobacco into the waters, as a tribute to an invisible people who dwelt under the waters, and who, in return for the tobacco, furnished the Indians with abundance of flint. The Mohawks said that these little people go to war in canoes like the Indians; and, as they are passionately fond of tobacco, the Mohawks gain their friendship by a generous tribute, and in return these people place large quantities of flint stone along the shore. The effect, however, which was produced, according to the Indian mind by mysterious agents, was caused by the natural action of the waves; as the lake was noted at this point for its violent storms, and, as flint abounded, the waves threw up quantities along the shore, and the water and friction gave them a polish that made them seem the work of intelligent hands.

The Mohawks had sentinels posted fifty or sixty miles from their town, watching for another French invasion, and they were surprised as well as pleased to find this peaceful band of missioners instead of a destroying army.

The Fathers were received with every mark of respect and honor in Gandaouague; and they immediately began their labors by visiting the Huron and Algonquin Christian captives, and adorning a little chapel where they might assemble them for morning and evening prayers. The Fathers were detained at this village some time by the Mohigans,[1] who were then at war with the Mohawks, but their time was not spent in mere waiting, as they were kept busy administering sacraments to the Christians, and instructing some Pagans.

The Fathers proceeded to the second[2] village, about five miles distant, where they were even more heartily welcomed than at Gandaouague; but they did not tarry here, as they wished to reach the capital of the nation. The capital, Tionnontoguen, had been destroyed the preceding year by the French, but had been rebuilt about half a mile from its former location. Here they were received some distance outside the village by two hundred warriors, who escorted[3] them to a place where they were formally welcomed by an eloquent orator. At their entrance to the town they were welcomed by the discharge of fire-arms from the cabins, and by the firing of two small cannons at opposite ends of the town. They were afterwards entertained at a banquet, in Indian style.

The feast of the Exaltation of the Holy Cross, September 14, was selected as the day for the presentation of their gifts, and the public explanation of their mission. The French opened the meeting with the singing of the *Veni Creator,* accompanied by a small musical instrument, which greatly pleased the Indians; then Father Fremin addressed the large assemblage on the subject of his mission. He spoke to them of the blessings of peace and the evils of war; and he told them they might now reap the fruits of peace, as they had suffered the

[1] These were the Loup Indians, and they are called in the Relations the Mohigans.
[2] See page 14.
[3] The young warriors led the line; the Ancients came next, and the Fathers were in the rear, as this was the place of honor in their processions.

horrors of war the year before in the destruction of their town. He reproached them for their perfidy, and for their barbarous cruelty towards French prisoners: and he said that his mission among them was to teach them to abandon these barbarities, to live more like human beings, and to adopt the faith and practices of Christianity. A Mohawk orator replied in the name of the nation, pledging his people to preserve the peace, offering the Fathers assistance in building their chapel,[1] and releasing several prisoners, who were friends of the French, as a proof of their sincerity.

The chapel was quickly built by the willing hands of the Mohawks, and was soon crowded by Iroquois, who came through curiosity, and by the old Huron Christians, who came with love and devotion; as the many years of their desolation had not lessened their fervor nor weakened their faith. The Fathers found ample reward for their hardships in the fidelity of these simple people.

In one of the villages Father Fremin found forty-five of these old Huron Christians, and he was astonished as well as delighted to find that after near twenty years of captivity, without a church or a pastor to enliven their faith, they still preserved all the attachment for their religion which they manifested in their old Huron home. The Indians, however, have very retentive memories, and often when these captives were free from the drudgery of Indian slave life they would assemble around some friendly fireside, whilst some well instructed chief would recount the teachings of the Fathers and the practices of the Church; or some pious matron would invite them to a retired nook in the forest to recite the rosary, which

---

[1] This mission was called "St. Mary's," Relations 1668.

106   THE IROQUOIS AND THE JESUITS.

they had learned from the sisters at Quebec, or from the Jesuits in their former home. One pious woman was selected to keep a record of the days, so they could know when the Sundays and holidays approached, to observe them in a religious manner. Father Fremin and Father Pierron labored successfully in the Mohawk villages, and in three months they had received about fifty persons into the Church: yet they encountered opposition and suffered abuse from the Iroquois, who often became deliriously drunk with the liquor obtained from the English[1] in exchange for their furs; and on these occasions entire villages became intoxicated and acted like so many demons.

The Rev. James Bruyas left Fathers Fremin and Pierron at Tionnontaguen, and proceeded to the Oneida Nation, where he arrived in September, 1667, to begin the work of evangelizing this small but insolent nation. Here a chapel was built by the Oneidas in which the Father was soon to say mass,[2] surrounded by the few Christians in the town. The missioner's time was principally occupied in instructing the sick and disposing them for the reception of the sacraments; and in this work he was ably assisted by Felix, a well-informed Huron, who earnestly invited the Oneidas to become Christians. In three months Father Bruyas added fifty-two members to his little congregation, and had bright prospects of future success; but he was obliged to proceed cautiously with adults, who very reluctantly relinquished their dream theories and loose marriages relations for the stricter discipline of Christianity.

Onondaga was the central nation of the Iroquois and

[1] The English had taken possession of New Holland in 1666.
[2] Shea, "The Catholic Church in Colonial Days." p. 285.

the capital of the league; and here every year delegates from the other nations assembled to discuss matters of state, to allay any internal dissensions, and to maintain the sovereignty of the league. It was here also that the Fathers had formed their first and most flourishing church about ten years before, and they longed to revisit the scene of their former labor and hasty flight, to revive the drooping spirit of charity and to relume the fading light of Faith. Father Julien Garnier, therefore, who had gone to Oneida to assist Father Bruyas, hastened to Onondaga, where he was most joyfully welcomed.[1] The famous Garakontie soon had a chapel[2] ready for the Father, and when he had provided everything necessary for this new mission he hastened to Quebec, with some other prominent men of his nation, to bring back another apostolic laborer for this promising field. After exchanging presents with the French, Garakontie returned to Onondaga in September with Father Stephen Carheil and Father Peter Millet.

In the meantime Father Garnier began his labors among the old Huron Christians, who formed the nucleus of his new congregation. The first fruit of this new mission shows the admirable fidelity of the Christians, and their firm attachment to the teachings of the Church. Father Garnier visited an Iroquois, who had been sick for two years, and had been gradually growing weaker, until, at the time of the priest's visit, he could scarcely speak; but to the oft-repeated questions of the Father he finally answered: "I can now die happy since God has granted me the favor I have been praying for so long." He had married a Huron Christian, who had instructed him in

[1] Garnier had merely gone to Onondaga to visit the Christians there, but Garakontie urged him to remain, at least until he could induce other Fathers to come from Quebec.
[2] The chapel was dedicated to St. John the Baptist.

the doctrines of the Church, and his only desire in life was to see a priest before death, so that he might leave the world as a follower of Christ. God evidently granted his prayer, as he died the next day, after receiving baptism from Father Garnier.

Father Stephen Carheil left his companion, Father Millet, at Onondaga to assist Father Garnier, and proceeded to the Cayuga villages, about seventy miles distant. The Cayugas had never, as a nation, borne arms against the French, but had manifested a friendly feeling towards them, and a disposition to accept the teachings of the missioners. The chief, who had been the host of Father Mesnard[1] ten years before, came with other prominent men of the nation to ask for a priest to bring back the light of faith to their homes. Father Carheil, accompanied by Father Garnier, reached the Cayuga nation November 6, 1668, and immediately began missionary labors by instructing and baptizing a female captive slave, who was that day burned at the stake and devoured by these cannibals.[2]

Father Garnier[3] gave two presents to the nation—one to ask for a chapel, another to invite them to accept Christianity. The chiefs replied by two presents, expressing their acceptance of the Faith, and their willingness to build a chapel. The chapel was ready by November 9, and was dedicated, by Father Carheil, to St. Joseph.

Father Carheil had a particular reverence for St.

---

[1] Mesnard died on the Algonquin mission in 1661. He told his friends before departing on this mission that he would never return, as his advanced years, and his delicate health, could not stand the severity of Indian missionary life; yet he would never be happy unless he went in obedience to the call of God.

[2] Relations 1669, p. 12.

[3] Father Garnier accompanied Father Carheil to Cayuga, and he also delivered the address, as he was better versed in their tongue.

Catherine, and on her feast day, November 25, many of the Cayugas came to be instructed in the Faith, so the Father looked upon this day as the birthday of his little church.

Many of the young men were absent on war, fishing, or hunting expeditions, but the rumors of an invasion by their old enemies, the Andastes, soon gathered them around their homes, when Father Carheil had an opportunity of explaining the Christian religion, and of gaining their affection by the courage he manifested in danger, and by his sympathy for their cause. He remained on guard with the sentinels at night, and as the Indians admired courage they manifested their gratitude for his interest in their cause, and their respect for his person, at a public banquet.

The Father turned their admiration for his courage to good account, as he went about among the people, telling them that good Christians had no reason to fear death. Why should they fear? They believed in God, they loved Him, and they obeyed Him; and after death they would be eternally happy in Heaven. But you, my friends, should fear death, because until now you have not known God, nor have you loved or obeyed Him; and should you die without baptism, without believing in, or loving God, you would be forever miserable. He told the warriors he would prefer death to seeing them die without baptism; and, as this was the eve of the expected battle, he said he would be on the field the next day to confer this grace upon the wounded, who wished to die as Christians.

Ambassadors from the Senecas came to Montreal November 10, 1668, to ask for priests to come and instruct their people; and they sent a beautiful gift to the

110   THE IROQUOIS AND THE JESUITS.

Governor, as an evidence of their good will. They had also sent representatives to Father Fremin in the Mohawk country, to induce him to come to dwell among them; and as Father Pierron had returned from Quebec, and as there were many Huron Christians among the Senecas Father Fremin left the Mohawk Valley early in October, 1668, for the Seneca Nation. The Seneca territory presented a vast field for the labors of the zealous missioners, as more than half of the population of the league dwelt in the valley of the Genesee; and there was an entire village[1] of Hurons and other captives[2] a few miles south of the present village of Victor, where there were many Christians, who still preserved the faith they had received in their old Huron homes, and who only needed the presence of a priest to revive their former fervor.

Father Fremin was the superior of all the Iroquois missions; and he visited the scenes of labor of all the other Fathers on his way to the Seneca Nation, which he reached on the first day of November, and was received with all the honor which these people are accustomed to bestow upon ambassadors of powerful nations. A chapel was soon built, and a little congregation of Huron Christians gathered around their pastor to renew their fervor and to revive their faith; but the great obstacle to the propagation of the Faith here, as in the other nations, was war; as then all the young men were absent and the

[1] Shea. "The Catholic Church in Colonial Days." It was called "Gandougaræ," but the Fathers named it St. Michaels, in honor of the old Huron village of the same name.

[2] There were three kinds of captives among the Iroquois: first, those captured in war, and who were treated as slaves, and could be killed at will; secondly, those who were captured in war, but who were liberated and adopted into some family; finally, those who came voluntarily to dwell in the land under the protection of the powerful confederacy, and these were entitled to most of the rights of the native Iroquois. The Hurons of Gandougaræ were principally of this third class, who had sought the protection of their conquerors after the dispersion of their own people.

older ones would not engage in any important affair, or listen to any matter affecting the life, traditions, and customs of their people without consulting the warriors of their race. The Senecas were then at war with the Ottawas, the Mohigans, and the Andastes; yet Father Fremin was kept busy encouraging the Christians, visiting and instructing some, and preparing the sick for baptism and a Christian death. In four months he baptised sixty persons; but most of these were the children of Christian parents, or sick and dying Pagans.

The chiefs built a chapel[1] for the missioner, and the people came in numbers to listen to his teaching. The Senecas were laboring to establish peace with the French, and they were willing, through motives of policy, to assist the Father in his work; but the sorcerers wielded all their vast influence to restrain the people from living according to the Christian law.

The Father's first care was for the sick; and, as one of the periodic epidemics was ravaging the towns, he was kept busy visiting the dying to prepare them for a Christian death.

In such a large field the duties were too onerous for one priest, so Father Garnier came from Onondaga to help his superior minister to the sick. As soon as the epidemic ceased the Fathers began to give instructions in their humble little chapel; but from the naturally stoic indifference of the Indian they could not tell whether their teachings made any impression upon the hearts of their hearers.

At the close of the year 1668 Jesuit priests were laboring in each of the Iroquois nations: in each nation there was an humble chapel where mass was said nearly

[1] This was probably at Gandachioragou, on the site of the present village of Lima.

every morning, and Sundays; and on the great festivals of the Church the mass was solemnized by the singing of hymns by these rude children of the forest; and in each nation there was a little congregation of old Huron Christians and Iroquois converts who learned the doctrines of the Church, and directed their lives according to the teaching of Christ. The Fathers gave instructions every day, and in some places twice a day, to the children and adults; and they found that the Indians were capable of understanding the great truths of Christianity.

Father Pierron, among the Mohawks, was very successful in conveying Christian ideas of death and judgment to the minds of the Indians by means of pictures; as they became very much interested in those pictorial representations of truth, and asked many questions concerning them, which gave the Father an opportunity of adapting his teaching to the intelligence of his hearers.

Every morning after mass the Fathers went through the villages to visit the sick, to instruct them, and to prepare them for baptism and consequent membership in the vast multitudes of the Church militant. Many of the greatest men among the Iroquois believed in the teachings of the Fathers, but they deferred their conversion to the last hour through fear of the taunts of their friends, or because they found difficulty in overcoming the Pagan vices of a life-time.

One of the most important duties of the Fathers was the salvation of the souls of prisoners destined for death. The Iroquois burned many of their prisoners at the stake; and their contact with Europeans had not, at that time, mitigated the cruelty or lessened the demoniac tortures they inflicted on their unhappy victims. It was the height of Indian heroism to bear these tortures without flinching,

A DICTIONARY OF THE LANGUAGE.

and to hurl defiance at their inhuman tormentors; but the Jesuits came, teaching the dying to be meek and humble, to forgive their enemies, and to prepare, even at that last hour, to meet their sovereign Judge. Often then, amid the roaring of the flames and the demoniac yells of these savage torturers, might have been heard the prayer of the victim imploring forgiveness for his own sins and mercy for his tormentors, whilst the Jesuit stood near to encourage the dying Christian to persevere, and to suggest thoughts and prayers in keeping with a Christian death.

The Fathers spent the evenings in their little cabins, preparing, with the light of pine knots, a dictionary of the language, or translating their instructions into the Indian tongue.

Although many of the prominent men of the Iroquois nations favored the teaching of Christiany, yet the Fathers encountered much opposition; for they had to contend against long-established practices that formed a part of the Indian social and religious life. The dream theory, or the necessity of fulfilling dreams, was observed in every village; the medicine men, or sorcerers, pretended by incantations and magic power to cure diseases, and to guide the weal of their fellow men; and very many were addicted to excessive drinking of liquor, which threatened the ruin of the entire league.

CHAPTER XIV.

THE MISSION IN 1669.

PIERRON AMONG THE MOHAWKS—PIETY OF CHRISTIANS—EXCESSIVE LIQUOR DRINKING—PIERRON PLEADS FOR TEMPERANCE—MOHAWK-MOHIGAN WAR—INSTRUCTING CAPTIVES—BRUYAS AT ONEIDA — ONEIDAS OPPOSED TO CHRISTIANITY — REVIVING FAITH AT ONONDAGA—DREAM WORSHIP—LABORS OF FATHERS—DEATH AT THE STAKE—CARHEIL AT CAYUGA—INDIAN MEDICAL SCIENCE—CAYUGAS DREAD BAPTISM—BUILDING A GRAND CHAPEL — FATHERS AMONG THE SENECAS — FIRST CHURCH COUNCIL—DANGER—NEW MISSION—PROGRESS OF CHRISTIANITY.

FATHER Pierron returned from Quebec October 7, 1668, and took charge of the Mohawk mission when Father Fremin started for the Seneca nation. There were seven[1] villages of the Mohawks, which he tried to visit each week, so that no sick person would be deprived of the benefit of his ministrations; but he found that one priest was insufficient to attend to the wants of these scattered people. Some of the well instructed Hurons assisted him in teaching Christian doctrine to the Iroquois; but they could not do all the work, so he was obliged to send to Quebec for another priest to help him in his work. Father Boniface, who had just arrived from France, was immediately sent to this promising field.

The Mohawks were at war, in 1669, with the numerous tribes of the Mohigans, whose territory extended from the Hudson River through several of the present Eastern States as far as Quebec; and many of the young

[1] Relations, 1669, p. 3.

Mohawk warriors could learn but little Christianity, as they were absent from their homes, roving in bands through the deep forests, and on the lakes and rivers, to attack their Indian foes.[1] Many of the Mohawk women, however, attended the instructions of the Fathers, and some of them acquired an extraordinary spirit of piety and devotion—reciting their rosary several times a day, and saying their prayers at early morning before they went to labor in the fields.

So great was the spirit of fervor that Father Pierron had the ceremonies of Holy Week observed as they are in France; and the festival of Easter was celebrated with great solemnity, and with piety and devotion, by these new Christians in their little bark chapel.[2]

Father Pierron translated the commandments of God and several prayers into rude Iroquois verse, so that they would be indelibly impressed on their memories by their habit of singing. They not only learned the Christian law but they observed its precepts, and gave examples of saintly Christian lives

The Europeans brought not only the light of civilization but also the curse of liquor drinking to the Indians; and the Mohawks were especially addicted to this evil, as they could easily barter their furs with the neighboring Dutch and English for supplies of strong drink.[3]

Often when a large quantity of liquor was obtained many of the adults of a village became intoxicated, and at such times the savage nature of the Indian asserted itself, and quarrels, and even murders, were not infrequent. The chief men of the nation recognized the ruin that this evil was working among their people, and, with the ad-

[1] Both the Mohawks and the Mohigans were then cannibals, and burned and devoured one another.   [2] Relations, 1669, p. 3.   [3] Relations, 1669, p. 4.

vice of Father Pierron, they sent a delegation to the Governor of the English colony at Manhattan,[1] requesting him to prohibit the sale of liquors to the Indians.[2] Governor Lovelace, in his reply, praised the Father for his zeal and good work among the Indians, but very diplomatically stated that he had taken all the care possible, and would continue to prohibit, under severe penalty, the excessive sale of liquor to the Indians. Notwithstanding the disorder reigning through intemperance, and the opposition of the sorcerers, the good missioners continued to add members to their little flock, and by the end of 1669 they had baptized more than one hundred and fifty; and although half of this number were persons in danger of death, yet the Fathers were effectively preaching the Gospel among the Mohawks.

The Mohigans continued their warfare on the Mohawk villages, and at early dawn on August 18, 1669, about three hundred of these warriors from the sea-coast near Boston, attacked Gandaouague; but after a spirited fight the inhabitants succeeded in repelling the invaders. The alarm soon spread to the other villages, and in a short time a large band of Mohawk warriors was in pursuit of their flying foes.

Father Pierron, who was then at Tionnontoguen, immediately hastened to the scene of the conflict, to comfort the wounded, to attend to their spiritual wants, and to instruct and baptize the captives destined for the stake.

The Mohawks sped rapidly down the river in their light canoes until the gloom of night was settling over

[1] New York.

[2] This was the first temperance movement in the State. Europeans had brought the blessings of civilization to the Indians, but they also brought many of its evils. One of the greatest of these evils was the custom of drinking intoxicating liquors, which the Indians readily adopted, and which degraded them lower than they were in their savage state, as it made them brutes.

the land, when they halted, and sent scouts ahead to reconnoiter the enemy's camp. When they learned that the enemy was strongly intrenched, they made a grand détour through the forest, and formed an ambush in a narrow defile through which the Mohigans must pass. Here they savagely attacked and repulsed the Mohigans; and the battle raged with varying success until the Mohigans escaped under cover of the friendly shades of the intervening night.

Father Pierron remained at Gandaouague during the battle, but as soon as he heard of the Mohawk victory he hastened to the scene, though it was twenty miles away; for some dying warrior might be consoled or saved by his presence, and the captives might be instructed before they fell victims to the enraged inhabitants of the town. The home journey was made in triumph; the Mohawks bore aloft on poles the scalps of the slain Mohigans, and the captives sang their death song of valiant deeds as they marched to their doom. As they crossed a brook the Father baptized the dying child of a female captive, and he found in this good deed a sufficient reward for the fatigue of the long journey.

When the Mohawks were wearied torturing the prisoners, and gave them a little respite, the Father led them to a cabin where he instructed them more at leisure, though some Mohawks objected, because they wished their enemies to be burned in Hell as well as at the stake. Father Pierron, however, convinced them that their hatred should not extend beyond the grave, as there is no place for enmity in Heaven; so they allowed him to save the souls of their captives whilst they tortured their bodies.

In the midst of these labors Father Pierron received a letter from his superior calling him to a conference at

Onondaga; and in ten days he traveled about two hundred and fifty miles, visiting his flock scattered through the six villages, to baptize those who might be in danger of death during his absence, and hastening through the dark and solitary forests to meet his brother priests.

The Oneidas were fierce, and proud, and the least tractable of all the Iroquois nations; they were not, therefore, well disposed to accept the Gospel which taught them to be meek and humble. The mission was dedicated to St. Francis Xavier, and it required all the zeal and patience of another such saint to make Christians out of these people; but Father Bruyas felt that his time was not spent in vain when he was able to baptize the sick and dying.

These people were passionately fond of life, and had recourse to many superstitions to obtain health for their sick; so they were not very well pleased with the teachings of the missioner, which brought the thought of death so prominently before their minds. Father Bruyas daily visited the cabins to instruct the sick, and, although he met with rebuffs and insults, especially from drunken Indians, he found much consolation in the saintly lives of some of his converts. Such fidelity in his converts, and the baptism of the dying, were the only reward the missioner could find for his life in the forest, deprived of the comforts of civilization, subsisting on water and parched corn,[1] and daily in danger of death.

Onondaga had been the most promising of the first missions established among the Iroquois, and as it was a large town, and the capital of the league, two Fathers, Rev. Julien Garnier and Rev. Peter Millet, were sent to revive the Faith and the spirit of piety in the nation; but

---

[1] Dried frogs were also a staple article of Indian fare.

THE OBSERVANCE OF DREAMS.

it was no easy matter to restore the fervor, which had become almost extinct after ten years without a priest or pastor. The greatest obstacle to the propagation of the Faith was the observance of dreams, which the Onondagas held to be a sacred duty; and as they attended with decorum the Catholic services they did not wish to be disturbed in their fatuous worship of dreams, as they believed their prosperity and life depended upon the fulfillment of the will of their maintou, which is revealed in dreams. It was not surprising that they should dream about the doctrines of Christianity, about Heaven or Hell; but one of their old men dreamed that he saw men falling from Heaven with hands and features mutilated, and a little man appeared to him and said that this was done in Heaven, where the Iroquois are made the captives and slaves of their old enemies, the Andastes.[1] The old man's dream was discussed in a public council, and many, no doubt, believed that the teachings of the Fathers would make them the slaves of their enemies.[2] Many, however, of their more intelligent men were favorably impressed with the dignity and beauty of the Christian law, and the superiority of civilized life over their barbarous customs.

The Fathers' time was occupied in visiting and instructing the sick adults; in watching over the sick children, lest any one should die without baptism; and in instructing the captives who were destined for a cruel death. The captives accepted willingly the Christian law, as this was the only ray of hope that beamed on their desolate state ; and they faithfully followed the instructions of the Fathers, repeating in their final hours

[1] Relations, 1669, p. 9.
[2] Another man related at this council that he dreamt he was in Heaven, where he had everything his heart could desire. This dream neutralized the effect of the dream of the Pagan.

the prayers they had learned, whilst the priests stood near to encourage and console them in their dreadful sufferings. To attend the captives in the time of torture was the most trying ordeal of the missioner's life. What could be more revolting to a refined sensitive nature than to witness an innocent fellow being undergoing the tortures of Indian cruelty! To smell the burning flesh of an innocent victim, to see their eyes or tongues torn out, to behold pieces of flesh cut from their living forms, to gaze upon the necklace of heated hatchet-heads burning to the bone, required the fortitude of a martyr and the self-sacrice of a saint. The torture often lasted two days and two nights; and during the greater part of this time the priest was present to instruct the victim, to console him, and to encourage him to die in a Christian manner.

The faithful Hurons at Onondaga, as at Oneida and among the Mohawks, had not forgotten their Christian education; and many of them gave testimony by their lives of the beauty of the Christian law. Many of the Onondaga converts gave evidence of singular piety and of holy lives, as they were led to imitate the example of the Christian Hurons from the Isle of Orleans.

Father Carheil's little congregation at Cayuga began to slowly increase in numbers, and it had not only women and children as members but some of the warriors also became humble followers of Christ. Two of the most celebrated chiefs at Cayuga attended the services in the chapel and the instructions of the Father, for the purpose of becoming members of his flock. Many learned the prayers and the commandments, but the priest would not admit adults to baptism without a long period of probation.

Besides the town of Cayuga,[1] which was the seat of

[1] See Chapter II.

the mission, there were two other villages in which the Father was obliged to labor, and which afforded him an ample field for his zeal. These other towns were situated on the Seneca River, ten and fifteen miles distant respectively from Cayuga, and were inhabited by Cayugas, and by captive Hurons and Andastes.

Father Carheil dwelt with the head chief of the nation, and though this chief was favorably disposed towards Christianity, yet he made the Father feel that his presence was not desirable. He had no personal dislike for Carheil, but as he had journeyed to Quebec to procure a particular priest for his people he was too proud to humbly accept a different one at the bidding of Garakontie. Garakontie, however, was too good a Christian to place any obstacle to the propagation of the Gospel; so he sent a present to the Cayuga chief to atone for any unintentional affront.

The Cayugas were very tenacious of the customs of their country and the traditions of their race, and they would not readily discard the superstitious and absurd method of healing the sick; so when Father Carheil refused to gorge himself with food to procure, as they believed, health for a sick Indian, they regarded his action as an insult to the family of the invalid. They attended the services of the Church in large numbers; they learned the commandments of God; and they learned to pray; but as they did not molest the Christians in their devotions, they did not wish to be disturbed in their sorcery and superstitions.

One day the Father entered the cabin to instruct and baptize a dying girl, the daughter of a Huron captive, but she would not listen to him. The father of the girl, addressing the priest, said: "You teach the same things that

Father Brobeuf formerly taught in our northern home; and as he brought death upon people by pouring water upon their heads you wish to kill us in the same manner." Although the priest was greatly discouraged, yet he did not retire, as he hoped to convince these people of their error. Shortly afterwards a sorcerer entered the cabin. This man was on friendly terms with the Father, and often visited the chapel to learn to pray; so he was ashamed to exercise his magic upon the dying girl in the presence of the priest, and he merely applied some simple remedy which could give no offense. The sorcerer only awaited the departure of the Father to apply his secret art; but as the latter did not seem inclined to leave, he was finally forced to go. Tears filled the eyes of the Father, and addressing the assemblage, he said: "Are you astonished, my brothers, at my grief? I lovingly hoped to save that soul; but now I see it shall suffer eternal loss —a loss which you do not understand, but which I know full well." Then the Father retired to the forest to seek consolation in prayer, and to deplore the loss of this soul. It was then that he seemed to partake of the grief of our Lord in the Garden over the loss of so many souls, who through all ages would refuse to profit by His proffered graces. Whilst in this deep reverie he was aroused by his host, who warned him not to walk in the direction of the cabin of the dead girl. He knew full well that this meant danger, and the burden of sorrow was removed from his heart, and he rejoiced to think that God might be pleased to crown his labors with a martyr's death. The Ancients assembled in council; their wise counsels prevailed, and no further attempts were made upon the life of the missioner.

The people readily learn the commandments, and

they willingly pray in the chapel and in their homes; but they have a horror of baptism, as they believe it is intimately associated with misfortune or death.

René, the companion of Father Carheil, was this year engaged in erecting a larger and a handsomer chapel, as the little chapel first built was not capable of containing the crowds that came for instruction. This new chapel was to be built in the style of European churches, but with the bark roof of the Indian chapel. Besides carpentry, René had a knowledge of medicine; and as he was kind and affable to the Indians he was a great help to the missioner, and by prescribing natural remedies for the sick he did much to convince the Cayugas of their folly in having recourse to the sorcerers and medicine men to be cured of their ills.

Father Fremin did not send any account of his mission work this year to the superior at Quebec, but from other sources it appears he met with the same success and opposition as the Fathers in the other nations. The people came in crowds to listen to the instructions, and to learn to pray; but the Fathers were not convinced that the adults were prepared for admission to the Church. The sorcerers advised the people not to abandon their ancient customs, and the young men were so busy preparing for war with the Algonquins that they could give but little attention to the Fathers.

Father Allouez, who was laboring among the Ottawa Algonquins, brought three Iroquois prisoners to Quebec to be restored to their homes; and this kindly act tended to avert the impending war between these two nations. The Senecas, however, had powerful enemies in the Mohigans and the Andastes; and the strife with these made them more peaceably disposed towards the French, and more willing to assist the Fathers in their work.

The Fathers made their home in one of the western villages;[1] and from this place they occasionally visited the other towns until they returned from the conference at Onondaga, when Father Fremin went to dwell at Gandougarae.

Early in August Father Fremin started for the Cayuga mission, which he reached on the tenth of the month;[2] and from this place, as superior of the Iroquois missions, he wrote to the Fathers laboring in the different nations to assemble at Onondaga for a conference[3] on their labors, and for a spiritual retreat for themselves. Father Carheil shortly afterward accompanied his superior to Onondaga, where they arrived August 20; and Father Fremin had leisure to examine his old mission[4] before the arrival of the other missioners.

All the Fathers had reached Onondaga by August 26, 1669, and they then spent a week in conference over their work, and in preparation and prayer for further success. As they were about to separate, to journey to their missions, word was brought of the killing by the French of seven Oneidas and one Seneca, near Montreal. This news caused a great commotion at Onondaga; and con-

[1] Most probably Gandachioragou, where there was a chapel. See chapter II.

[2] Some historian—with senses keen enough to perceive evil in every act of the Jesuits—rashly asserted that Father Fremin designedly left his mission at this time to incommode LaSalle, and many other writers repeated the statement without taking the trouble to investigate its truth. Marshall and Winsor say that Fremin left the Seneca town the same day that LaSalle arrived at Irondequoit Bay. Winsor, in his latest work, "From Cartier to Frontenac," with an utter disregard for dates, says that Fremin and Garnier left their posts August 26, 1669.

Fremin was at Cayuga August 10, the day that LaSalle reached Irondequoit Bay, and he could not have made the journey in less than two days. Fremin would not have called the Fathers from the Mohawk and Oneida missions to inconvenience LaSalle, nor would he have left his lay companion among the Senecas if he wished to hamper the explorer in his work.

[3] This was the first ecclesiastical council held in the State.

[4] Fremin had been at Onondaga with the French colony in 1657.

sidering the revengeful spirit of the Indians, the Fathers looked upon themselves as certain victims of retaliation. Belts, however, were immediately sent from Montreal to allay the perturbed spirit of the Oneidas and the Senecas, and the Fathers were allowed to depart in peace.

As Fremin and Garnier were passing through Gandagaro,[1] the large eastern Seneca village, on their return, a young warrior savagely attacked Garnier, and threatened to kill him, and would, no doubt, have made good his threat had not others intervened to save the missioner's life. They reached Gandachioragou, however, in safety the seventh day of September, and soon after Father Garnier took charge of this mission.

Father Fremin was delayed some time on account of sickness, but on September 27, 1669, he started for Gandougarae, where he was to make his future home. The old Hurons were delighted to have a priest dwell among them, and they even gently reproved him for tarrying so long with the Pagans of the western towns whilst there were so many Christians at Gandougarae anxiously awaiting his coming. The good Christians began the erection of a pretty little chapel, where they might hear mass and the Word of God; and Father Fremin went about among his flock to learn their wants and the condition of his mission. The chapel was ready Sunday, November 3, and it was filled with Christians, who came to revive their faith, and with Pagans, who came to satisfy their curiosity. The oldest of the Huron Christians taught catechism, and the children vied with their parents in bringing their companions to pray.

[1] LaSalle and his party visited the Senecas during the absence of the Fathers, in search of a guide to the unknown seas and lands of the West. LaSalle, with Galinee and some men visited Gandagaro, and remained in the vicinity some weeks; but they did not succeed in obtaining a guide. Father Dollier remained with the rest of the party at Irondequoit Bay, where he said mass in one of the boats as often as the weather permitted.

It was not by the number of baptisms alone that the propagation of Christianity among these people could be judged; for the Indian is naturally phlegmatic, knowing well how to conceal his thoughts; and often when they seemed indifferent to the teachings of the Fathers they were storing deep in their hearts the thoughts of God, of Heaven, and of Hell, and it was only when approaching death brought them closer to these that those thoughts became acts, and they manifested an earnest desire before leaving this world to be consoled by the presence of the priest, and fortified by the sacraments of the Church. All, moreover, had respect for the chapel; and even in their drunken orgies,[1] which were very common, they kept away from the house of God.

It could not be expected that the pure and spiritual doctrines of Christianity would, in a few years, take the place in the affections of these people of the carnal vices they had practiced, and the superstitions they had observed from time immemorial; yet the patience, perseverance, and love, of the missionaries triumphed over the prejudices of the Indians, and in many of the villages every adult was sufficiently instructed to receive the sacraments at the hour of death. Many of them believed, but did not wish to become Christians, because they did not care to abandon their vices.

The Fathers had prayers every morning and evening in the chapel, and instructions at some convenient hour; while the Christians were faithful in attending church, and receiving the sacraments on Sundays.

---

[1] These drunken riots lasted as long as the liquor, which they obtained from the Dutch, held out—sometimes continuing two weeks. See Relations, 1671.

CHAPTER XV:

THE MISSIONS IN THE YEAR 1670.

BRIGHT PROSPECTS—PEACE COUNCIL AT QUEBEC—BAPTISM OF GARAKONTIE—OPPOSITION OF THE DUTCH—INDIANS DEFEND THEIR FAITH—PIERRON ASSAILS MOHAWK CUSTOMS—MOHAWKS REPLY—RENOUNCE WORSHIP OF AGRESKOUE—DRUNKEN REVELRY AT ONEIDA—ZEAL OF MILLET AT ONONDAGA—GARAKONTIE'S COUNSEL—GOOD EFFECTS—HURON CHRISTIANS—PAGAN PREJUDICES AT CAYUGA—DREAM THEORY—HURON CHRISTIANS OF GANDOUGARAE—EXAMPLES OF PIETY—INDIAN IDEA OF HEAVEN —DREAMS.

IN writing this year to the Provincial in France, Father LeMercier[1] stated that the Iroquois missions "never presented brighter prospects than at the present time; all the nations have chapels and priests; all listen with interest to the teachings of the Fathers; and all seem to be on the eve of their Christian regeneration."[2]

The success of the missions depended upon peaceful relations between the Iroquois and French, so the latter were careful to strengthen the ties of friendship which bound them to their dusky allies; and a council was held at Montreal to adjust some differences existing between the Iroquois and Algonquins. A party of Iroquois had pillaged a defenceless village of the Algonquins; and this act of hostility threatened a war, which would also involve the French but for the wisdom and prompt action of

[1] LeMercier was the superior of the Jesuits in New France.
[2] The Recollects returned this year to Canada, and brought great relief to the overworked Jesuits.

the great Garakontie who immediately sent wampum belts to the Iroquois nations to restrain the young warriors from further hostile acts, and to invite them to send delegates to Montreal where they would meet the Algonquins, and settle their difficulties in a peaceful manner before the Governor of the French.

The Iroquois party reached Montreal about the same time that four hundred Algonquins came down the river for their annual barter of furs. The Governor invited the Indians to Quebec, and twenty from each nation were selected as delegates to the council. They arrived at Quebec towards the end of July, and three meetings were held to adjust their differences. At the first session the delegates merely exchanged compliments and kindly greetings. The next day the Algonquin orators offered their gifts, and eloquently proclaimed the desire of their nation to preserve the peace which had been so ruthlessly broken by the Seneca warriors; and they called upon the Governor to punish those who violated the treaty he had sanctioned.

The decision given by Onontio the next day was very satisfactory to the delegates, who had assembled to listen to the peaceful solution of questions which they had long sought to settle by the scalping knife, or the tomahawk. He had ordered, he said, some Frenchmen to be put to death because they had broken the peace by the murder of three Iroquois; and now he would deal in a similar manner with the Senecas who had given cause for war by their wanton attack on the Algonquins. Peace, he said, would bring prosperity and happiness to all; and he urged the Indians to accept the blessings the missioners would bring, by teaching them the truths of Christianity and the customs of civilized life. An old Huron chief thanked the Governor for advancing the temporal interests of the Indians, and for opening the paths for the missioners to bear the light of Faith to distant nations.[1]

Garakontie then arose, and delivered an eloquent oration in favor of the Faith. He publicly proclaimed his belief in Christianity, renounced all Pagan practices, and expressed a desire to be baptized. He had already asked in his own home to be received into the Church, but Father Garnier wished to further test the sincerity of the chief; but on this occasion he spoke with such love and zeal for Christianity, and expressed such an ardent desire for baptism that the Bishop, who had learned of his good works and good life, resolved to grant his request, and to give all the pomp possible to his solemn baptism. The Governor of New France and the daughter of the Intendant stood sponsors for the Indian chief; and the Bishop administered the sacrament in the cathedral of Quebec, which was crowded with French and representatives from nearly every Indian tribe in New France. When asked if he wished to be baptized he said he had long since desired this grace; and he returned thanks to the Bishop for making him a child of the Church and an heir of Heaven.

He was afterwards conducted to the residence of the Governor, where he was received with firing of cannon by the soldiers, and was entertained at a grand banquet given in his honor. Garakontie was one of the greatest Indians of his age, and one of the wisest and the most influential among the Iroquois chiefs; and his adoption of Christianity showed that the missioners were making a deep impression on the minds of the most intelligent Indians.

[1] According to Indian official etiquette it was not proper to reply to any proposition the same day it was offered, and the French observed this rule in dealing with Indian statesmen.

The influence and acts of the Dutch retarded the spread of Christianity among the Mohawks; as they not only sold large quantities of intoxicating drink to these Indians, but they also tried to turn into ridicule the religious truths and practices which the Iroquois had learned from the French missioners. The Christian Indians had to contend against the taunts and the arguments of their Pagan brethren in the practice of their faith; but they had to overcome a greater difficulty in the attacks of the Dutch, who brought all the subtilty of educated minds, and all the malice of heretics, to bear on these simple people to induce them to relinquish their Catholic faith. Some of the intelligent and well instructed Indians could give reasons for their belief, and could defend their faith against these attacks; but the existence of religious dissensions among Europeans would necessarily lessen the confidence which they would have in the doctrines of Christianity.

The fervent Christians were accustomed to carry their beads, a little cross, or a medal, around their necks; and the Dutch tried to persuade them that this was idolatry. On one occasion, when some Dutch traders assailed these customs, an intelligent Christian replied: "You manifest very little intelligence when you attack us in this manner, or you imagine we are not well instructed in our faith. You are mistaken when you imagine we honor the Blessed Virgin as the master of life. We know too well the honor which belongs to God to bestow it upon any creature. We well know that God alone created all things, and that He alone is to be honored as our sovereign Master; but as He deigned to become man to save us, and as He chose Mary for His Mother, is it not proper to honor her as such? If Jesus Christ, her Son, exalted her to the highest degree of honor, if the angels and saints in Heaven offer her their homage, why should not we honor her upon earth? This little chaplet of beads enables us to offer her a certain number of acts of homage every day; and her image, which we have frequently before our eyes, awakens in our hearts the love and respect we should have for the Mother of our Saviour."[1] "We do not pray to the wood of the cross," another one said, "because it has not ears to hear us, nor life to help us; and God, the Master of Life, is a pure spirit who cannot be seen with bodily eyes; but we carry the cross about our necks to remind us that Jesus Christ died for us on the cross, and He died a temporal death to procure for us eternal life."

The Indians not only gave reasons for their pious practices, but as they were ruthlessly attacked, they became the aggressors, and accused the Dutch of teaching them evil. "You tell us," said Marie Tsiaouentes, "not to listen to the voice of those who preach to us the word of God; but you have always taught us evil. You seek only our furs, and you do not care for our souls. You even chase us from your place of worship, as if we profaned it by our presence. You come to this land only to promote your own interests, and not for our spiritual welfare. The Fathers, who instruct us, have come to teach us the truth, and the way to Heaven; and they left their own homes and their friends to teach us the way to Heaven. They do not seek our furs, or our wampum, but they teach us that our real treasures are in Heaven; and as they give us the goods of Heaven without demanding in return those of earth, we beleive they are true and you are false. They teach us what is good for our souls,

[1] Relations, 1670.

and you only try to corrupt us; and on this account you will be punished in Hell, like other wicked people."

On another occasion four disreputable Dutchmen invited Marie to a party, for the purpose of getting her drunk. When she was urged to drink like the others she firmly refused, aud said that she may have been guilty of many follies before baptism; but she knew more now, and would not willfully offend God. Threats, or even force, could not alter her determination, as the only thing she feared in this world was sin. She was as uncompromising with the Pagan Indians as with the Dutch, and whenever they proposed any magic rite for the healing of the sick, or the sorcerers entered a cabin to exercise their art, she would immediately leave the company, loudly proclaiming that it was no place for a Christian.

These humble Christians encountered much opposition to their faith, but they found consolation in the life of the Saviour, and in the history of the early Christians. Many of the native Mohawk converts looked for relief from these petty persecutions of the Dutch and their Pagan fellow countrymen in exile; and their hearts anxiously yearned for a new home on the St. Lawrence, under the protection of the French.

The Iroquois had already learned that the Fathers did not seek any temporal gain by laboring amongst them, but came for their moral and religious improvement, and they consequently believed in their teaching, and lived Christian lives, though they were often obliged to suffer persecution in the observance of the Christian law.

Father Pierron would not receive any adults into the Church unless they were free from every sinful habit, and would abandon the superstitious practices of their race; but drunkenness was so common and superstitions so

THE GREAT FESTIVAL OF THE DEAD.   133

generally followed that he baptized very few adults, and his prayers and labors for their conversion seemed to be in vain, yet he did not weary in trying various methods to teach them Christianity: at one time instructing them in the art of reading and writing, so they might be able to learn Christian doctrine from books; at another time teaching them a play in which the sacraments, the commandments, the chief truths of Christianity, and the end of man, were represented by painted toys which pleased the fancy and enlightened the mind.[1]

An event occurred in March, 1670, in the town of Gandaouague which advanced these people far in their progress towards civilization and Christianity, and which was of vast importance to the Mohawks and to the Iroquois nations. Delegates from the other nations had assembled to take part in the great festival of the dead, and Father Pierron was invited to witness the ceremony, which began with a narration of the fables and superstitions which formed the theoretic part of their religious belief. Father Pierron was very strict and intolerant in everything pertaining to religion, and considered their fables as foolish and their sorcery as the work of the devil; so when he spoke he told them their history was lies, and their superstitions were the work of demons. One of the chiefs reproached the Father for what seemed to him, a wanton insult to his race, and he said that these things had been practiced and believed by his people from time immemorial. Father Pierron, believing he was doing the work of God, and secure in the hold he had in the esteem of these people, became more bold at the reproach of the chief, and replied that because the Iroquois had practiced these things did not prove that they were good, as they also practiced

[1] Relations, 1670, p. 35.

drunkenness, debauchery, and thievery, yet they did not believe that these things were good; and he said it was his duty to teach them to abandon their superstitions as well as their vices. The chief made no reply, but told the Father to leave the assembly room as they wished to sing their songs and observe their rites; but as the Father did not wish to yield, it was only to avoid disturbance that he reluctantly withdrew. Rumor soon spread through the town that Father Pierron had been insulted at the meeting and would leave the country; and as the people loved him and feared the resentment of the French, much feeling was manifested towards the chief who had ordered him to leave the assembly. This chief was a friend of the missioner and willingly came to apologize for his rudeness, and he also offered to do all he could to induce the entire nation to become Christians. He proposed that a council of the chief men of the nation should be held, then the Father should give a present to each of the three clans of the Mohawks, and he should publicly invite them to abandon their old traditions and become Christians.

This chief, who had great authority among the Mohawks, assembled the leading men of the nation in the cabin of Father Pierron, where the missioner addressed them on the folly of their superstitions and fables, and on the beauty and benefit of Christian truths. The Mohawks had frequently said that they were one body and one soul with the French; but Father Pierron said that they could not be one soul as long as the French believed that the soul was immortal and made to the image and likeness of God, whilst the Iroquois believed that it was a wolf, a serpent, a fish, or a bird, or some other animal, which appeared to them in a dream. He told them that

Agreskoue, whom they called the master of life, was only a slave, a demon of Hell; that God alone who created all things, was the Master of life. He then gave them a large belt of wampum inviting them to renounce Agreskoue, and all superstitious practices connected with this worship, and to adore God, and observe His law.

Great applause followed this proposition, and Father Pierron was delighted with the prospects of success. He presented another belt to urge the sorcerers to cease invoking the demons in healing the sick; but to use the remedies which Nature supplied, and whose efficacy they had learned through the kindness and skill of the French.

Two days[1] afterwards a council was held for the purpose of replying to the propositions of Father Pierron. The great Onondaga chief, Garakontie, was present and had labored, no doubt, earnestly and effectively, during the interval between the councils, to influence the Mohawks in favor of Christianity, though the Mohawk orator said it was not Garakontie but Father Pierron who had changed their minds and hearts in regard to their religious belief.[2] The orator repeated faithfully and eloquently all the arguments Father Pierron had advanced against the superstitious practices of the Iroquois, and he also gave presents as pledges of their belief in the propositions of Father Pierron. Garakontie also spoke, and said he was pleased that the Mohawks had more faith in the words of a man like Father Pierron, who sacrificed so much for their salvation, and who brought them the word of God, than they had in his own; and they showed their wisdom in accepting these truths, because they would promote their happiness in this world and in Eternity.

[1] The Indians never gave an immediate answer to any mportant proposition, as this would seem to indicate indifference or hasty judgment.
[2] Relations, 1670; p. 43.

The next day the Ancients again assembled, and gave a more definite and satisfactory answer to the propositions of Father Pierron. The chief who first proposed this council spoke for his people, saying: "It is not an easy matter to give up customs we have observed since childhood, and to renounce traditions that have been the guide of our race since the beginning of the world; but as we have resolved to please you in all things, and to show the great pleasure we have in listening to you, we make you absolute master of our bodies and souls; and there is no obstacle which we will not overcome to render ourselves worthy of the honor which you wish to procure for us. Instruct us, because we wish to believe what you believe, to condemn what you condemn, and to renounce whatever is displeasing to you. If any benighted person should hereafter invoke Agreskoue, know that it will not be with our authority or consent. Had we the authority over our young people which old men should have, then we could assure you that your wishes would be universally obeyed. We commend our sick to your care, as you have deprived us of the only means, which up to this time, we have employed to restore their health. Enlarge your chapel, so that there will be room for all of us to go to receive the instructions which we believe to be the will of God."[1]

Father Pierron thanked the Ancients for their favorable reply; and then hastened to the chapel to return thanks to God for having blessed his labors in such a signal manner. A few days after the Father was still more pleased to see the sorcerers casting the shells, and other instruments of their mysteries, into the fire. The Ancients led the young to the chapel to be instructed and to learn

[1] Relations 1670, p. 44.

to pray; and although the French had often learned to mistrust the Iroquois, yet there was good evidence that Christianity had obtained a strong foothold among the Mohawks.

The great desire these people manifested to learn the truths of Christianity claimed more time and attention than Father Pierron could give to this work, and in July he went to Quebec to get other missioners to help him in this promising field, and the Rev. Thiery Beschefer and the Rev. Louis Nocolas returned with him to the Mohawk country.

Drunkenness was the great obstacle to the propagation of the Faith among the Oneidas, as it was in the valley of the Mohawk, and during the time of their drunken revelry even the life of the missionary was not safe. A party of Oneidas returned from the Dutch settlement August 16, 1669, with sixty casks of liquor; and from that time till the middle of November a great many of the adults were drunk every day, and would not come near the chapel except to commit some outrage.[1] When the liquor gave out Father Bruyas went through the town calling upon the inhabitants to come to listen to the truths of Christianity. Many attended his instructions, but he did not receive any healthy adult into the Church till Christmas, 1669, when he baptized an exemplary female who had repeatedly asked to be baptized. His time, however, was fully occupied in visiting the sick and in instructing his little Christian flock.

Garakontie came from Onondaga to encourage the Oneidas to visit the chapel, and to learn the truths of the Christian faith.

[1] When Father Bruyas went to the conference at Onondaga his companion, a layman, was obliged to fly from the village for safety.

The Onondaga mission was dedicated to St. John the Baptist, and Father Millet imitated the example of this great saint by going about through the town and through the forest, crying out "Do penance, for the kingdom of God is at hand; prepare ye the way of the Lord;" and in this way he gathered the people around him at the chapel where he gave them a short instruction on some of the important truths of Christianity. He ridiculed their superstitions and sorcery, their dream theory, and the worship of Agreskoue. He also attended their banquets to invoke God's blessing on the feast, where formerly the Indians called on the demons or their manitous to preside on these festive occasions.

Garakontie was a great source of comfort to the missioners by his holy life, and a great assistance to them in their labors. He advised Father Millet to pay more attention to the old people, and to have a special instruction for them on Sundays, as the Indians have great respect for the aged, and the influence of their example would react favorably upon the young; so the Father gave a banquet on the following Sunday, to which Garakontie invited the Ancients of the nation, so they might become better acquainted with the missioner and with the doctrines he taught. As it was customary for the Indians to sing about their fables or their history at these feasts, Father Millet sang the goodness of God towards his people, the birth of the Saviour of the world and His victory over the demons; and to make a deeper impression on the minds of these people he placed the Bible, representing the will and the word of God, on a little table, and above it the image of the Saviour, with the symbols of Indian sorcery and superstition at his feet, to show the triumph of Christianity.

Father Millet spoke to them about the unity of God and the creation of the world by His power; about the Redemption of mankind through the Incarnation, by which the Son of God became man to teach all the way to Heaven by word and example. As the Saviour returned to Heaven He left His teachings in the Bible, and He commanded His Apostles to teach His word and His will to every race and nation in the world. This was his mission among them; as he and his companions had left their pleasant homes in France to bring the Gospel to the Indians of the New World, in obedience to the command of the Saviour. The chiefs seemed very much pleased with the address, and they thanked the Father for his entertainment and for the light he shed upon his mission. The Father's preaching evidently had a good effect on the minds of the Ancients, as the chapel was soon too small to accommodate the numbers that came for instructions, and it was necessary to divide them into two bands, using the little bell to call the children to the chapel, and ringing the large old bell, which had done missionary duty in the town for fourteen years, to warn the adults of the time for the sermon and prayer. The children began to sing, and to repeat their catechism lessons by the fireside and in the streets, and in a short time many were heard to say: "There is but one God, who is the Master of life;" and those who were already Christians began to show greater piety and charity in their lives, and to imitate the holiness of the early Christians.

The good disposion of the Indians inspired the Father to make another attack on their superstitions, and especially on the observance of dreams. He again assembled the Ancients in council, and told them they should abandon their feasts of impurity and gluttony, and their observance of dreams, for these dreams are often either wicked or foolish, and it must be wrong to fulfill them. As the belief in dreams was universal among the Iroquois, Father Millet was doubtful of the issue, but he considered this step necessary for the good of religion, and to test the faith of some who were addicted to these practices, but who wished to be admitted to the Church. A long conference on these subjects was held among the Indians after the departure of Father Millet from the council, and when he was recalled, Garakontie gave the reply of his nation to the propositions of the Father. He said that his countrymen were convinced of the truth of the Father's words; that they would renounce the superstitions he had prescribed; they would no longer believe in, or obey the dream spirit; they had already forsaken the worship of Agreskoue, whose spirit was no longer invoked at their feasts, but the missioner, himself, was invited on these occasions to pray, and when he was absent some chief took his place in asking God not only for the blessings of earth, but also for the joys of Heaven. He said he hoped soon to see the entire nation attending the chapel; and, as a pledge of the sincerity of his people, he gave the Father the usual belt of Wampum.[1] It could hardly be expected that the entire nation would immediately abandon its ancient customs; or that the young men, who enjoyed such liberty of action, would give up their vices to become Christians. Father Millet, however, took advantage of their promises to assail the practices of the sorcerers and medicine men, as he hoped by destroying the influence of these men to wean the people from their superstitions and imperceptibly lead them to adopt Christian customs. The Indians could

[1] Relations, 1670; p. 53.

more easily give up these outward forms than they could overcome their passions, and hatred of an enemy, which with them was the greatest virtue, could not readily be exchanged for Christian love. They very unwillingly, therefore, permitted the Father to prepare their captives for a Christian death and consequent happiness in Heaven; for they savagely burned these captives in this world, and they wished them to burn eternally in hell; but their opposition did not prevent the missioner from instructing and baptizing nearly every one of their victims.

The Church among the Onondagas was composed principally of Hurons and other nations that had been conquered by the Iroquois, for although some of the latter were baptized, yet Father Millet did not wish to receive any adults into the Church whilst such general depravity existed around them. Those who had been received into the Church led very edifying lives, and were faithful in their attendance at the chapel and prompt in their prayers in the cabin and in the field. Garakontie, especially, gave testimony by his life to the efficacy and beauty of Christian teaching, and he tried to induce his countrymen to abandon their superstitions and vices, and regulate their lives according to the law of Christ.

Father[1] Carheil writes from Cayuga June 10, 1670, that his time was fully occupied in teaching Christian doctrine to young and old, in baptizing children and adults, and in visiting the sick and dying. The country was placed under the protection of St. Joseph, and each of the villages[2] was dedicated to some saint. He had baptized twenty-five children and twelve adults since the preceding autumn, although many objected to the sacrament, prejudiced, no doubt, by the malicious stories circulated

[1] Relations, 1670. [2] See Chapter II.

by Pagan Indians. They claimed that nations decayed as they adopted Christianity, and death soon followed the reception of baptism. One instance of obstinacy will suffice to show the trials of the missionary. He visited a Seneca woman who was sick, and spoke to her of God, of the soul, and eternal life; but she would not listen to him, and prejudiced all her friends against him, so that all maintained profound silence when he entered the cabin, or were indifferent to his presence. He said mass for her, and prayed that God would give her the grace of faith; but she still remained obstinate and threw her shoe at him when he attempted to address her. The Father did not lose hope, but returned to the cabin at evening and spoke to those present of the teachings of Christ. Finally, a Christian woman told the sick Seneca that she was dying, and should listen to the missionary and prepare for the meeting with God. She yielded; told the missionary she believed all he had taught her, and asked to be baptized.

The Huron Christians gave great consolation to the Father, and a noble example to the Pagans, by their fidelity to the Faith, by their devout demeanor, frequent reception of the sacraments, and the purity of their lives.

A very large number attended the instructions which were given every day in the chapel, nearly one hundred coming the first day; but it was almost impossible to induce them to abandon their religious theory of dreams. Although they did not believe that a dream was a divinity yet they held that a genius, or demi-god, they call Agatkonchoria, appears to them in dreams, and commands them to do what he thus reveals; and they faithfully follow the mandates of this mysterious power, as happiness and prosperity depend upon obedience, and misfortune and evil will come from refusal or neglect to obey. The principal of these genii is Tharoniawagon, who is also the chief divinity and the master of life.

The young men delight in hunting, fishing, and in war; and when they are successful in these they become insolent and despise Christianity, as the foundation of faith is the spirit of humility, and this virtue is directly opposed to all the savage believed to be good or great. It is very difficult, therefore, to make an Indian die a saint who has lived all his life a savage.

Father Fremin found his greatest consolation among the Senecas in his little congregation of old Huron Christians at Gandougarae. These Christians had not forgotten the doctrines they had been taught in their old homes, and they came again to the foot of the altar to renew their faith, and to thank God for the presence of a priest. They made open profession of their faith, and the purity of their lives made a very favorable impression upon the minds of the Pagans.

Many of the Christian Hurons were very exemplary, and even saintly in their lives; and through the long years of their desolation they kept alive the spirit of faith by repeating the truths taught them by the Jesuits in their old home, by acts of piety, and by prayers. Two of the old men were especially noted for their holy lives, and the Pagans as well as the Christians were edified by their good example. One of these old men, James Atondo, was noted for his spirit of prayer, and for his zeal in proclaiming the name of God. He accepted the law of God as the guide of his life, and he sought to convince his Pagan friends of the benefits to be derived from prayer. He told the Pagans that they gave banquets and presents, and went to much trouble to propitiate the dream spirit so they might be successful in fishing, in hunting, and in war; yet they were in misery and in want, whilst disease and war carried off some of their finest men. He did not believe in fulfilling dreams, but prayed to God for guidance and help, and God blessed him with a vigorous old age, and an abundant supply of fish and game. He was comfortably situated in this world, and hoped to be happy with God in the next; whilst they would only be released from present ills to fall victims to greater sufferings after death.

Francis Tehoronhionga was another noted and exemplary member of Father Fremin's little flock. He was intelligent, and well instructed, as he was formerly the host of Father LeMoyne; and he taught the doctrine of the Church to every member of his household. For more than twenty years he never neglected his daily prayers; and every day he besought God to preserve his life until he could again see a priest, and receive the sacraments of the Church. He had the firmest hope that his prayers would be heard. He could not believe that God would call him to Christianity and allow him to die without its blessings, because then all his prayers would have been in vain, and the spiritual character of baptism would be a mark of dishonor instead of a symbol of glory. When he heard of the arrival of Father Fremin he exclaimed: "God has at length heard my prayer." In speaking of his dead relatives he said: "Why should I grieve over their departure? My mother died shortly after receiving baptism, and most of my near relatives received the sacraments before death; and I hope they are now happy in Heaven." Every member of his family, who died when a priest was not near, made, at least, a confession of sin, and endeavored to excite in his heart perfect sorrow for the past. The greatest affliction of his life, he said, was caused by the bad conduct of one of his sons, who led a very bad life and died without having been reconciled with God. He had then but one son living, and, although this one had gone on the war path, yet, as he had received the sacrament of penance from Father Fremin before his departure, if death should come it would not find him entirely unprepared.

Francis knew many of the Bible narratives, and the miracles and parables of the Gospel, and he delighted to recite these for the edification of his neighbors and friends, and in this manner he paved the way for the teaching of the Fathers.

It was a very difficult and tedious task to imbue the minds of these savages with pure and thorough Christian principles, as these were contrary to all their traditions, modes of life, and forms of thought; and they were apt to confound their Indian belief with Catholic truth. As an instance of this confusion of Pagan opinion with Christian truth, Father Fremin relates the peculiar notion an Iroquois woman had of Heaven.[1] The daughter of this woman died a Christian, and, as the family was quite prominent in the nation, the girl had twenty slaves to do her bidding; so she was never obliged to carry wood or water, or do any manual labor in this world; and as she was the only member of the family in Heaven, she would there be compelled to cook for herself, and do all the drudgery; so this kind mother requested the missioner to baptize a female slave, who was dying, so that she might be a servant to her child in Heaven.

The Senecas seem to be more firmly attached to the dream theory than the other Iroquois, and they consider

[1] Relations, 1670.

any one guilty of a grevious crime who would not fulfill the obligations thus revealed. The dreamer is not deterred from fulfilling every feature of the dream, how rediculous soever or difficult it may be. One, for instance, dreamed of taking a bath, and as soon as he awoke in the morning he ran naked to the neighboring cabins, and compelled the inmates to pour kettles of water over his body. Another dreamed he was taken captive and burned at the stake; so he had his friends bind him to a stake, and light the faggots around him until he was quite severely burned, as he hoped in this way to escape a real captivity, and a horrid death. Another made the long and toilsome journey to Quebec to obtain a dog, which she dreamed she had purchased from the French.

The missionary, therefore, is in constant danger, as one of these Indians may dream that it is his duty to mutilate or kill the minister of Christ.[1] There were, however, many bright examples of beautiful lives and saintly deaths among the Christians to console and encourage the Fathers, even in the midst of these dangers.

[1] Relations, 1670.

CHAPTER XVI.

THE IROQUOIS MISSIONS IN 1671.

MANY BAPTISMS—EXAMPLES OF PIETY—GARAKONTIE'S FAITH—CONDEMNS DREAM FOLLY—HATRED OF SIN—GANDOUGARAE DESTROYED—LIQUOR DRINKING—OBSTACLES TO FAITH—DELAYED CONVERSIONS—BAPTISM OF SAONCHIOGWA—COUNCIL AT QUEBEC—IROQUOIS EXILES.

THIS was a peaceful and a comparatively uneventful year on the Iroquois missions; and the Fathers continued their work of instructing, civilizing, and receiving into the Church, these savage people. About three hundred were baptized during the year, and although the greater part of these were the sick, and the prisoners who were burned at the stake, yet these baptisms do not represent the extent of the labors of the Fathers among the Iroquois, as their instructions were far-reaching and of great importance; and the Indians were gradually abandoning their vices and superstitions, and were unconsciously adopting civilized and Christian customs.

More than eighty were baptized on the Mohawk missions and many of these manifested by their lives and by their words before death, that they had the true Christian spirit, and were well instructed in their religion. One faithful woman had been repeatedly solicited by a chief to do evil, but she repressed his importunities by declaring that, as a Christian, her soul was precious in the sight of God, and she would not offend Him by defiling her soul with sin.

Father Bruyas, who had charge of the mission of St. Francis Xavier among the Oneidas, relates several instances of the faithful and enlightened Christian spirit manifested on different occasions by members of his flock. An old Christian Huron, Joseph Ondessonka, requested the Father to tell him when he would be near death, so he might give his whole attention to the care of his soul. He made a general confession[1] of his whole life, and continually called upon God to be merciful to him and to forgive him. Shortly before death he asked the priest to assemble the Christians in his cabin so he might exort them to be faithful to their religion, and thus they would one day be united in Heaven. He died with the name of Jesus on his lips, calling upon the Saviour to receive his soul.[2] Shortly after the death of Joseph another prominent member of the little church at Oneida was called to her reward. She had been a model of the true Christian in her life, and she edified her friends by her saintly death. She thanked God for the full use of her senses during her last illness, so that she could devote the last hours of her life to prayer and preparation for eternity.

Such holy lives and saintly deaths were the only consolation the Fathers found among these people, and the only visible reward for their labor.

At Onondaga Garakontie publicly proclaimed his Christian faith, and gave in his life a beautiful example

---

[1] He could not write, nor was he versed in the science of numbers; but he adopted an effective method of portraying the number and different kinds of sin. He formed little heaps of grains of corn to represent the several times he had committed any sin, and the different heaps showed the various species of sin.

[2] Relations 1671, p. 15.

of the efficacy of Christianity in overcoming evil and of leading its professors into the path of virtue. Before accepting the Faith he had a plurality of wives, and was addicted to many of the superstitions of his race, but he abandoned all these on the threshold of the Church. In a speech at a public banquet he said that he had filled many important offices in his country; he had been kind to the poor and to the widows, helping them in their time of need; and all these things he had done through natural inclination, or a sense of honor; he would continue to do in the future as he had in the past, but henceforth he would act through higher motives, because his religion taught him that these good deeds were pleasing to God.

They must not, however, expect him to countenance the belief in dreams, or to participate in any of the superstitious practices of their forefathers; because all these things were forbidden by the law of God. An occasion soon came in which his fidelity was put to a severe test. The Iroquois celebrate in the spring time the feast of dreams,[1] during which they expect that Thoroniawagon, the master of life, will reveal to them their good or evil fortune during the coming year; and, as the feast is celebrated in his honor, they hope he will grant them success in the hunt, and victory in war. The chief of the town is expected to appoint the time and suggest the preparations for the feast. Garakontie held this position, and when his attention was called to the matter at a council he replied that he was a Christian and could not sanction any such superstition.[2]

The action of Garakontie displeased the Pagans, but it encouraged the Christians to publicly profess their belief;

[1] Called Onnonhouaroia.   [2] Relations 1671, p. 17.

and it gave the sanction of the greatest living Iroquois to the teaching of the Fathers.

The great chief fearlessly proclaimed his faith before the Dutch at Albany, and he told them that they could not hope for success in their peace negotiations with the Iroquois because they sought to discredit the teachings of the Jesuits. "When we treat with Onontio,"[1] he said, "he tells us we must honor God and keep His holy law, and we must respect and believe those who teach us what is good for our souls; but you turn us away from the worship of God, and ridicule the practices taught us by the Black Robes."

The uncompromising faith of this great chief had a salutary effect upon the Christians at Onondaga; and they renounced old customs which were immoral, and they abstained from liquor, which was bringing disgrace and ruin upon their race. When one of the members of the little flock gave scandal by excessive liquor drinking, she was excluded from the church until she had made reparation by public penance: but so highly did these people prize the rules of their church that they willingly bore the penalties inflicted for public sin; nor was their respect for these laws weakened by the taunts, or the sneers, of their Pagan friends.

Father Carheil baptized sixty-two in his different missions this year, and of this number thirty-five died shortly after receiving this first sacrament of the Church.

He met with some difficulty in eliciting true sorrow from the adults for past sins; as many of these had been addicted to vices which, with the natural light of reason, they knew to be wrong; but when the greater light of revelation and grace discovered these things to them in

[1] The French Governor.

the enormity of sins, their souls were disturbed with the consciousness of guilt, and a special grace was required to enable them to conquer. In such cases the missioners had recourse to prayer; and they generally were pleased to find such persons manifesting every outward mark of sincere sorrow. As an instance of the difficulty of awakening sorrow for sin in the hearts of these people, Father Carheil relates the case of a young woman who was a regular attendant at the instructions in the chapel. She was amiable in disposition and refined in manners, and her conversation showed more of European culture than of savage breeding. She gradually learned the doctrines of Christianity, and the missioner considered her a well disposed subject for baptism. In making his daily visits to the cabins, the Father found this woman quite seriously ill, and piteously begging for some remedy to restore her health. He spoke to her of the spiritual healing of the soul, and of the dispositions necessary for receiving the sacraments; and she listened with pleasure to his instructions upon the nature and effects of baptism; but when he told her that the pouring of water alone was not sufficient to merit the graces of this sacrament, but that true sorrow and a firm resolve to sin no more were also necessary, she refused to accept his teaching. The saving of a soul was too important a work to be abandoned on account of a rebuff, so the Father resumed his instructions as soon as she would allow him to enter her cabin, and her dislike of Christianity was soon changed to love. The solicitude which the Father manifested for her spiritual and corporal welfare won her confidence, and she soon learned that deep sorrow for sin brought true joy to the soul.

Father Garnier relates examples of individual piety

and holiness of life manifested by his little flock; but, as a nation, the Senecas did not seem to be any more disposed to adopt Christianity than their brethren of the Cayugas, and it was only in the time of humiliation or defeat that they hastened to the chapel. The town of Gandougarae, St. Michael's, was entirely destroyed by fire in the spring of 1670, and the inhabitants lost all their provisions and personal property, yet their greatest loss seemed to be the chapel. They said the destruction of their own homes was a merited punishment for their opposition to the Gospel, and they promised to erect a handsome chapel for the Father, as soon as they could provide shelter for themselves, and protection against their enemies.

Drunkenness was very common among the Senecas whenever they could obtain liquor from the Dutch or French, and at such times the orgies continued until all the liquor was consumed. Often twenty or thirty small casks of strong drink were brought from the settlement at Albany, and the entire Pagan population of a town would begin a drunken debauch, which would last for many weeks. It was at such times, especially, that the Christians showed the influence of their faith upon their lives. They took no part in these excesses, and were obliged to hide away in the forests to escape from the riotous rabble; and they would steal their way to the chapel, under the mantle of morning twilight, to pray in peace.

The Senecas were as fully fascinated with the dream folly as the other nations, and they celebrated the feast every spring time with all the fervor of religious enthusiasts. Some of the Christians, however, firmly protested against this folly, and refused to take part in the dream feast. One old Huron, at St. Michael's, went through the town, and also through the neighboring village of St. James', crying out against the custom, and warning the Pagans not to approach his cabin to seek his aid in furthering their folly.

The Father says these people manifest great aversion to the Faith, and the conversion of a Savage must be the work of grace. The unrestrained liberty of their life made them averse to any law which restricted their will, or fettered the freedom of passion's sway. Pride, also, prevented many from yielding submission to the Christian law; for this vice reigned in the cabins of the Iroquois as well as in the palaces of Europe, and a few furs, or a number of scalps, were sufficient to fill an Indian's mind with exalted thoughts of his own importance. Their moralty was not in accord with the Christain code, and they could not be induced to abandon the practices of a licentious life for the moral virtues of the Gospel. Some of their amusements were immoral, but they were a source of sensual pleasure which the young people would not willingly forego at the command of the priest.

Insurmountable as these obstacles seemed, yet the Fathers[1] overcame them by untiring efforts; and their zeal, their patience, and their sweetness, won the respect and good will of many of these people.

The Fathers knew the language well, and every day they preached to large numbers in the chapel. All the Senecas were sufficiently well instructed to receive baptism; but human considerations or sinful lives kept them out of the Church, and many delayed their conversion until they found death approaching.

[1] Father Fremin left the Seneca mission this year to take charge of the little congregation at Prarie de la Madelaine.

The Senecas were also very much attached to the observance of superstitious customs, which they very reluctantly abandoned to adopt Christianity; but as all were well instructed very few died without being received into the Church. Many of the Senecas put off their conversion to the hour of death, because they did not wish to abandon their vices or renounce the customs of their race; but when they realized that life was drawing to its close they urgently sent for the priest, and requested to be baptized so they might enter the Christian Heaven. It was difficult, however, for them to overcome in a moment the habits of a life-time. Father Garnier relates the peculiar case of one of his converts who persisted in believing in dreams. This man dreamed, shortly after baptism, that he was in Heaven, where he was received by the French with the cry which the Indians utter when they meet a prisoner who is destined for the stake; and he accused the Father of deceiving him, as baptism was, according to his dream, only a mark by which the French in Heaven might know those who were to be burned.

Morning and evening prayers were said in the different villages, by Pagans as well as Christians, and Father Garnier was kept so busy instructing and baptizing that he was obliged to send for help to assist him in his work.

Following the example of Garakontie, Saonchiogwa, the great chief of the Cayugas, was received into the Church at Quebec, with all the ceremony and honor which the prelate and Governor could bestow upon so distinguished a convert.

The Senecas and Cayugas were near neighbors and firm friends, and were closely allied in peace and war; so when the former decided to send a delegation on important business to Quebec, in 1671, they selected Saonchiogwa, the Cayuga chief, as their ambassador.

The French Governor labored to put an end to the war between the Iroquois and Algonquins; and he threatened to invade the land of the Senecas unless they buried the hatchet and released the captives they had taken. The proud Senecas were very indignant at this unjust assumption of French alliance with all the Indian nations who were at war with the Iroquois, merely because these nations traded with the French, or because French Fathers preached the Gospel among them.[1] The French furnished arms to these nations to fight the Iroquois, and at the same time they ordered the Senecas to lay down their arms. Many of the young warriors were in favor of resenting this insult by attacking the French settlements; but the wiser ones feared the French might make good their threat, and that their homes would be made desolate, as were the towns of their Mohawk brethren some years before by the army of DeTracy. In this dilemma they resorted to their usual peace strategy, and they resolved to send some of their less important captives to Quebec, as a peace offering to Onontio. To more effectually conceal their duplicity, they placed these prisoners in the hands of Saonchiogwa, who had always been friendly towards the French, and whose sincerity would not be questioned at the council.

Saonchiogwa willingly undertook this embassy, as he had long cherished the desire of entering the Church; and his visit to Quebec would bring him near his old friend, Chaumonot,[2] who would instruct him, and pre-

[1] Relations, 1671.
[2] Saonchiogwa represented the Cayuga nation at the first council, held at Onondaga in 1656, to consider the treaty of peace with the French, and the adoption of Christianity by the Iroquois; and he was one of the chiefs who replied favorably on this occasion to the proposals of Fathers Chaumonot and Dablon.

pare him for baptism at the hands of the Bishop. As soon as he had fulfilled his duties as delegate to the council he gave his time and attention to the care of his soul, and placed himself in the hands of Father Chaumonot for instructions. As he had been the host of Mesnard and Carheil, at Cayuga, and had carefully listened to the truths they had taught, he was prepared in a very short time for admission to the Church.

So sincere seemed Saonchiogwa in his resolution, and so comprehensive was his knowledge of Catholic teaching, that the Bishop did not hesitate to confer on him the sacrament of baptism in the Cathedral, where he renounced the Pagan practices of his race. Talon, the Intendant, was his sponsor at baptism, when he received the Christian name of Louis. Talon then gave a grand banquet in honor of the neophyte, who was allowed to invite as his guests all the Iroquois, Hurons, and Algonquins, at Quebec.

Many other Iroquois followed the example of Saonchiogwa, and came to Quebec where they could be instructed in Christianity without fear of molestation from their Pagan friends; and some of these remained there, in the new Indian community, after their reception into the Church, so they might practice their religion in peace. Christianity sank deep into their hearts when they could sacrifice the love and esteem of friends and fellow countrymen, and could abandon their native land to follow the light of Faith. One generous Christian widow, who held a high hereditary rank[1] of importance among the

---

[1] These were called Oianders by the French, and their office was of the same importance as that of the Ancients among the men. The office was hereditary, but it was retained only by common consent of the clans, and by the merit of the individual. They held councils to discuss state affairs, and their opinions were generally respected by the councils of the league.

Mohawks, left her home and kindred to seek more religious liberty among the French, and to have the opportunity of satisfying her spirit of piety and devotion in a Christian community. She was degraded from her rank, because she had renounced the customs of her country; but she did not grieve over this loss, as she prized more highly the name of Christian than the title of Oiander.

CHAPTER XVII.

MISSIONS IN THE IROQUOIS COUNTRY--Continued.

FEW CONVERTS—CATHOLIC IROQUOIS EMIGRATE—FERVOR AMONG THE MOHAWKS—BRUYAS AT TIONNONTOGUEN—DRUNKENNESS—CONFERENCES AT ONEIDA—INFLUENCE OF SORCERERS—PAGAN BELIEF—GARAKONTIE'S EXAMPLE—OBSTACLES TO CONVERSION—PRACTICE OF MEDICINE—RAFFEIX CHARMED WITH CAYUGA—PIETY AT CAYUGA—CHAPELS AMONG THE SENECAS—FALSE NOTIONS—OMENS OF EVIL.

FATHER Bruyas, who had labored for nearly five years among the Oneidas, was made Superior of all the Iroquois missions, and, with Father Boniface, he attended to the spiritual wants of the Mohawks, who, though they were once the most bitter foes of the French, were now the most docile and submissive among the nations. The number, however, of healthy adults who became Christians was small, as this step to them seemed a renunciation of the cherished customs and the traditions of their race; and those who did embrace the Faith felt obliged to leave their homes in the pleasant valley and emigrate to some of the Catholic Indian settlements on the St. Lawrence. This year fifteen Christians left for the Huron settlements of Notre Dame de Foi, and about fifty more had their canoes ready for the journey when the entreaties of their relatives and friends, and the conviction that their departure would weaken their country in the war with the Mohigans, induced them to remain.[1] Father Pierron was called to labor among the Iroquois at

[1] Relations 1672, p. 18.

the new mission of St. Francis Xavier on the St. Lawrence, Father Fremin, the Superior, having gone to France in the interests of his Catholic Indian settlement.

Father Boniface had his little chapel at Gandougarae, and he also attended the neighboring village of Gannagaro. His people were very devoted to the Church, and surpassed all the missions among the Iroquois in their fervor and zeal. This was the land[1] which had been bathed in the blood of the first martyrs among the Iroquois, and the missioner ascribed the fruit of his labors to the blessings of this goodly seed.

Father Bruyas began the formation of a little church at Tionnontoguen, which also included the neighboring hamlets, but he did not meet with the same success which crowned the zeal of Father Boniface in the adjoining towns. The Christians here were few in numbers and void of influence, being mostly slaves; and the Pagans seemed more inclined to follow the counsels of the Dutch than to accept the teaching of the Jesuit.

Bruyas gave his leisure hours to the preparation of a work[2] on the language, which would enable him to acquire a more exact knowledge of the dialect spoken by the Mohawks, and which might serve as a guide to future missionaries.

The doctrines of Christianity were so generally accepted in Father Boniface's mission, and the people were animated by such a Catholic spirit, that he began receiving the adults into the Church who were not in immediate danger of death. In ten months he solemnly baptized

[1] The villages had been removed to other sites, probably twice since the deaths of René Goupil and Father Jogues; but these were practically the same people who had crowned the lives of these saintly persons with a martyr's death.

[2] This was called, "Mohawk Radicals," and was the first work of the kind ever written on this branch of the great Iroquois-Huron tongue.

about thirty adults;[1] and though this may not seem a very large number, yet they were persons upon whose fidelity he could depend, and their adoption of Christianity showed that the zeal of the Father was gradually weaning the Mohawks from the Pagan rites. Christian maidens refused to accept in marriage Pagan youths who were known to be opposed to the Christian law, and even wives left their husbands when they were not allowed to practice their religion in peace. When Christians heard of the illness of one of their brethren they assembled at his cabin to pray with him for a speedy recovery or a happy death.

At Christmas time Father Boniface built a little crib in his chapel, representing the Infant Jesus at Bethlehem, and around this the children came, and sang the hymns they learned, in honor of the Saviour.

The Mohawks of Tionnontoguen did not respond so generously to the efforts of Father Bruyas, but he found an ample field for his zeal in reclaiming the old Christians who had relapsed into the vices and customs of the Pagans.

Peace was proclaimed between the Mohigans and the Mohawks, but this was more disastrous to the latter than war. War compelled the Mohawks to abstain from liquor, because the ways to the Dutch settlement were beset with armed bands; and they feared, moreover, that their drunken carousals would leave them an easy prey to their wily enemies. As soon as the war ceased liquor was again brought to the towns, and a drunken revelry began which ended only when a fatal epidemic swept over the nation. The disease carried off its victims in a few days; and the Fathers were kept busy instructing the sick and baptizing the dying.

[1] The celebrated chief, Assendase, was converted this year, and he edified the Christians by his good example.

THE FOLLY OF THEIR FABLES. 161

In the Autumn of 1671 whilst the young men of the Oneida nation were on the war-path or the hunt, Father Bruyas invited the Ancients to meet every day, at a convenient hour, to listen to his explanation of Christianity, and to learn the folly of their fables. Many came to these conferences through curiosity, others came to pass away the time, and others came to learn something of Christianity. One of the Oneidas, who was versed in the tradition of the nation, requested the honor of opening the first conference with a recital of the teachings of his forefathers in regard to the creation of the world. The fanciful fables which were held as important truths by these people were easily refuted by the Father, and the doctrines of Christianity were placed in such a strong light that the Oneidas came more willingly to be instructed. At the end of each conference Bruyas made a prayer begging of God the grace to know Him, to believe in Him, and to keep His commandments. The good effect of the Father's labors was manifest in the warm welcome accorded him in the cabins, when he came to visit the sick. The sorcerers, however, remained obstinately inimical to the introduction of Christianity, and their example greatly retarded the spread of the Gospel. Death did not always terminate the opposition of this class to the Faith, for after the earthly career of these men was ended their spirit seemed to hover over the people, like an evil genius impelling to evil. One of the Ancients called a meeting of the councilors to discuss a dream he had, in which a famous sorcerer appeared to him, and gave him advice regarding the defense of the nation. The Andastes, he said, intended soon to invade the land with a great army, and the only hope of safety for the nation consisted in placing his body in the path over which the enemy should pass. Such great faith did the people have in this sorcerer's power during life that they easily believed after death he could guide the nation to weal or woe; so they exhumed his body, and placed it in a grand mausoleum built on the path leading to the home of the Andastes.

Father Millet replaced Father Bruyas at Oneida, and he was very favorably impressed with the good dispositions which the people manifested towards his teaching. The conferences of Father Bruyas were generally discussed, and many were convinced of the reality of the pains of Hell for the wicked and the joys of Heaven for the just, and they desired to escape the one and enjoy the other by being enrolled among the members of the Church. Many Pagans believed in the efficacy of confession; and about forty made a general acknowledgment of their faults to the Father, who took advantage of this favorable symptom to guide them to the practice of moral virtues which would soon lead them to the adoption of Christian belief.

The Oneidas, like the Mohawks, were gradually abandoning the worship of Agreskoué. At their feasts and banquets the priest was generally invited to invoke the blessing of God, where formerly they besought Agreskoué, or some demon, or manitou, to preside on the occasion.

Many of the more intelligent Oneida Pagans believed in a kind of metempsychosis, in which their souls would again appear in this world in some of their descendants. They believed that after death the soul would go to the happy hunting ground, to the home of Thoronhiawagon; but they were so attached to the scenes and pursuits of this life that they hoped to return after death to hunt the deer and fight their foes, and this desire became a part of their belief. Many others believed they could not go to

Heaven without the assistance of the Black Robes. These were anxious to see the priest when they were ill, and they carefully prepared for the reception of the sacraments.

Father Millet began to receive healthy adults into the Church, and he had bright prospects of making faithful Christians out of the greater part of the nation.

The example of Garakontie gave many of his countrymen more confidence in Christianity, and they attended more assiduously the instructions of the Fathers, and manifested a better religious spirit in their last hours. Garakontie would not take part in any of the superstitious rites of his country, and openly proclaimed his adherence to the Christian faith. He was dangerously ill, and his old Pagan friends endeavored to persuade him that it would not be wrong to try the old method of healing. He refused, however, to allow the medicine men to use their mysterious arts in restoring his health; and he protested in the presence of the ancients of the nation, who had assembled to bid him farewell, against the use of any superstitious rites. He afterwards told Father Millet that he was too firmly attached to his faith to do anything forbidden by the commandments of God.[1] Having recovered his health, he was sometime afterwards sent to Montreal, as an ambassador from the Iroquois, to attend a council of the Algonquins and French: and here in the presence of five hundred savages of different nations he proclaimed his Christian faith, and told them he once lived like themselves in ignorance of the true God and a worshiper of dreams; but now he was happy in the faith of God and the hope of eternal life, and he exhorted them to follow his example and abandon their foolish superstitions.

[1] The medicine men did perform some of their superstitious rites at this time in his cabin, but it was without his knowledge or consent, and he expressed his regret to Father Millet that such a rite had been performed in his home.

When Garakontie returned from Quebec he found one of his Pagan relatives very ill, and he hastened to the Father to seek a remedy for the disease. De Lamberville told him that his body was past healing, but he would give him a remedy for his spiritual malady. This man was pleased with the candor of the Father, and although he wished to go to the country of souls, where he believed his ancestors to be, yet he was convinced of the truth of the Christian faith, and was soon admitted to the Church.

The genius of the Indian, de Lamberville says, is to follow no law but his own will, and to do only what his interests or wants suggest. He cannot, consequently, be made a Christian by argument; as the motives of credibility seem to make no impression on his mind. He can only be converted by two means: by gold and by iron; he must be won by presents, and held by force. The fear of a French army, or the hope of temporal gain has more influence upon his mind than the arguments of the Fathers. The Iroquois were not slow to perceive the difference in religion between the French, the English, and the Dutch; and as these Europeans had different beliefs, the Indians concluded they were all wrong. There were many, however, who understood and appreciated Christianity; who became members of the Church, and led exemplary lives. This was especially true of women, who had more time to learn the Christian doctrine, and a greater inclination to practice its precepts; yet there were many able men, like Garakontie, who were equally exemplary in their lives and firm in their attachment to the Church.

The prominent men among the Iroquois who became Catholics must necessarily be sincere, as they were obliged

THE PRACTICE OF MEDICINE.　165

to renounce the traditions of their race, and their action created a feeling against themselves which often resulted in temporal loss or social dishonor.

Father de Lamberville understood something of the practice of medicine, and he was often able to render valuable aid to the sick Onondagas. He relates that on one occasion the medicine men were endeavoring to dispel the pain of a toothache with their magic art, as they said that some demons had taken possession of the tooth and must be driven out, when the Father extracted the tooth and relieved the patient, to the great surprise of an admiring throng.

They held very strange notions about the causes of disease. They believed that evil spirits, or Otki, placed small pieces of wood, or pebbles, in the parts of the body where pain was located, or which was the seat of disease. Hence, cancer was a pebble inserted in the flesh by an enemy, or an Otki; rheumatism, or paralysis, was a long stick running through the joints and the nerves; and the skill of the medicine men and sorcerers was directed towards expelling these substances by counteracting the power which had inserted them. Sometimes the Onondagas sacrificed a dog to Agreskoué, or they threw tobacco into the fire, to propitiate the demons, and to induce them to cease tormenting the sick.

Garakontie gave valuable advice to the Father about the character and disposition of the people who sought admission to the Church, and was a guide and councilor to the missioner in his dealings with the people.

Father Carheil[1] went to Quebec on account of poor health, in 1671, and Father Raffeix took his place at Cayuga. Father Raffeix was charmed with the beauty of the

[1] Father Carheil made a pilgrimage to St. Ann, at Beaupre, which was even at that time celebrated. Shea, p. 294.

Cayuga country, the most delightful he had seen in America, and was pleased with the inhabitants, whom he thought more tractable than the Onondagas or the Oneidas; but he did not think that they were yet prepared, or disposed, to enter the Church. He adopted a new method of teaching Christianity, by setting the articles of faith to music; and, as the Indians had good voices, correct ears, and a love for music, they readily learned to sing these truths, and also the morning and evening prayers. Although he had no consolation or society, but a sense of duty and the presence of God, yet he requested his superiors to allow him to remain at Cayuga; but, as Father Carheil returned to his mission from Quebec, he proceeded to the Seneca country to assist Father Garnier.

Father Carheil began, in 1673, to administer the sacrament of baptism to persons who were not in danger of death. He believed the nation was favorably disposed towards Christianity, and there was already a sufficient number of fervent Christians to encourage the neophytes to persevere. He was more disposed, also, to baptize healthy adults from the fact that many of these people believed that baptism was a seal of death, for many of the people died soon after receiving the sacrament.

Examples of holy lives and true Christian spirit were to be found at Cayuga as well as among the other Iroquois nations; and these instances were not confined to the old men or the women of the nation, but the young warriors also showed they could appreciate the beauty and worth of Christianity. Such lives formed the greatest consolation and the only visible reward for the Father's zeal in this otherwise dreary life.

There were three missions among the Senecas, although there were only two Fathers to attend them.

Father Raffeix took charge of the missions of the Immaculate Conception towards the end of July, 1672, and Father Garnier attended St. Michael's and St. James'. There was no chapel at St. James' in 1672, though it was the largest of the villages, and many of the people there were obliged to go to St. Michael's on Sundays for instruction and mass.

The year 1673 was one of the most peaceful and prosperous the missioners enjoyed in the Seneca country. The Christians were faithful in attending the chapels and in receiving the sacraments. The Pagans also came to hear the sermons and to pray, and many of them would, no doubt, become members of the Church, but they would not abandon the superstitious practices of their race, and especially the magic of the medicine men, as they knew no other way of healing the sick.

Garnier was so busy at St. Michael's that he had little time to attend St. James', so he asked for another Father to take charge of the latter mission; and the Rev. James Pierron came as the first resident missioner to this populous town.

Father Garnier says that "it is not immorality or vice, but their false ideas of Christianity, that keeps many of the Senecas out of the Church;" for he knows more than two hundred families who lead comparatively good lives, and who would make exemplary Christians. Faith is a gift of God, and the Father continually prays that it will be given to these people.

The Hurons of St. Michael's believed that peace between the Iroquois and French could not be permanent, for the distant rumblings of war were already heard; and they desired to leave the Seneca country and join their brethren near Quebec, or unite with their fellow Christians at the new settlement near Montreal, in forming an Indian Catholic colony.

The confraternity of the Holy Family[1] was established in all of the missions, and effected much good, as it taught the neophytes how to form the family life according to the model Christian home.

The conversions, however, were not very numerous among these people, and there was an undercurrent of ill will towards the missionaries and their teaching that might break into open violence at any moment. Some[2] think this hostility arose from the defeat of the Iroquois by the Andastes, while others[3] ascribe it to the influence of the Dutch at Albany, who in 1673 recovered New York from the English, and, desiring to preserve their ascendency over the Five Nations, openly advised them to drive the missionaries from their country, and to take up arms against the French.

The Pagan Indians persecuted the missionaries, and labored to render their teachings and their mission odious; and their action prevented many from embracing Christianity who were well instructed, and who were free from the vices of their race.

When the English regained New York, they claimed also the territory of the Five Nations, and the Fathers realized that their missions among the Iroquois must soon come to an end.

From 1668 to 1678 the missionaries had baptized 2221 Indians,[4] but as the greater number of these were the sick and dying they did not very notably increase the Christian congregations in the Iroquois villages.

---

[1] History repeats itself, and after two hundred years we find the Bishops of the province of New York urging the pastors to establish this confraternity in their parishes.
[2] Relations.   [3] Shea.   [4] Shea, p. 304.

CHAPTER XVIII.

THE MISSIONS IN THE IROQUOIS COUNTRY--Continued.

FATHER BONIFACE RETIRES—CHIEF ASSENDASE—STATUE OF BLESSED VIRGIN—BRUYAS GOES TO ONONDAGA—PAGANS DOMINANT AT ONEIDA—CHRISTIAN FAMILY LIFE—CONVERTS BECOME APOSTLES—HEALING THE SICK—DEATH OF GARAKONTIE—CARHEIL'S PATIENCE—INTEREST IN SORCERY—PAGAN PREACHES CHRISTIANITY—SLAVES WILLING CONVERTS—IROQUOIS INVITED TO MEET GOVERNOR FRONTENAC—FORT CATAROQUOI—THE LIQUOR EVIL—RUMBLINGS OF WAR.

THE mission had attained a state of settled sameness; and year by year they presented the same features, varied only by the greater or less element of danger in the lives of the missioners, or by the conversion of some noted chief. The congregations did not seemingly increase in numbers, for many of the faithful Catholics left every year for the Prarie or Lorette, and many others went to join their white brethren in Heaven.

Father Boniface,[1] among the Mohawks, was worn out with this rude life and excessive labors, and he was obliged to relinquish his work to seek rest among his brothers at Quebec. The Rev. James de Lamberville came to the lower Mohawk towns, and his pleasant manner and ardent zeal enabled him to continue the success of his predecessor.

When Father Bruyas had formed his little congregation at Tionnontoguen, by recalling the old Christians to

[1] Father Boniface never entirely recovered, and he died September 17, 1674.

their duty, the Pagans also came to the chapel to listen to the word of God. The knowledge of Christianity gradually spread among the people and many were convinced of its truth, and they were charmed with the beautiful lives which were formed according to the Father's teaching. Among the prominent Pagans who were pleased with the new life was the chief Assendasé, who resolved to cast his lot with the little band of Christians at Tionnontoguen. His relatives were very much displeased with his determination to become a Christian, and they even threatened to kill him unless he desisted, but he was too fearless a warrior to be deterred by threats, and he told those who assailed him to kill him if they pleased, he would only be too happy to die in such a cause. The day after his baptism he publicly renounced belief in dreams and the evil customs which, as a Pagan, he had practiced, and he even refused to attend the gatherings at which dreams were discussed. He would not allow the medicine men or sorcerers to attend him when he was ill. His life, he said, was in the hands of God, and whenever God was pleased to call him he was ready to go. His death in August, 1675, was most edifying, and it added another name to the list of prominent Mohawks who entered the Church.

Father Bruyas had been making some progress at Tionnontoguen, and to encourage the Christians in their devotions he obtained a statue of the Blessed Virgin, which he set up in his little chapel. The statue was unveiled on the feast of the Immaculate Conception, December 8, 1676, and the Christians sang the Litany of the Blessed Virgin and some hymns in the Mohawk tongue. The presence of the statue awakened unusual interest among the Pagans, and an extraordinary spirit of fervor among the Christians, and the latter came three times to the chapel the first day to sing their hymns and manifest their love for the Mother of God. After this event the Pagans manifested a more friendly feeling towards the Christians, and they came in greater numbers to listen to the word of God.

Father Bruyas was superior of all the Iroquois missions, and his duties required him to exercise a supervision over the other missioners, and to direct them in times of difficulty or danger. When concerted action, therefore, was necessary he could more quickly communicate with the different Fathers from a central point like Onondaga than he could from his remote Mohawk home; so he removed in 1678 to the capital of the league, and Father Vaillant took his place at Tionnontoguen.

The instructions given by Bruyas at Oneida, and afterwards continued by Millet, had been made so interesting that large numbers attended, and the knowledge of Christianity was quite generally diffused among all classes. Pagan influence was still dominant, however, and it was not easy for the Christians to avoid the contagion of bad example which everywhere surrounded them. Like their brethren among the Mohawks, some of the Oneida converts believed they could not bring up their families in a proper manner in the midst of vice; so they looked anxiously towards LaPrarie or Lorette as their haven of hope. They had the example of their pious countrywoman, Catherine Ganneaktena, to urge them to seek a new home, and only very great interest or family ties could induce them to remain in a Pagan land. One Christian woman had three daughters, whose lives she wished to shield from the vices practiced by Pagan youth. They must necessarily mingle at Oneida with depraved

Pagans, and it would be very difficult to keep their young lives pure in the midst of immoralities; so she took her daughters, her mat, and some food, and fled, like Lot and his family from the ancient Sodam.

Father Bruyas labored earnestly to instill into the minds of all the virtues of Christian family life, and to teach Pagan youth the value of virtue and the sanctity of marriage. He introduced the society of the Holy Family so they might have a model to guide them in establishing the sacredness of home. The more intelligent Oneidas were pleased with the lives led by the good Christians, and many were convinced that the teaching of the Father would promote their interests in time and eternity; and in 1676 Chief Saonresé, with many other prominent persons, became members of the Church. The converts to Christianity were very anxious to have their Pagan brethren enjoy the blessings which the new life brought to themselves; and whenever they heard of a dying child or a sick adult the priest was notified so that he might visit the sick to instruct or baptize, for few at that hour would refuse his ministrations. Many a time would the Father be forced to travel miles to find in the forest some dying Pagan, or visit some distant fishing station to baptize a child.

The Iroquois clung to the sorcerers because they believed these could cure them when they were ill, but when they found that the sorcerers were powerless to help them they turned to the priest for consolation. At Onondaga a sick chief had tried in vain the art of the sorcerers to regain his health, and then he turned in despair to the priest for the same purpose. Father de-Lamberville told him that his body was past healing, but his soul was also sick, and it must be healed if he wished to be at peace with the Master of Life and be happy after death. The chief was pleased with the Father's frankness, and he began to make immediate preparations for death. The thought of death did not disturb him, for he believed, with the Father's guidance and care, he would reach the Christian Heaven.

There were many noble models of Christian lives at Onondaga to encourage the neophytes to persevere, and to console them for the sacrifices they made in the practice of their faith. Some of the converts had left their homes to dwell at LaPrarie, but the chiefs, and their friends, tried to induce them to return. One Onondaga Christian, who had been living for some time at LaPrarie, followed her husband to their old home, whither he had returned at the solicitation of his friends. This man had been a catechumen at LaPrarie, but at Onondaga he joined the Pagans in their drunken orgies, and soon fell back into their old vices and beliefs. They had one son, and to save this child from the liquor habit, and from the degrading vices of the Pagans, the Christian mother fled again to LaPrarie, and left her husband to his fate.

The Onondaga mission lost its most famous and most faithful convert in 1676, in the death of Garakontie. He was then far advanced in years, and he contracted a severe cold by coming some distance, in a storm, to attend the midnight mass.[1] When he realized that his end was near he begged Father deLamberville to prepare him for death. He gave his farewell banquet; and advised the nation to maintain peace with the French, to abandon their superstitions, and to become Christians.[2] He wished to be buried like the French, in a plain coffin; and he requested the Father to have a large cross erected over his

[1] Shea, "The Catholic Church in Colonial Days." [2] Relations 1673-9.

grave to remind the nations that he died a Christian. Whenever deLamberville visited him, during his illness, they prayed together, and his soul passed away amid the prayers of his friends. Scarcely a sin sullied his soul after he entered the Church, so exact was he in the observance of the law of God; and once, when he became slightly inebriated with wine, he made a public apology for his unconscious fault.[1] DeLamberville delivered an address at his grave, extolling his virtues, and urging his hearers to imitate the example of their most eloquent and influential chief.

Father Carheil possessed one of the greatest virtues of the Iroquois missioner—the virtue of patience—and this enabled him to gain many obstinate souls to God. He would visit the sick every day in a friendly or social manner for many months, doing deeds of kindness, and performing the most menial offices, until he gained the good will of the sufferer. It was only when he had won the affection of the patient that he spoke of the soul, and of the necessity of preparing for eternity. He visited a sick woman every day for two months, and she seemed pleased with his kindly interest in her welfare, but as soon as he spoke to her about religion she became angry and would no longer listen to him. The Father continued his good offices, however, and one day when she seemed to be in a pleasant mood he ventured to introduce the tabooed question; she immediately became excited, and attempted to scratch the Father's face, but her weak condition rendered her attack harmless. Carheil returned the next day and told the sick woman she had only a short time to live; she should, therefore, repent of her sins, and should prepare for baptism. Patience triumphed over

[1] He believed that brandy alone was intoxicating, and had never before tasted wine.

obstinacy, and the persistent zeal of the Father was rewarded by the conversion of an obdurate soul.[1]

The happy death of their converts was the Fathers' sole reward for months of patient waiting and care. Father Carheil, at Cayuga, found in the happy Christian death of a young warrior ample compensation for months of self-sacrifice and toil. This young man had faithfully followed the instructions of the Father, and he was gifted with an extraordinary spirit of prayer. During his last illness he wished to have Father Carheil constantly at his side so they might converse on holy things and pray together; and when his soul passed away it was accompanied with the prayers of his teacher and friend.

Father Garnier had convinced the people of Gandougarae of the evil of liquor drinking, and drunkenness was very rare in the town; but the Pagans still clung to their immoral dances and sorcery, and attachment to these customs withheld many from the Church. The Pagans knew no other method of overcoming disease than by sorcery, and the medicine men and sorcerers made a comfortable living by this means of healing; so they would not readily abandon these customs for Christianity which offered them no pecuniary compensation in return. Thorough conviction, therefore, of the truth of Christianity, and a spirit of self-sacrifice were necessary in the people to lead them to the new life.

Some believed but were not ready to make the sacrifice which their conviction enjoined. An intelligent Seneca, for instance, urged his sick relatives to become Christians, because then they would be worthy of Heaven. He was not a Christian himself, he said, but he had examined the teachings of the Black Robes, and he was

[1] Relations 1673-9.

convinced that they taught the truth. He was not yet prepared to abandon his old habits, but some day he would enter the Church. The Fathers found their most fertile field among the captives and slaves; because the lives of these were not linked with the traditions of their masters, nor were their habits formed by the customs of the Iroquois. They had not the opposition of relatives and friends to encounter in embracing Christianity, nor would they lose prestige by their new life. Christianity, moreover, consoled them in their present miserable life and promised them happiness in the future.

Intelligent men among the Senecas believed in the doctrines taught by the missioners, but they knew it would be well nigh impossible to live up to this teaching amid dissolute Pagan environments. Those who resolved to accept the Gospel looked to a life at one of the Catholic settlements on the St. Lawrence as their only hope; but this meant the loss of their rights as members of the Seneca nation and the Iroquois league, and few were willing to make this sacrifice.

The Iroquois finally vanquished the Andastes, after a long and stubbornly contested war, and the subsequent peace gave the victorious Senecas leisure to look about for new enemies to conquer. They looked with disfavor upon the encroachments of the French. They had not forgotten that Onontio sailed up the river with an armed band to show them the feasibility of an invasion, and the new fort at Cataroquoi seemed a menace to their liberties.

LaSalle was sent by the Governor, in May, 1673, to Onondaga[1] to allay any fear the Iroquois might have that the new fort was designed as an instrument of war. He

---

[1] LaSalle was advised to visit the other nations also, if he considered his presence in these places necessary. He visited the Senecas, and spent some time in their towns.

THE NEW GOVERNOR. 177

was instructed to invite the Iroquois to send delegates to meet the Governor at Keute,[1] where they could greet the new Governor, and could ratify all the treaties made with the former representatives of the King of France. About two hundred Iroquois came; and at the meeting in July, 1673, the Governor told them he intended to build a storehouse on the spot which would serve as a trading post, where they could exchange their furs for French merchandise. He also advised them as a father to accept the teaching of the Black Robes who dwelt in their towns, and to become Christians, so they might be more intimately associated with the interests of the French.

The object of this assembly was evidently to gain the good will of the Iroquois, and to divert their trade from the Dutch and English at Albany to the French merchants, who would establish their stores on the site of the new fort.

The following year the French transferred the title of the fort[2] to LaSalle, on condition that he should indemnify the government for the amount already expended, should keep a garrison[3] of twenty men, and should build a church within two years. The fort became another one of those trading posts which wrought such demoralization among the Pagans.

The custom of drinking strong liquor was the greatest evil introduced by Europeans to the Indians of North America. The Indians depended upon the hunt for the furs which supplied their families with comfortable cloth-

[1] There was a Sulpician mission at Keute. The council was not held here, however; the Governor changed the meeting place to the site of the new fort.
[2] The place was first called Fort Cataroquoi, but LaSalle changed this to Frontenac in honor of his patron.
[3] Frontenac had no soldiers to garrison the fort, hence the king of French was more willing to transfer it to laymen, and relieve the colonists from this unnecessary burden and expense.

ing, and which formed the chief staple of trade; but when they began to barter their furs for liquor their families began to suffer, and want and crime increased in the land. Not only furs but everything of marketable value was given for drink: the hunt was abandoned for they had no arms; the fishing was neglected, because the time was spent in drunken riot.

The Fathers fought strenuously against the liquor traffic with the Dutch; and they succeeded in restraining the Christians from this habit, and they even lessened the evil among the Pagans, but they encountered a formidable obstacle in the French traders. The Dutch were not Catholics, and they were not supposed to refrain from selling liquor to Indians at the command of priests; but the French Catholic merchants pursued the traffic in defiance of the Church, and their example weakened the force of the priests' counsel against the practice, and the evil spread through the land. In vain did the Bishop of Quebec plead with these merchants to desist, and he even inflicted the penalties of the Church when they refused to obey: the trade had the sanction of the civil authorities, and it would continue to flourish as long as there were large profits and a ready market. The *Coureurs du Bois* were, in many cases, itinerant rum-sellers, who carried liquor to the dwellings of the Indians when they were unable to reach the trading posts. The only restraint upon the Iroquois in the liquor evil was the influence of the Fathers, and this was on the wane, because the younger warriors were opposed to the encroachments of French domination.

The great Garakontie had ever been the steadfast friend of France. In the Iroquois councils he had ever pleaded for alliance with the French; but now that his voice was still in death France had no friend to champion her cause among the Five Nations. Opposition to the presence of the Fathers had been increasing; they had been maltreated on several occasions, and they began to prepare for the coming storm.

CHAPTER XIX.

CONCLUSION OF THE MISSIONS IN THE IROQUOIS COUNTRY.

DUTCH INDIFFERENT TO INDIAN ADVANCEMENT—ENGLAND AND FRANCE RIVAL POWERS FOR DOMINION—THE FUR TRADE—FRENCH MISSIONARIES DIVERT TRADE FROM THE ENGLISH—EFFORTS TO COUNTERACT THE MISSIONERS' INFLUENCE—DONGAN PROMISES ENGLISH PRIESTS IF IROQUOIS WILL BANISH FRENCH—IROQUOIS VALUABLE ALLIES—BOTH ENGLISH AND FRENCH CLAIM TERRITORY OF THE IROQUOIS—IROQUOIS DIVIDED IN FEALTY—CHRISTIAN IROQUOIS LEAVE THEIR HOMES—MISSIONERS LEAVE THE MOHAWKS—CLOSE OF THE MISSION—SENECAS' INTERESTS PROMOTED BY ALLIANCE WITH ENGLISH—DECEIVED BY LA SALLE—GOVERNOR DE LA BARRE INVITES IROQUOIS TO A COUNCIL—GOVERNOR DONGAN INVITES THEM TO ENGLISH COUNCIL—THREATENED WAR FORCES FATHERS TO LEAVE—DE LAMBERVILLE THE INNOCENT INSTRUMENT OF DECEIT—DENONVILLE INVADES SENECA COUNTRY—SENECAS RETALIATE—IROQUOIS UNITE WITH ENGLISH IN WAR AGAINST FRANCE—MILLET PRISONER AT ONEIDA—PEACE—IROQUOIS REQUEST MISSIONERS TO RETURN—CATHOLIC PRIESTS BANISHED FROM NEW YORK STATE BY ENGLISH LAW—FATHERS RETURN—CLOSE OF MISSIONS.

WHEN the Dutch took possession of the country between the Iroquois region and the sea, and established trading posts at Manhattan[1] and Renselaerswick,[2] they entered into an alliance with the Iroquois, which continued firm and friendly until Dutch power was supplanted by British rule. The honest Hollanders were content to barter their rum, their fire-arms, and their trinkets, with the Iroquois for the valuable furs

[1] New York. [2] Albany.

which these obtained in the hunt; and they did not exert themselves to teach the Indians the arts of civilized life, or the religion of Christ.

When the French missionaries, therefore, first came to the Iroquois cantons the easy going Dutch were indifferent to their presence, except to make some disparaging remarks to the Indians about the work and teachings of the Fathers, or to intercede for them when they were captives in danger of death.

The English got possession of New York in 1664, and they immediately gained the good-will of the Iroquois by acts of kindness, and by a treaty which was never directly broken.

England and France were the great rival powers of Europe; and they were at continual war for supremacy and an extension of their sway. They brought their quarrels with them to the New World, and both nations struggled and intrigued for the allegiance and friendship of the Iroquois Indians. The English resorted to diplomacy and intrigue to attain their end; whilst the French tried to overawe the Iroquois with their power, and to reduce them to subjection by force of arms.[1] The benefit which England and France hoped to obtain from alliance with the Iroquois, was a monopoly of trade with those nations in time of peace, and their support in war.

Explorers and discoverers, after Columbus, had visited different parts of the New World in search of wealth and fame, and they soon found that the most accessible riches were the valuable furs they could purchase from the various Indian nations, with the cheap commodities of civilized life. French enterprise soon secured a monopoly of the trade. Along the waters of the St.

[1] Colden.

Lawrence and the Ottawa rivers for hundreds of miles, their daring traders sped in search of furs, whilst the missioners kept pace with them in quest of souls. The Indians soon learned the importance of the fur trade, and every stream leading to the French trading posts, that would carry their light bark canoes on its bosom, bore many a load of rich furs destined for the European markets. The only way of transporting these goods was by the rivers and lakes that led to the trading posts that had been established along the banks of the St. Lawrence and the Hudson rivers. Often they encountered falls in the rivers, or they came to an end of the lake; but their canoes were light, and two men could carry them on their shoulders over the portages, whilst some of the party carried the furs in the same manner. The transportation of large quantities of furs would have been impossible except by the Indian method along the water routes, as there were no beasts of burden in the country, nor any roadways but the narrow trail through the forests that the Indian used in hunting or in war.

The French early established trading posts at Quebec, at Three Rivers, and at Montreal, and these were the most convenient points of barter for large quantities of furs in the New World. To these places every year with their fur-laden canoes came the Abnakis of the present Eastern States; the great Algonquin family, whose numerous tribes extended from the Atlantic to the Mississippi.; the Montagnais of Lower Canada; the Hurons from Georgian Bay; the Nippisiriens, the Ottawas, the Petuns and the Tionnontates of the North and West; and an occasional Iroquois party, bent more on taking scalps than bartering peltry.

The most valuable fur was the beaver; and, as these

were rare in the land of the Iroquois, large bands of well-armed warriors from the different nations of the league invaded the territory of their neighbors in search of the valuable beaver.

Other nations were not disposed to submit tamely to these encroachments of the Iroquois on their hunting grounds, but attempted to repel these poachers by force. This led to many petty wars; and as the French had secured the friendship of the most important fur-trading tribes, they became involved in these quarrels, as they furnished arms to their allies to protect their trade in furs.

The Iroquois sold their deer and bear skins to the Dutch or the English at Albany; and these encouraged them in their depredations on the beaver territory of their neighbors; and, consequently, prejudiced them against the French.

The English wished to secure this trade, as they could sell the stronds and duffels of the Indian trade much cheaper than the French; but the acute diplomacy of the latter kept the fur-trading nations at war with the Iroquois, so that they could not bring their furs to Albany, through the territory of their enemies.

The French missioners wielded considerable influence over the actions of the Indians, and they would naturally counsel the Iroquois to trade with their fellow-countrymen along the St. Lawrence. The English and the Dutch believed that the presence of the French missionaries was an obstacle to their trade with the Indians, and they used means to banish them from the Iroquois country.

Governor Dongan of New York asked authority from the King of England to erect forts upon the Delaware, the Susquehanna, and the Niagara rivers; to assist the

Iroquois in their forays upon the beaver territory of their neighbors; to protect the Indians who wished to trade with the English; and to secure British right to these regions. He says the French claim as far as the Bay of Mexico: "For which they have no other argument, than that they had possession this twenty years, by their Fathers living so long among the Indians. They have Fathers still among the Five Nations, and have converted many of them to the Christian faith, and done their utmost to draw them to Canada, where there are already six or seven hundred, and more like to go, to the great prejudice of this government if not prevented. I have prevailed with the Indians to consent to come back from Canada, on condition that I procure for them a piece of land, and furnish them with priests. I have procured the land and have promised the Indians that they shall have priests, and that I will build them a church.

"By that means the French priests will be obliged to retire to Canada whereby the French will be divested of their pretence to the country, and then we shall enjoy that trade without any fear of being diverted."[1]

The[2] priests promised by Dongan never came, but in their stead came some Protestant ministers, who labored for a time, with indifferent success, among the Iroquois.

England and France were rival powers in Europe, and, on several occasions, their hostilities had been transferred to their colonies in the New World. At such times each government employed the Indians as guides to lead them through the forests, or as scouts to discover the hidden strongholds or ambushes of the enemy, and as the Indians learned the use of fire-arms they became valuable allies or most formidable foes.

[1] Governor Dongan's report on the state of the Province.
[2] Dongan asked for priests, and three English Jesuits were sent to New York, where they started a Latin school. Doc. Hist. N. Y.

The Iroquois were the most powerful and warlike of all the North American Indians, and their supremacy was acknowledged by all the nations within hundreds of miles of their homes. Their territory lay between the English possessions in the South and the French colonies of Canada, and their friendship would be very valuable in the event of war between these two nations. The English feared the ascendency of French influence over the Iroquois through the presence of the French priests, and they began to discredit their mission, and to intrigue for their banishment from the Iroquois country. The Fathers induced the Iroquois to make peace with the Indian allies of the French, so that these would be free to bring their furs to the French trading posts; whilst the English wished them to make war on these Indians, to destroy this trade and to divert the Iroquois from attacking the English colonies of Maryland and Virginia.

Shortly after Dongan became Governor of New York, he claimed all south of the lakes as English territory, and wished to make the Iroquois acknowledge allegiance to the Crown of England. He well knew that Indian independence would not brook such a burden, so he taught them that English supremacy was necessary to protect them from the attacks and rapacity of the French. He had the arms of the Duke of York placed over the castles of the Iroquois, and he told them the French would not dare to attack their towns while they bore the symbol of British rule.[1] Though a Catholic himself, he advised the Iroquois to expel the French Jesuits from their land, and he would send them English priests to teach them Christianity.[2] He also urged them to bring back their breth-

[1] Colden.
[2] O'Callaghan thinks Dongan was sincere in promising English priests, as the English register of the Jusuits shows that the priests of the order were in New York in 1685-6.

ren from the Catholic settlements on the St. Lawrence; and he offered them assistance and protection if they would settle near the waters of Saratoga Lake.

Although the Christian Iroquois had the greatest faith in their missionaries, and the greatest love and reverence for their persons; yet the Pagans cherished the memory of many hostile deeds against the French, and they were disposed to cast their lot with the English, and banish the French Fathers from their land.

Some Frenchmen had murdered and robbed six Iroquois—three men, two women, and a child—near Montreal, on account of the valuable furs they possessed, and shortly after some soldiers murdered and robbed a Seneca chief for the same reasons; and although the Governor had these murderers put to death, yet the Iroquois did not forget these deeds, and they attacked a French fort in Illinois.

The Mohawks and the Senecas seemed to be more especially under the influence of English agents, while the other nations were disposed to side with the French.

The Christian Iroquois could not preserve their faith in the presence of the bad example, and the vices of their Pagan brethren, and in the face of the opposition of the English and Dutch when the missionaries would be driven from the field; so the Fathers induced many of their spiritual children to abandon their homes, and, in many cases, their kindred, and to emigrate to the new Catholic Indian settlements near Montreal, where they would be free to practice their religion and worship God.

Large numbers from the different nations settled at these places and formed communities which gave to the Church many saintly lives, and to the world noble examples of eminent virtue. This desertion of the Catholic

Iroquois from their country aroused the anger of the Pagans against the Fathers, because it weakened the power of their race, and was opposed to the policy of the league.[1]

The English, also, actuated by motives of self-interest, urged the Iroquois to oppose this emigration, and to treat the deserters as traitors to their race.

The Mohawks were more directly under the influence of the English than the other Iroquois, and it was from this nation also that the greatest number of defections took place. The wife of Kryn, the great Mohawk chief, became a Christian, and to escape the anger of her lord she went to live at the new mission at Prarie le Madeleine. Kryn wandered away through the forest, part in anger, part in sorrow, till he came to the new community on the St. Lawrence, where he was so enchanted with the strange and beautiful lives of these neophytes that he, too, begged to be received as a member. After receiving baptism he returned to the Mohawk country, where he induced about forty of his fellow-countrymen, mostly Christians, to leave their native land and emigrate to the Prarie. There were very few Christians left in the Mohawk country in 1679, and Father Bruyas, the superior of the Iroquois missions, found that prejudice was so strong against him that his influene was destroyed, and as he was in danger of death, with the Rev. James de Lamberville, he retired to Onondaga. The Rev. Francis Vaillant de Gueslis, however, remained at Tionnnontaguen until 1681, when the inimical influence of the Enlish forced him to leave. Most of the Christians had abandoned their Mohawk homes for the new Catholic settlements along the St. Lawrence River, and with the

[1] It was the policy of the league to increase their numbers by the adoption of captives.

departure of the Fathers the Mohawk mission of Our Lady of Martyrs was closed forever.

The Seneca towns were the most distant from the French settlements, and as the Senecas did not engage very extensively in the fur trade they did not often come in friendly contact with the French, and they were, consequently, but lightly swayed by the brilliant authority of Onontio.[1]

The Seneca region was very fertile, producing immense quantities of corn, which the Senecas bartered with the neighboring nations for the furs which were so rare in their own land. They made war upon the Indian nations that traded with the French, and as these obtained their fire-arms at Quebec and Montreal, the Senecas naturally looked upon the French as the enemies of their race. The Senecas made war upon the fur-trading nations of Western and Northern Canada, and intercepted their rich fur-laden canoes on their way to the trading posts on the St. Lawrence.

The English encouraged the Senecas in this warfare, and furnished them with fire-arms at a mere nominal cost, to weaken the influence of the French, and to destroy their fur-trade, or divert part of it to the English posts on the Hudson.

When LaSalle came to the Niagara River in 1678, with Father Hennepin and a number of men, to build the first vessel to sail the upper lakes, he sought by treaty or by guile to secure permission from the Senecas to erect a fort on the river to protect his prospective trade with the West. He soon learned that the Senecas would not allow a fort to be erected on their domain; so he beguiled them with the belief that he merely intended to

[1] The Indian name for the Governor of Canada.

erect a shop in which they might find a blacksmith, who would repair their guns and manufacture for them the iron implements of war. He erected a building, but it was intended for a storehouse, which could easily be converted into a fort if he were successful in his expedition on the upper lakes. The Senecas viewed with alarm the building of the Griffon, which appeared to them as an immense war canoe; as they saw in this an extension of the power of the French and an enlargement of their trade with the western nations, so they attempted more than once to burn the vessel before it was complete. No blacksmith remained to repair their guns when the Griffon sailed; and when they saw they were deceived, they retaliated, some time after, by burning the quarters LaSalle intended for a fort.

A Seneca chief had been wantonly robbed and murdered by French soldiers, and although the soldiers were shot yet the Senecas manifested their spirit of resentment by attacking a French fort in Illinois.

With the memory of these different grievances rankling in their hearts, the Senecas were not disposed to be friendly towards the Fathers, and they began to show in many ways that the missioners were not wanted in their land.

Governor de le Barre made preparations in 1683 to humble this haughty race, and to punish them for their interference with the fur trade, and for their repeated attacks upon the Indian friends of the French. The Fathers well knew that their lives would not be safe in the event of war; so they quietly made preparations to leave their little bark chapels in the hands of the Christians, and retire from the field, in which they had not reaped an overabundant harvest, with the hope of returning when the storms had passed.

Governor de le Barre came to Cataroquoi in 1684 with an army of French and Indians, to defeat the Senecas, but as an epidemic broke out among the soldiers he decided to agree upon terms of peace with the Iroquois. All the nations were invited to send delegates to the council at Cataroquoi, but only representatives from Oneida, Onondaga, and Cayuga, came, as these cantons were still under the influence of the French priests.[1] The Mohawks and the Senecas were induced by the English not to send their representatives to the council.

Governor Dongan held a council of the Iroquois in July, 1684, to induce them to make a treaty of peace with Lord Howard, the English Governor of Virginia, in favor of his colony in the South. Dongan advised the Iroquois on this occasion to place their towns under the protection of the royal arms of England, and he also counseled them to bring back to their old homes the Christian Iroquois who had emigrated to the settlements near Montreal, or if they would not return to treat them as traitors to their race.[2]

The threatened invasion of the French, and the influence of the English, so incited the Cayuga Pagans against the French that they began to ill-treat Father Carheil; and they finally robbed him and forced him to leave the canton. About the same time Father Millet left his mission among the Oneidas, and proceeded to the camp of the French governor at Cataroquoi.

The Fathers had now closed all the missions in the Iroquois country except the chapel at Onondaga; and here the two brothers, Fathers James and John de Lamberville still labored, enjoying the confidence of this nation which remained faithful to French interests.

[1] Colden. [2] Colden, p. 52.

MARQUIS DEMONVILLE AS GOVERNOR. 191

De la Barre had patched up a sort of peace with the Iroquois, but it was never ratified by the Senecas, nor respected by the other nations, and after the council at Albany a force of Iroquois started on the war-path against the Ottawas, friends of the French.

The Marquis Demonville succeeded De le Barre as Governor of Canada in 1685, and he determined to subjugate the Iroquois as the only means of securing peace for the French and prosperity for their trade. Colonel Dongan, Governor of New York, was in the meantime inciting the Iroquois against the French, and he endeavored to obtain possession of Father James de Lamberville, the only priest[1] then among the Five Nations; but the Onondagas would not allow him to leave until an act of base deception on the part of Denonville compelled the last priest to leave the Iroquois country. Denonville was secretly preparing to attack the Senecas, and, to more thoroughly conceal his designs, he invited, through Father de Lamberville,[2] delegates from the Iroquois to meet him at Cataroquoi. The nations sent their delegates, chiefs, and orators, to meet the new Governor, who, with barbarous treachery, of which the Indians would scarcely be capable, cast them into prison and sent them to France as galley slaves, or as captives to the French King.

Father de Lamberville had been made the innocent instrument of this cruel deception, but it cost him his mission, and it nearly cost him his life. The Onondagas had the utmost confidence in his integrity, and they believed him when he told them that he was not aware of the evil designs of Denonville when he invited their delegates to the council; but they decided that he should

[1] Father John de Lamberville had gone to Canada.
[2] Father John who had replaced his brother.

leave their land. They allowed him to depart in peace, and thus the last missioner left the country of the Iroquois, and the missions were closed after twenty years of successful existence.

Denonville made preparations in the early spring of 1687 for his expedition against the Senecas, and June 13th he set out from Montreal with about sixteen hundred French soldiers and four hundred Indians,[1] and started up the river in small boats and canoes towards the land of the Senecas. July 1st they reached Cataroquoi, where they remained until July 4th, when they proceeded to Irondequoit Bay, where they were to meet the French and the Indians from the West. Thence they continued their march along the Indian trail through the oak forest, on the western shore of the bay to Gannagaro,[2] the first of the Seneca villages where they gave battle to a force of the Senecas and defeated them. The Senecas fled, and the French and their Indian allies burned and demolished the cabins in the different towns, and destroyed immense quantities of corn.[3] Having completed the work of destruction, Denonville proceeded to the Niagara River where he built a fort, and left a garrison of one hundred men with Father de Lamberville as chaplain; but a sickness broke out among the men by which nearly all perished, and the fort was abandoned.

The Iroquois retaliated for this wanton destruction of their homes and property by a renewal of their old system of warfare against the French, and they also waged war on the Christian Iroquois near Montreal, who had fought with Denonville in the invasion of their country.

---

[1] Among the Indians were about one hundred and fifty Christian Iroquois from the settlements near Montreal, who went to fight against their former fellow-countrymen.
[2] St. James. See p. 12.
[3] Denonville estimates that they destroyed 1,200,000 bushels. (Marshall).

SENECAS ATTACK THE CANADIAN COLONY.

Love for their old homes and kindred was still strong among the Christian Iroquois, and many of them were inclined to leave Caughnawaga, or the Two Mountains, and cast their lot with their own race; but Kryn, the Mohawk chief vehemently opposed removal, as it meant a probable loss of faith, and the missions were saved.

In July, 1688, the Senecas attacked the Canadian colony at La Chine and killed two hundred; and they also attacked the Christian Iroquois at Two Mountains and at Caughnawaga, and forced them to fly to Montreal for protection. As the English had instigated this attack, Kryn, the Mohawk chief, with some Iroquois and French, retaliated by attacking the English settlement at Schenectady and killing many of the inhabitants.

These acts of hostility tended to exasperate the representatives of the English and French powers, and Governor Dongan called a council of the Five Nations at Albany, and advised them not to allow any more French priests to enter their territory, as they worked against the interests of the Iroquois and of England.

Frontenac succeeded Denonville as Governor of New France in 1689, and he immediately tried to patch up a peace with the Iroquois through the chiefs whom he had brought back with him from France; but the Iroquois were too much under the influence of the English to yield to any terms submitted by the French. War broke out the next year between England and France, and the Iroquois joined the ranks of their English neighbors.

After leaving the fort on the Niagara River built by Denonville, Father Millet went to Cataroquoi, where he labored among the neighboring Indians, and assisted as chaplain at the fort. In June, 1689, a band of Iroquois approached the fort, declared that peace had been made at Montreal, and asked for a priest and a physician to attend to their sick and wounded. Father Millet and the resident physician went out to meet this band, on an errand of mercy, when they were immediately seized as prisoners of war, and were carried off to the home of the Iroquois.

There were some Oneidas among this band of warriors who were well acquainted with Father Millet, and they were also aware of the love their own people had for this priest; so they protected him from any harm and brought him to their own canton, where he was adopted as a member of the nation and was made a sachem of one of the clans.[1] He had no sacred vestments, nor sacred vessels for the altar, and could not celebrate mass; but the few Christians still living here, and some from the other nations, gathered around him to converse with him and to receive the sacrament of penance. He had a little chapel in a grotto, dedicated to the Dying Saviour, and here he recited prayers on Sunday and at morning and evening, for those who chose to come, and he also taught them, unmolested, the doctrines he had taught in their town as an accredited minister of Christ.

The English feared the influence of his presence, and they sought by strategy to bring him to the Mohawk country where he would be in their power. They sent some Mohawk messengers to invite him to their towns to attend to the Christians there; but his Oneida friends would not allow him to depart as they feared treachery, and they told the Mohawks he could always be found in his little chapel at Oneida.[2]

Millet remained here until 1694, when peace was concluded and he returned to Quebec. War broke out

[1] Colden. [2] Lettre du Pere Millet.

again the next year, and Frontenac led a force of over two thousand French and Indians into the country of the Onondagas and the Oneidas, and compelled them to sue for peace.

Hostilities between the English and French ceased with the peace of Ryswick in 1697, and prosperity once more appeared in the land. The husbandman was allowed to till the soil, and the trader to traffic in furs.

The Iroquois also made friendly overtures to the French shortly after, and the prospects seemed bright for a renewal of the former successful missions among these people; but the hatred engendered by religious differences now arose to prevent the return of Catholic priests.

The English Governor, Bellomont, had a law passed by the New York Legislature, in 1700, making it a penal offense for any priest to be found in the territory subject to the king, and punishable with perpetual imprisonment; and anyone who harbored a Catholic priest was subject to a fine of two hundred and fifty pounds.[1] In the latter part of August the Governor called the Five Nations to a council, at which he told them he had sent for ministers to come to instruct them; and he advised them to capture any Jesuits they found in their land and bring them to Albany.

Father Bruyas went to Onondaga with the French representative, after the peace of Ryswick, to negotiate the exchange of prisoners, and during the council he gave a belt as a pledge that he would come back to them, to live amongst them as a missionary; but the Iroquois council would not accept the belt, as they had already accepted one from the English Governor, who promised to send Protestant ministers to instruct them.[2] Father

[1] Shea, p. 357.   [2] Colden, p. 201.

Bruyas attended the Iroquois council again in 1701, and endeavored to relume the fading light of faith, but how willing soever the Indians may have been to see the Fathers among them once more they feared the power and authority of the English Governor, who exerted all his energies to prevent a revival of the missions.

The next year, 1702, the Iroquois of their own accord responded to the invitation of Father Bruyas, and asked the missionaries to come again to their people.

Father James de Lamberville was selected for Onondaga, whilst Revs. Julian Garnier and Vaillant de Gueslis proceeded to the Seneca villages near the Genesee. In October, 1702, the chapels were again opened and the word of God was announced to these erratic children of the forest.[1]

The English did not view with any good will the presence of the missionaries among the Iroquois, and they began secretly to prejudice the minds of the Indians against the French in general, and the Fathers in particular. They succeeded, finally, in 1709, in forcing them to leave the Iroquois country forever, and to relinquish the field which had been so productive of joy and sorrow, of pleasure and pain; which had sent so many saints to Heaven, yet in which, through the enmities of civilized powers, the harvest was never fully reaped. English influence over the Iroquois practically excluded the French missionaries from their country, and many of the Indians fell back into Paganism, or listened with indifference and incredulity to the preaching of some paid preachers of Protestantism, who abandoned the field as soon as their salary ceased; whilst many others preserved the faith even in their wanderings, and when deprived of all external aids, till love through death supplanted faith and hope.

[1] N. Y., Vol. Doc. IX., p. 737, and Charlevoix History of New France, p. 153.

CHAPTER XX.

RESULT OF THE MISSIONS.

CANNIBALISM ABANDONED—HATRED SUPPLANTED BY LOVE—CHRISTIAN TRUTHS ADOPTED BY IROQUOIS—RELIGIOUS STRIFE OF EUROPEANS OBSTACLE TO FAITH—SACRIFICES OF CHRISTIAN INDIANS — INDIAN MARTYRS — PIOUS EXAMPLES — KIND AND PIOUS LADIES OF FRANCE HELP TO EDUCATE INDIANS—JESUITS START SEMINARY AT QUEBEC—URSULINES OPEN CONVENT FOR INDIANS—INDIANS PREFER FOREST FREEDOM TO CONVENT WALLS—IROQUOIS GIRLS MOST TRACTABLE—CHRISTIAN INDIANS PRIZED CATHOLIC BOOKS—SCHOOLS IN THE FORESTS —SCHOOLS AT THE CATHOLIC SETTLEMENTS.

BEFORE the advent of the missionaries the Iroquois were cannibals, and often had the Fathers witnessed the cruel spectacle of some unfortunate slave, or one of their own captive companions, being roasted on the spit, or thrown into a large caldron of boiling water to be cooked and devoured by these savages. The Fathers taught them the sacredness of human life, and the abomination of devouring the flesh of their fellow beings; and in deference to this teaching of the missionaries, and the wishes of the French, they buried the caldron, and promised to renounce this barbarous practice forever. To hate an enemy the Iroquois considered one of the noblest virtues, but as they were taught that men are all brothers and children of the same eternal Father, they learned to have, at least, a moderate degree of love for their fellow beings, and were known to forgive and even to pray for their enemies. The Indian had but a very confused notion of God or of the soul, and his idea of God, the highest being, Master of life, did not include any religious relations towards the Supreme Being, any moral obligations towards his fellow-man, or accountability for his acts. His mind did not rise above nature, and he recognized no moral restraint except the advice of the Ancients, or the power of an enemy; nor did he know any force except the visible and animal of this world. When the waters, therefore, devastated their fields it was because some evil okki had destroyed their dams; and when a storm arose it was because some unknown animals, living in the caverns and dens of the earth, had removed the opening from the caves of winds and allowed them to fly over forest, lake, and moorland. Though the greater part of the Iroquois did not become Christians, yet they seemed to have generally adopted the ideas of God as taught by the missionaries, as a new name, Haw-wen-ne-yu, was adopted to express the new belief; and Thoronhiawagon, their old deity, was relegated to the class of genii, or spirits; while the name and worship of Agreskoue, the sun, had entirely disappeared years before the Fathers had left the field. They[1] also seemed to have unconsciously adopted many of the truths of Christianity and principles of morality as taught by the missionaries; as they were found many years afterwards advocating these truths as a part of their traditions, and practicing works of piety which they could only have learned from the Jesuits. At one of their councils, held at Tonawanda, chief John Skye made a very long speech on moral matters, and on the religious traditions of his race. In conclusion, he said: "You must not do bad, you must not speak bad, you must not think bad; for the

[1] Alden, Missions.

Great Spirit knows your thoughts as well as your words and deeds."

Some of them were accustomed to rise during the night to pray.[1]

This teaching and this custom must have been some of the lingering rays of the light spread through their land by their first teachers, the Jesuits.

The missionaries also endeavored to teach them the arts of civilized life, as they became Christians, and would undoubtedly have succeeded in both had not the English, Dutch, and French, transferred their political and religious strife to American soil, and so bewildered the poor Indians by their conflicting interests and theories that they could not place implicit confidence in the words of any of the Europeans.[2]

The Indians of North America might long since have been a civilized and Christian race if the governments of Europe, through their agents, had not interfered, with the Catholic missionaries in their work of redeeming these savage children of the forest. The missionaries were always sincere and unselfish in their dealings with the Indians; and their presence and labors among these dusky tribes were the noblest, and almost the only, redeeming feature in the relations of the two races, whose history on the part of the whites is but a narrative of debauchery, of treachery, and of deceit. Thousands of the Iroquois blessed the coming of the Catholic missionaries, as through them they subdued their passions, triumphed over the vices of their race, and obtained the happiness of Heaven;[3] whilst even the Pagans held the Black Robes

[1] Alden.   [2] Parkman.
[3] Dablon. The relations only continued to 1672, but Father Dablon, who was superior of the mission, wrote an account of their labors from 1672 to 1679, which was published in 1860.

in reverence, although they did not profit by their presence, but were whirled along with the great mass of their race, without grace or God, like so many of their white brethren, towards the happy hunting ground, where they believed they would hunt the deer and fight their foes.

Many of the adult Christians gave strong proof of the firmness of their faith, not only by assisting the Fathers to instruct the catechumens, but by leaving home and kindred and emigrating to the new settlements near Montreal, where they could preserve and practice their faith.

Many individual examples could be given which would show that the Iroquois Christians realized and appreciated the truth and beauty of Christianity; as they sacrificed their lives for the faith with all the fervor, resignation, and love, displayed by the early martyrs of the Church. Among the Christian Iroquois who had emigrated to the Sault was Stephan Te Ganonakoa, and his young family. In August, 1690, he set out with a party of friends for the usual fall hunt, but shortly after they were attacked by a band of Cayugas, and Stephan and his wife were led captives to Onondaga.[1] Here they were tortured with all the cruelty which these people inflict upon the enemies of their race, because they had abandoned their country for Christianity. They inflicted upon him the most cruel tortures to compel him to renounce Christianity and return to his native home; but he remained firm and endured the torments until death, with the stoicism of the Indian and the fortitude of the Christian martyr. He begged only for time to pray; and then he urged them to proceed with their torments, for his sins

---

[1] Kip. p. 121. Kip was a Protestant bishop, who admired the self sacrifice and devotion of the missionaries and the heroic virtues of the Catholic Iroquois.

deserved punishment, and the more severe were his sufferings here the greater would be his reward in Heaven.

Two years later Frances Ganannhatenha, an Iroquois living at the Sault, was captured and taken to Onondaga where the nails were torn from her hands; the sign of the cross was cut on her bosom with a tomahawk; she was burned at the stake; her scalp was torn off, and hot ashes were placed on her head; yet, whilst the savages were inflicting these cruelties, she prayed and advised her tormentors to become Christians.

The next year a young Indian woman of twenty-four years, whose home was at the Sault, was captured by the Pagans; and when she realized what cruelty awaited her she cried out that her sins merited whatever punishment they could inflict on her; and she prayed the Lord would give her strength to suffer for her sins. She was burned at the stake, and as the fierce flames arose around her frail form, with her dying breath she gently murmured the names of Jesus, Mary, and Joseph.[1]

Stephan Aonwentsiatewet, a young man who dwelt at the Sault, was captured by the Mohawks, and was hurried off to their towns to be tortured. He had influential friends among the Mohawks, and his life was saved. He was urged to live like the Pagans, to adopt their customs and practice their vices, but he refused. He saw that it was impossible for him to practice his faith among Pagans, so he resolved to escape. He was recaptured, and, after a prayer for his friends and for his torturers, he was put to death.[2]

The humble Mohawk maiden, Catherine Tekakwitha, led a most remarkable life of fervor and devotion, and she added lustre to the glory of the Church in the New World

[1] Kip, p. 129. [2] Burtin, "Vie de Catherine Tekakwitha."

by the virtues which adorned her soul. Her life was proof that children of the forest, reared amid Pagan surroundings, are as capable of the highest degree of Christian perfection as those who enjoy the advantages of refined education and civilized society. Her tomb at the Sault became a shrine to which thousands of her own race as well as Europeans came to pay their tribute of respect to a holy virgin, whose beautiful life entitled her name to be enrolled among the number of the saints. Many also came with their sorrows. and their ills, and through her intercession they obtained miraculous favors.[1]

The missioners baptized more than 4,000[2] adults and children during the years they labored in the Iroquois country. Fully 1,500 emigrated from the Iroquois cantons to the Catholic settlements on the St. Lawrence River, where they have practiced their religion with fidelity to the present day.

The King of France had early expressed a desire to have the children of New France educated like the children of Europeans, and to adopt the manners and customs of civilized life. Many of the wealthy nobles and the pious ladies of France had contributed generously towards the establishment of seminaries of learning at Quebec, for the training of Indian boys and girls. The king hoped by this means to make the Indians loyal subjects of France, and the pious ladies wished to see them faithful children of the Church.

The Jesuits believed that the Christian education of some of the Huron youths would greatly facilitate their work in converting these people, so they started at Quebec, in 1635, a little seminary which they called the "Seminaire des Hurons." Father Daniel and Father

[1] Kip, p. 114.   [2] Dablon.

Nicoll brought some promising children from the Huron country and placed them in this seminary; but some soon died, and the others fled from the institution. Some Algonquins and some Montagnais were also admitted, but they did not take kindly to the study of books.

The Ursulines came to Quebec in 1639, and they immediately began the work of educating all the girls, of whatever race, that they could induce to come within the sacred precinct of their convent walls. They especially desired to educate and civilize the Huron and Algonquin girls, who were amenable to their teaching. The celebrated Marie de l' Incarnation, the superior of the convent, was well fitted for this work, as she knew the Huron and Algonquin languages well, and was devoted to the enlightenment and elevation of the Indian girls.

From the time the seminaries were established at Quebec and Montreal the Fathers had sent some of the brightest young Indian boys and girls they could find in their respective missions to these schools, so that they might be instructed in the arts of civilization, and taught the truths of Christianity; and then when they graduated from these seminaries, and returned to their forest homes, they might also become missioners in civilizing and Christianizing the Indian nations. Peace with the Iroquois gave the Fathers an opportunity of placing many of the young boys from the Five Nations in the seminaries at Montreal and Quebec, and several of the girls in the convent of the Ursuline nuns; and in this way they hoped to spread the light of progress and of faith among these benighted people, and teach them to adopt the customs and practices of civilized life.

The Indians could not be expected to pay anything for an education they did not appreciate, and the work of sustaining these institutions devolved on the pious ladies of France, who religiously and generously contributed towards the conversion of these savages. There was an inherent charm in the untrammeled freedom of Indian life that firmly wedded these people to their forest homes. No inducements of civilized life could lead them from the traditional customs and occupations of their race. The commercial activity of civilized communities was for them an intolerable prison life, whilst they utterly despised the tillers of the soil. They gloried only in the hunt or in war, and when they visited the Europeans it was to barter their furs for arms and ammunition or for rum, or to lie on the ground and gaze in idle curiosity and scorn at the busy lives of the merchants and traders.

The children of these people could not brook the restraint of convent life, and when they seemed content with their surroundings, at an unguarded moment, they would scale the walls and fly like deers to their forest homes.[1]

Marie de l' Incarnation says that it was almost impossible to civilize them, as scarcely one out of a hundred children who passed through their hands would adopt the manners and customs of European life.

The Iroquois were the most implacable foes of the French, yet, paradoxical as it may seem, their girls were the most docile pupils of the convent. When the Catholic Iroquois began to settle on the St. Lawrence, some of their girls went to live with the sisters, where they learned the arts and sciences of civilized life; and some of them joined the community and became exemplary and saintly nuns.

[1] The Montagnais, at the Bay of Chaleurs, were taught by the Jesuits to read and write near two centuries ago, and they have preserved the knowledge thus acquired to the present day by teaching their children the contents of the books that were printed in their language.

SCHOOLS FOR THE INDIANS. 205

As the Indian converts learned more of Christianity they valued education more highly, because they found that books were an important factor in the preservation of their faith. Little works on Christian doctrine were published in the Huron, Iroquois, and Algonquin, languages, and schools were started in the Catholic Indian settlements, in which all who wished could learn to read and write in their own tongue.[1]

The first schools for Indians were located in large towns, but as these were not successful many thought they would be more prosperous if they were placed in the country, away from the turmoil of the town, where the Indian youth could have the fields and the forests to engage in the pastimes of their homes. There were three little isles in the St. Lawrence at Gentilly, above LaChine, called the Isles of Courcelles; and these were given by the Governor to the Abbe Fenelon in January, 1673, for the purpose of establishing a seminary for Indian boys.

Schools were started at the different Indian Catholic settlements, in which the Indians were taught to read and write, and other branches were added when they could be induced to remain; and these schools have continued without interruption to the present day.

There are now four excellent schools for the Catholic Iroquois at St. Regis, two at Caughnawaga, and one at Two Mountains,[2] in which the pupils learn all that is generally taught in our grammar, or common schools. It is a general complaint, however, that parents do not realize that much benefit is conferred by such an education, and they still prefer to see their boys learn to hunt or fish, or lazily till the soil; whilst some few serve as pilots

[1] Letter of Bishop of Quebec to Bishop Timon.
[2] Canadian report of Indian affairs, 1893.

to guide steamers through the dangerous rapids of the St. Lawrence, whose every rock has been known to their race for many ages.

CHAPTER XXI.

LA SALLE AND FATHER HENNEPIN.

LA SALLE LEARNS TOPOGRAPHY OF COUNTRY FROM IROQUOIS—WATER ROUTE TO EAST INDIES—EXPEDITION FOR FAITH AND FAME—VISIT SENECAS—VISITORS REGALED WITH ROAST DOG—VISIT NIAGARA RIVER—DOLLIER AND GALINEE BUILD FIRST CHAPEL ON LAKE ERIE—WINTER SOJOURN IN THE FOREST—LAKE STORM ENDS MISSIONARY ENTERPRISE—SECOND EXPEDITION—BUILDING OF THE GRIFFON—TE DEUM AT NIAGARA—FIRST RECORD OF MASS AT NIAGARA—HENNEPIN'S MIDWINTER JOURNEY TO SENECAS—WHERE THE GRIFFON WAS BUILT—GRIFFON ANCHORED AT SQUAW ISLAND—FIRST RELIGIOUS SERVICE IN BUFFALO—LOSS OF THE GRIFFON.

SOME other Reverend Fathers visited the homes of the Iroquois during the period of the missions, and, although they did not directly labor to propagate the Gospel among the Indians, yet they performed religious services in this region, and their deeds form a part of the early Church history of this part of the country.

The Cavalier[1] La Salle had learned from some Iroquois at Montreal that there were vast forests and prairies to the westward, teeming with game; that there were vast lakes, on the borders of which were inexhaustible mines; and that there was a river to the west of their country which flowed into a great sea. The discovery of a northwest passage to the East Indies was the highest ambition of the early explorers, and La Salle thought this might be the route that would solve the problem, and bring him

[1] Marshall, p. 191.

wealth and fame. In the summer, therefore, of 1669, with two Sulpitians, Revs. Francois Dollier de Casson, and Rene de Brehart de Galinee, he organized a joint expedition,—the Cavalier to make discoveries, and the missionaries to preach the Gospel and bring the light of faith to the unknown nations and tribes beyond the lakes and along the extensive valley of the Mississippi.[1] The party was composed of about twenty-five men, and started from La Chine,[2] July 6, 1669, ascended the St. Lawrence to Lake Ontario, and skirted along its southern shore to Irondequoit Bay. Thence they proceeded to the Seneca village of Gannagaro, or St. James, in order to obtain a guide to conduct them through the wilderness to the Ohio River. They were received with great pomp by the Seneca chiefs and ancients; and a banquet was prepared for them, at which the principal dish was roast dog.

They were detained here for three weeks, expecting to obtain a captive, or slave, as a guide; but they were obliged to depart without one. They returned to Irondequoit Bay, where Father Dollier and some companions had remained, and where mass was celebrated on the shore, in a little chapel made of the oars and the sails of their canoes. They proceeded along the southern shore of the lake towards Niagara River, where they landed, and very probably said mass. Here they learned from the Indians about the great falls, which they did not visit but accurately described from the account given them. They went to Burlington Bay, and thence overland to an Indian village, situated between the head of the Bay and Grand River, where Father Dollier said mass and all the company received Holy Communion. Here La Salle left

[1] The Relations of 1670 give this name to the river.
[2] So called, perhaps, from its being the supposed starting point to China. Marshall.

THE LOSS OF THE CHALICE. 209

the party, and the Sulpitians proceeded down the Grand River to Lake Erie. As the season was far advanced,[1] the missionaries decided to remain in this beautiful region until spring; so they built a chapel[2] a short distance from the lake; gathered nuts and killed game for food; gathered the wild grapes which were here in great abundance, and pressed them to serve as wine for the altar; and thus this little congregation of French Christians spent the winter of 1669-70, worshiping on Sundays in the first chapel erected on the borders of Lake Erie. They made preparations to continue their westward journey on the lake, March 26, 1670, but during the night a violent storm arose which submerged one of their canoes, and their ammunition was destroyed; but the greatest loss was the chalice, without which they could not celebrate mass or administer the sacrament of the Holy Eucharist, and their grand missionary enterprise came to a sudden end, and they reluctantly made their way to the nearest settlement of French.

They[3] said mass in their travels in more than 200 places where mass had never been celebrated before, Father Dollier celebrating at least three times every week.

LaSalle was not discouraged by the failure of his first attempt to explore the vast region of the West, but made preparations for another expedition over the lakes and waterways to discover new lands, and to buy peltry from the Indians. For this purpose he sent a party of carpenters and artisans to build a fort at Niagara and a vessel

1 It was then October 15.
2. Margry Decouverts. On M. Galinee's map there was a Presque Isle on the Canadian shore above Grand River, which was very large. This is now Long Point, and the chapel was a little inward of this, probably on Big Creek, at or near Spring Arbor. General Clark, however, holds that they wintered at Dover, thirty-five miles west of the mouth of Grand River.
3 Journal of Galinee in Margry.

above the Falls.[1] He had received a grant of land near the present site of Kingston, Ont., where he built a fort which he named Frontenac, and here he also built a brigantine of ten tons, which he loaded with materials for the new vessel and with supplies and provisions for his explorations on the upper lakes.

The companions of LaSalle in this enterprise were Father Louis Hennepin, a Flemish Franciscan, the Chevelier Henry de Tonty, the Sieur la Motte de Lussiere, and sixteen men.[2] Father Hennepin possessed something of the venturesome spirit of LaSalle, and he accompanied the party not only to attend to their spiritual wants but also to take part in the exploration of the vast region of the West. Their exploring party embarked in their little brigantine at Fort Frontenac November 18, 1678, and on the sixth of December, the feast of St. Nicholas, they entered the beautiful river Niagara, "Into which no bark similar to ours had ever sailed."[3] The grand strains of that noble hymn of the Church, the Te Deum, arose from the deck of the vessel, and resounded along either shore of this romantic region, so interesting and pregnant with events of importance to Church and State. The next day a party with Father Hennepin ascended the river in a canoe and landed on the Canadian shore, near the old suspension bridge, ascended Queenstown Heights and followed the river as far as Chippewa Creek, where they encamped for the night. The next day they returned to the mouth of the river, and on the eleventh of December Father Hennepin said mass on the American shore, presumably the first ever said in this vicinity.[4]

LaSalle had not arrived from Fort Frontenac, and, as

---

[1] Margry "Decouvertes." Vol. I.   [2] Marshall.   [3] Hennepin N. D., p. 74.
[4] Marshall.

the Indians objected to the building of a fort, LaMotte invited Father Hennepin to accompany him to the Seneca villages near the Genesee River, to obtain from the chiefs a sanction for their work. They started from the Niagara River on Christmas day, 1678, and journeyed five days along the ridge road trail to the Genesee, through the snow in the wilderness, with parched corn, or some wild game killed by their Indian companions, for food, and some large oak or lofty pine for a shelter at night, until they reached the large village of Tagarondies.[1] On the first day of the year Father Hennepin said mass[2] in this village and preached to the Iroquois, in the presence of Fathers Garnier and Raffeix, S. J. They were kindly received and generously treated by the Senecas; but their mission was fruitless, and they returned to their companions on January 14th.

In the meantime the brigantine had been towed up the river to the present site of Lewiston, at the bottom of the footpath near the old bridge,[3] and the men awaited the coming of LaSalle to begin work. LaSalle selected a site for his shipyard about five miles above the Falls, on Cayuga Creek,[4] where two bark cabins were built, one for a work shop, and the other for a chapel where mass was said every day, and where Father Hennepin preached on Sundays whilst the devout Frenchmen made the forests resound with the strains of the Gregorian chant for high mass. LaSalle was obliged to return to Fort Frontenac for supplies for his expedition, and Father Hennepin accompanied him as far as Niagara (Youngstown), where a site was selected for a fort; but to avoid giving

[1] Gandachloragou.
[2] Father Hennepin always carried his portable altar on his back during these journeys, and, consequently, said mass in many places not recorded.
[3] Roseel. [4] Locality in doubt, Remington.

offence to the Senecas the French pretended that it was to be a blacksmith shop which LaSalle had promised them.

The vessel, which was completed in May, 1679, was called the Griffon, in compliment to Count Frontenac, and was blessed by Father Hennepin; and the first vessel of the upper lakes floated out with the Te Deum over the waters of the Cayuga Creek to the Niagara River. The Griffon soon after sailed up the river to the foot of Squaw Island, about two and one-half miles from the lake,[1] where she was anchored and remained nearly three months awaiting the return of Father Hennepin and LaSalle, who went to Fort Frontenac for supplies and for other priests to assist them in the work.

After the return of Father Hennepin mass was daily celebrated on the vessel, and the word of God was preached on Sundays from the deck of the Griffon to the men ranged along the shore.

This was the first religious service that was held in the present city of Buffalo, and the first time the Gospel was announced in a place which is now adorned with many beautiful temples dedicated to the worship of God.

The Griffon sailed up the lakes on August 7, 1679, and Father Melithon remained as chaplain to the little band which LaSalle left at the stocks[2] where the vessel was built, to carry the furs he expected to bring on his

[1] At the foot of Austin street, Buffalo.

[2] There is some difference of opinion among authorities in regard to the location of the chapel and the cabins of Father Melithon and his companions, after the sailing of the Griffon. The cabin above the Falls seems to have been a mere temporary structure, but the one at the mouth of the river was intended for a permanent storehouse and fort. Denonville, in his act of possession, in 1688, says the stocks above the Falls still exist, but the *quarters* which La Salle had built at the mouth of the river had been burned by the Senecas.

The quarters, or fort, at the mouth of the river, were large and commodious, and it was here, most probably, that Father Melithon and his companions dwelt.

return from this place to the lower lake. The Griffon was lost in a storm; the Senecas burned the storehouse at Lewiston; the French with Father Melithon soon after returned to Fort Frontenac, and thus disappeared the first Catholic house of worship along the banks of the Niagara River.

CHAPTER XXII.

GARACONTIE.

GREAT ORATOR—HEARS THE ELOQUENT CHAUMONOT—ENCOURAGES CHRISTIANS—FRIEND OF THE FRENCH—GIVES HIS CABIN FOR A CHAPEL—TEMPERANCE ADVOCATE—EULOGY OF LE MOYNE—GARACONTIE AT THE GREAT COUNCIL—HIS BAPTISM—HIS PIETY AND ZEAL—PUBLICLY PROFESSES CHRISTIANITY—FAREWELL BANQUETS—PREPARING FOR THE END—HAPPY DEATH.

GARACONTIE was born, in all probability, before any Europeans entered the State of New York, about the year 1600; and he must have been quite a youth when he heard the warriors or the sachems tell of the strange race of pale faces, that had come to Manhatta[1] in their great canoes, or had appeared near the lake of the invisible nation at the head of a band of Quatoghies,[2] and had slaughtered the Mohawks with their wonderful arms. He was a man of considerable influence in his country when the Iroquois first came into friendly contact with the French; and, as a great orator and nephew of the Sagochieendaguate,[3] the head sachem of the league, he occupied an important position in the country. He was as celebrated in his day as Red Jacket was among the modern Senecas; and whenever an embassy was to be sent to the neighboring nations, and especially to the Europeans, all eyes turned to Garacontie as the representative of his race. He had listened in mute astonishment to the wonderful eloquence of the saintly

[1] New York City.   [2] Hurons.   [3] To-do-da-ho.   214

Chaumonot, portraying the beauties and truths of Christianity to the assembled nations; but with true Indian stoicism he remained apparently indifferent, and did not manifest any inclination to accept the Faith. The truths he had heard from the missioners had evidently made a deep impression on his mind, for, after the marvelous flight of the French colony from Onondaga in 1658, he became the protector of the Christians and the friend of the French.

In 1662 he was in the Mohawk country, and whilst there he saw a large crucifix, two feet in height, which had been carried off by them in one of their raids on Quebec, and knowing the reverence the Christians had for this emblem of their faith, he bought it from the Mohawk Pagans and brought it to Onondaga.[1] He hung it up in the deserted chapel, and then he invited the French captives and the Christian Indians to come there to pray. The mission bell was still at the chapel, after the flight of the French colony, and Garacontie had it rung every morning and evening to call the Christians together; and he encouraged them with banquets to maintain their devotion and the practices of their faith. He openly advocated alliance with the French, at a time when all the Iroquois nations were secretly plotting their destruction, and he became the friend of the French captives, securing their ransom by his influence, or saving them from the horrors of Indian torture by his eloquent pleading

In July, 1661, two canoes came down the St. Lawrence with a delegation of Cayugas and Onondagas, to make a treaty of peace with the French, and to bring back the light of Faith to the Iroquois cantons. The Cayuga chief, who had entertained the Fathers at his own home

[1] Faillon, Vol. 3, p. 2.

five years before, was at the head of the embassy, and he offered his presents, but positively demanded the return of the missioners to the Iroquois country. As an evidence of the good will of the Iroquois towards the Faith, he said that the chapels were kept in repair, and that Garacontie at Onondaga did the work of a missioner, when no priest was in the land.

Father LaMoyne returned with this party to Onondaga, where he was received with great honor by Garacontie, who placed his own home at the disposal of the priest for the services of the Church.[1] Through the influence of Garacontie, the mission of Father LeMoyne was, at least, a partial success, as he returned to Montreal the following summer with eighteen captives, after having baptised about two hundred at Cayuga and Onondaga.

Garacontie saw with sorrow the havoc that the excessive drinking of strong liquor was working among his people, and he also saw that the missioners were the only Europeans that condemned and tried to prevent its sale to the Indians; so he openly declared that the teaching of the Fathers was the only salvation of his race. He looked upon the missioners, therefore, as the benefactors of his race long before he professed his faith in their religion, and at every opportunity he employed his wonderful eloquence to bring them back to the Iroquois cantons.

He prevailed upon his people, in 1665, to send a delegation to Quebec to make peace with the French. At the meeting with the Governor, De Tracy, he made a speech which displayed all the ability and eloquence of an educated statesman. Father LeMoyne had died a short time before in the wilderness, and Garacontie apostraphized his spirit in Indian style: "Ondessonk,[2] listen,

[1] Relations, 1661. [2] The Indian name of Father LeMoyne.

I implore thee, from the land of the dead whither thou too soon hast gone. Many times hast thou placed thy head upon the death scaffolds of the Mohawks, thou hast fearlessly leaped into their fires to snatch the French from the embers; peace and happiness followed thy footsteps, and friendship thrived in thy presence. We have seen thee upon our council mats decide for peace or war, our cabins were too small when thou entered, and our towns too restricted when thou camest, so great were the crowds that wished to hear thy words. I will not disturb thy repose with this untimely speech. So often hast thou taught us that this life of misery shall be followed by one of eternal joy; and as thou art now in the possession of this, why should we deplore thy death?

"We mourn for thee because in thy death we lost a father and a friend. We are consoled, however, because thou hast found that life of infinite joy of which thou hast so often spoken."[1] He averted war from his own nation; peace soon followed, and he was pleased to see the Father again laboring among the Iroquois.

Peace with the Indian allies of the French was not pleasing to the young Iroquois warriors, and their wanton attack, in 1670, upon a defenseless Algonquin village threatened to involve the whole country in war, but for the prompt action of Garacontie. He immediately sent belts of wampum to the different Iroquois nations to restrain the impetuosity of their warriors who were preparing for the struggle, and advised them to send their delegates to Montreal where they would meet the Algonquins, and they could amicably settle their differences by the arbitration of the Governor.

The delegates from many Indian nations assembled at

[1] Relations, 1666, p. 5.

Quebec, in July, 1670, and Garacontie spoke in the name of his country in favor of peace; and then he addressed the multitudes, with the zeal of an apostle and the fiery eloquence of the great orator, in favor of the Christian law. Although not a Christian himself, yet he had been living for some years according to the Christian law, and had renounced polygamy, the folly of dreams, and all the superstitions of his race. He advised all the Indian nations to follow his example and become Christians, and he publicly requested the Bishop to receive him into the Church.

The Bishop learned from the missioners that the Iroquois chief was worthy of baptism, and as he had labored to ransom the captives in his own land it was proper that the Church should free him from the slavery of Satan.

The Governor and the daughter of the Intendant were his sponsors, whilst the Bishop solemnly conferred the sacrament in the Cathedral, in the presence of many hundreds of dusky warriors from different tribes and nations.

He humbly thanked the Bishop for granting him the favor he had long since desired, and for having opened for him by baptism the gates of the Church. He was afterwards entertained at a grand banquet, given in his honor by the Governor, at the fort, where he was received by the soldiers with military honors.

The effects of the sacrament of confirmation, which he received on this occasion, were visible in the greater zeal he manifested for the propagation of the Gospel among his people and in the efforts he made to overthrow the superstitions of his race. He advised the Fathers in regard to the manner of preaching the Gospel to the Indians, and he encouraged his people to adopt Christianity. He attended mass every morning at the little chapel, though his home was more than a mile distant; and his holy life gained the admiration of his people, although the Pagans were disposed to blame him for abandoning the customs and traditions of his race. He carried his rosary with him in his travels, and recited it with devotion; and he ordered the public banquets to be opened with prayer.

After his return from Quubec, at a solemn celebration, addressing his brethren, he said he had always labored for the general weal, raising his voice when the interests of his country required him to speak, and risking his life for his people in times of danger. "Is there a poor family in the town," he said, "or a poor widow who can say that I did not use my authority to provide the help necessary to cultivate their fields and to gather their harvests? When fire destroyed their homes and consumed their goods, did I not help them to rebuild and to replenish their stores? If I have done these things, he said, "in the past, through natural inclination and through a motive of honor, I will continue to perform such honorable deeds through a higher motive, because I thus obey the express command of the Sovereign Master of Life."[1] He was not pharisaical in relating the good he had done, for he also told of the evil deeds he had committed and of the scandal he had given the young by his lewd life before he adopted the Christian law; but he hoped that his good life for the future would make amends for his past wickedness. They must not expect that he would sanction the observance of dreams, or favor the superstitions of his race. His example favorably influenced many towards Christianity, as they had the greatest confidence in his intelligence and honor.

[1] Relations, 1671, p. 16.

Garacontie was an old man at this time, and visions of the future life were continually hovering before his view, but it was the Heaven of the Christian, and not the happy hunting ground of the Indian, to which he aspired; so when sickness came his first care was for his soul. In 1676 he gathered his friends about him, and gave three farewell banquets, at which he expressed his opinion on important matters, and revealed his last wishes to his friends. In the first banquet he condemned the doctrine of dreams, which he thought was inimical to the best interests of his race. In the second banquet he denounced those feasts in which the guests were compelled to devour all the food placed before them, or to indulge in other unbecoming or indecent deeds. In the third banquet he sang his death song in Indian style, and recounted the glorious deeds of his life for the benefit of his family and friends, and in the interests of his race. It was in the evening of life, especially, that the enlightened and Christian spirit of Garacontie was revealed. He saluted God as the Sovereign Lord and Master of Life, in whose hands are our lives, as well as the destiny of the world. He saluted the Bishop of Canada, who had received him into the Church, and in whose presence he had made the solemn promises of baptism which he had striven faithfully to observe. He called upon the Bishop to pray for him, that he might die a good Christian and appear worthy in the sight of God. He made a public profession of his faith, and condemned all the errors and superstitions of his Pagan life.

He recovered sufficiently to attend the midnight mass at Christmas; but the weather was very cold and a pulmonary disease attacked his feeble frame, and, kneeling there in the little chapel he told Father de Lamberville that his death was near, and he fervently made his confession. During his last illness he frequently prayed, or he had some pious Iroquois recite the rosary for him until he peacefully departed. "The great Catholic chief of Onondaga, Daniel Garacontie, stands in history as one of the most extraordinary men of the Iroquois League."[1]

[1] Shea.

CHAPTER XXIII.

CATHERINE TEGAKOUITA.

PAGAN INDIANS IMMORAL—HIDDEN VIRTUES OF CONVERTS—CATHERINE'S BIRTH PLACE—HER PARENTS—SMALL POX RAVAGES—CHANGE OF HOME—FIRST MEETING WITH MISSIONERS—DESIRES TO BECOME A CHRISTIAN—HER BAPTISM—PERSECUTION—FLIGHT—LIFE AT THE SAULT—VOWS VIRGINITY—FAILING HEALTH—HONORED AS A SAINT—HER RELICS.

THE Iroquois had many noble traits of character, which served on occasions as the ground-work for Christian sanctity; and though they were addicted to cruelty and many forms of vice, through ignorance of any higher law than instinct or pleasure, yet they needed but to be shown the beauty and worth of Christian virtue to be led on to the highest degree of holiness. The Indian maiden's first step towards Christianity was in the path of holy purity. This virtue was not known among the Pagan Indians, nor was it ever practised before the advent of the Christian missioners. Its inculcation by the Fathers was a strange revelation to people long abandoned to unrestrained lust; but the women were not slow to perceive that the new doctrine was an honor to their sex, and its practice would confer upon them a dignity they had not before enjoyed.

Many deeds of eminent virtue were performed by the Iroquois converts unknown to the world, and many holy lives were spent in the forests, like the flowers of the desert, whose beauty and whose fragrance were not

CATHERINE TEGAKOUITA.

even perceived by the world; but some examples have been recorded which show the effect of Catholic teaching upon the souls of these simple children of nature. The life of Tegakouita, a Mohawk maiden, was written by Father Chauchetiere, who was her spiritual director at the Iroquois settlement of the Sault, near Montreal, and gives us an idea of the effect of Christian morality upon the lives of the Indians.

Situated upon a slight eminence on the south bank of the Mohawk River, a short distance west of the Schoharie, was the first village of the Mohawks, near which Renè Goupil was slain in 1642, for having taught an Indian child to make the sign of the cross. The same people also put the saintly Father Jogues to death a few years later, when he came among them to announce the Gospel. The blood of martyrs is the seed of Christians, and the most beautiful flower which sprang from the soil sanctified by the blood of these holy martyrs was Tegakouita, who was born in this village[1] in 1656, and who has been revered by different generations as the most saintly person of her race.

Her father was a Mohawk Pagan, but her mother was an Algonquin captive who had been instructed and received into the Church by the French at Three Rivers, before the Iroquois invaded her home and carried her from her native land. The light of faith began to shine over the benighted Iroquois about the time of Tegakouita's birth, when Father LeMoyne visited the Mohawk villages as ambassador and as missioner; but he never met the Algonquin Christian mother, nor did he baptize her infant child.

In the winter of 1659-60, small-pox ravaged the Mo-

[1] The village had been removed to a different site shortly after Goupil's death.

hawk villages and numbered among its victims the father and mother of Tegakouita, and left its indelible mark upon her features, and nearly destroyed her vision. She was taken in charge by her uncle, who was the leading chief of the village; and her aunt taught her the arts of Indian embroidery, and all the work of an Indian maiden. As the small-pox had left her weak eyes she was not inclined to take part in the games of the Mohawk youth, and she was thus saved from some of the vices of her race.

After the small-pox scourge had swept over the village, in 1660, the site was abandoned and another town was built farther up the valley, on the bank of Auries Creek. DeTracy came with a French army in 1666, destroyed the Mohawk towns and the large stores of provisions, and compelled the Indians to sue for peace. The next spring the Mohawks requested the French priests to come to dwell among them, impelled more through the necessity of pleasing the French than through any desire of learning the teachings of Christianity. After the destruction of their towns by DeTracy, the Mohawks rebuilt on the north banks of the river, and the town in which Tegakouita dwelt was known as Gandaouge, or Caughnawaga, which means the Rapids, because here the sparkling waters of the river gurgled in swift flowing waves over the rocky decline of the river.

When Fathers Fremin, Pierron, and Bruyas, came in 1667 as the first missioners to the Mohawks, they tarried at Gandaouge, the first village on the route from Montreal; and they became the guests of Tegakouita's uncle, as the chief man of the town. They only remained here two days, and Tegakouita was too timid to learn much of the faith of her mother. A church was built in the village, and a faithful little congregation was formed;

TEGAKOUITA BECOMES A CHRISTIAN.

but Tegakouita was not among the number, as she feared the displeasure of her uncle, who was hostile to the religion of the French. She only awaited a favorable opportunity, however, to manifest her desire of becoming a Christian. The opportunity came in the autumn of 1675, when she was about nineteen years of age. She had accidently injured her foot, and was obliged to remain in her cabin with some decrepit old people, whilst her companions were in the field gathering the new corn for the winter's store. Father Lamberville was making his round of the village when he entered the cabin of Tegakouita, who at once expressed her desire of becoming a Christian. She had often heard some of her companions singing the hymns that Father Boniface had taught them; she had beheld, no doubt, the beautiful ceremonies in the little chapel at Christmas; and she had often listened to the teachings of the Fathers; so her present declaration was not a sudden impulse, but a serious resolution she had long since formed. She was enrolled among the number of catecumens, and began to attend the chapel instructions to prepare for the sacrament of baptism. All through the winter she learned the doctrine taught by the Fathers, and anxiously awaited the moment when she would be received into the Church of her Algonquin mother. The missioners did not receive many adults into the Church, as there was always so much danger that they would lapse into their old vices and Pagan practices; but Tegakouita was so reserved and modest and the people spoke so well of her, that Father de Lamberville decided to baptize her on Easter Sunday. In baptism she took the name of Catherine; and she immediately began a life of prayer, of self-denial, and of eminent virtue, such as she saw manifested in the lives of the saintly missionaries. Persecution and calumny assailed her; the Pagans attempted to lead her into their life of sin, or slay her, but she remained steadfast, and was satisfied to suffer persecution for the sake of her Saviour. She would not marry at the command of her guardians, because she had given her heart entirely to God. Most of the adult Christians had fled from the valley of the Mohawk on account of persecution, and the eyes of Catherine wistfully turned towards the new Christian Caughnawaga on the banks of the River St. Lawrence. Father de Lamberville advised her to flee from her persecutors, as death seemed to await her in the Mohawk valley.

Garonhiague, or Hot Ashes, a noted Mohawk chief, who had joined the little band of Christian Iroquois at the Sault, returned to his old home in 1677, with one of Catherine's relatives, for a visit; and Catherine immediately prepared her plans for escape. Discovery meant death, but Garonhiague was a brave as well as a wise warrior, and he made a successful arrangement for the flight of his young Christian protegée. Catherine fled through the forest on unbeaten paths, in company with her Christian relative, whilst her Pagan uncle followed in hot haste, uttering dire threats of vengeance; but she managed to elude her pursuer, and reached in safety her new Christian home.

There was a model Indian Christian community at the Sault, and in the little chapel Catherine spent all the hours she could spare from her daily life before the Blessed Sacrament. She lived with her relatives and engaged in all the labors of the other Indian maidens; but she would not marry, though she had many favorable offers, because she wished to live a virgin, as she believed this state more perfect and pleasing to God.

When leaving her Mohawk home, Father de Lamberville sent a note with her to the pastor at the Sault, in which he wrote: "Catherine Tegakouita goes to live at the Sault. I pray you to take the charge of her direction. You will soon know the treasure we are giving you. Keep it well, therefore, and may it profit in your hands to God's glory and to the salvation of a soul assuredly very dear to Him."[1] The people at the Sault, as well as the Fathers, soon learned that they had received a spiritual jewel of great value in the advent of Catherine, as she led a life of such remarkable holiness and piety that she was a model and an inspiration to the people of her race.

She prepared assiduously for her first communion, which she received in the little chapel at Christmas; and ever after she strove to receive the Holy Eucharist every Sunday. The greatest affliction came when she was separated from the little chapel, the place she cherished most on earth, as she was obliged to accompany a hunting party into the deep forests to obtain their annual supply of food; but even then, like the saintly Jogues on the Mohawk, she erected, in a retired nook, a little bark screen where she could pray without molestation, and could bring vividly before her mind the presence of our Divine Lord in the tabernacle of the chapel on the St. Lawrence. She could never again be induced to join a hunting party, but she was willing to perform any kind of drudgery or toil if she could be near the house of God.

Catherine had an intimate friend at the Sault, a young girl, from whom many of the holy deeds performed by this saintly maiden were learned. She made a vow of perpetual virginity in March, 1679, and when she was

[1] Messenger of the Sacred Heart.

asked afterwards by her relatives why she did not marry she could truly say she was not her own, as she had dedicated her life entirely to God. Father Chauchetiere, who knew her well, says that her life at the Sault was like that of St. Catherine of Sienna, and might well serve as a model for the most fervent Christians of Europe.

Her health began to fail in 1679; she would not, however, relinquish any possible works of virtue, but became more zealous and fervid as the reflected vision of God became more luminous and distinct in the approaching light of eternity.

Father Fremin gave her the last sacraments in April, 1680, and he requested her to address those who gathered around her in the cabin, for she had unconsciously been the source of much fervor during her short life, and he wished to perpetuate the memory of her beautiful life among her people. She died in Holy Week, when the Church was commemorating the sad mysteries of the passion of our Lord, which she often strove to imitate by the severe penances and scourages which she inflicted upon her own innocent body.

The Indians came to kiss her hands as a tribute of respect to her holy life. Her reputation for virtue soon spread abroad, and her grave became a holy shrine whither the devout faithful of Canada went as pilgrims to pray. Bishop Laval came with the Marquis Denonville to pray at the tomb, as he said, of the "Genevieve of Canada."

The Fathers of the third Plenary Council at Baltimore solicited from the Holy See the introduction of the cause of her canonization;[1] and members of different Indian tribes[2] sent an humble petition to Rome in favor of this most illustrious child of their race.

[1] Shea.   [2] Walworth Kateri Tegakouita.

Her relics were eagerly sought, and many were carried away by devout pilgrims, but some still remain on the banks of the St. Lawrence, which had so often witnessed the struggles of her people against the encroachments of civilized foes. Her body was first buried near the cross on the banks of the river but it was later removed to a resting place beneath the chapel. When the village site was removed, the precious relics were deposited in the new chapel as one of its treasures. Part of her body was brought to St. Regis, where the new colony was formed, and the remainder is still preserved in the vaults of the little church at Caughnawaga,[1] on the St. Lawrence River, a few miles above Montreal. A granite monument was erected to her memory in 1890 by the Rev. Clarence Walworth of Albany. This monument was blessed by the Bishop of Albany in July, 1890, in the presence of the Archbishop of Montreal and a large assemblage of priests and people. A large cross was placed over the tomb, which stands as a mute memorial of the triumphs of Christianity in transforming this savage child of the forest into a gentle Christian saint.

[1] The writer had the pleasure of beholding these relics in the summer of 1894.

CHAPTER XXIV.

FATHER JOGUES.

AT COLLEGE—ON THE HURON MISSION—JOURNEY TO QUEBEC—CAPTURE—TORTURE—CAPTIVITY—ESCAPE—AMBASSADOR TO MOHAWKS—THE MYSTERIOUS BOX—FIRST MISSIONER TO MOHAWKS—DANGER—DEATH—CHAPEL ERECTED TO HIS MEMORY—PILGRIM SHRINE.

FATHER Isaac Jogues was the first missioner among the Iroquois, and he was the first to seal his work with a martyr's death. He was born in 1607, at Orleans, France, of pious Catholic parents. He early attended a Jesuit college, where he was soon inspired with the desire of an Indian missioner's life. During his college course he met three famous Huron missionaries, Brebeuf, Lalemant, and Masse, who were forced to return to France in 1629, when the English took possession of the French posts in the New World. He came to Canada in 1636, to assist his brethren among the Hurons, and he immediately experienced the hardships of the Indian missionary's life, in the long journey up the Ottawa River to the country of the Hurons. Here he labored with the zeal of an apostle, and looked forward for the martyr's death as the reward of his toil. He knelt before the Blessed Sacrament one day and besought our Lord to grant him the grace of a martyr's death, and he seemed to hear a voice saying: "Thy prayer is heard."

Father Lalemant selected him in 1642 for the hazardous journey to Quebec, to bring back supplies and goods

FATHER ISAAC JOGUES S J

for the numerous missions around Georgian Bay. The Iroquois were at war with the Hurons, and small bands lay concealed in some favorable ambush for days at a time, along the banks of the Ottawa River, waiting to attack the Huron trading parties along the route. Jogues and his party reached Quebec in safety, but were attacked and plundered, and some were slain on the return voyage, and the priest with others of his party was led a captive to the Mohawk towns.[1] There were about forty persons in the Huron party, and all of these looked to Father Jogues for spiritual consolation in their hour of need. He not only comforted his little flock, but he gave them courage by the heroic fortitude he displayed in bearing patiently the cruel tortures inflicted on him. The bones of his fingers were crunched between the teeth of a Mohawk warrior; his thumb was cut off, and the nails were torn from his fingers; yet he did not complain, but asked God to forgive him, and even rejoiced that he was found worthy to suffer for Christ.

Then began his long and dreary captivity as a slave; but even the burdens of this life were lightened by the good he was occasionally able to do for his fellow Christian captives; and the knowledge he acquired of the people and their language also relieved the monotony of toil, as he hoped some day to put this knowledge to good use as a missioner among them.

In the summer of 1643 Father Jogues was with a fishing party on the Hudson River, a few miles below the Dutch trading post, when he heard of the cruel torture of some Huron captives in the Mohawk villages, and he desired to return to administer spiritual consolation to these poor unfortunates before death. The Mohawks had been

[1] See Chapter II.

prowling around Fort Richelieu, and as an excuse for their presence they induced Father Jogues to write a note to the commandant. The bearer of the message never returned; and his party was fired upon by the French, who, no doubt, suspected some evil design from the presence of the enemy. The Mohawks attributed this attack to the letter of Father Jogues, and they resolved to put him to death. The Dutch commander[1] was aware of the evil design of the Iroquois, and he induced the Father to steal away at night from his Indian captors, so that he might escape to France in a vessel which was then lying in the harbor. He reached the vessel in safety; but the Iroquois soon discovered their loss, and they threatened to destroy the trading post unless he were restored to them. It was only after long weeks of hiding and negotiations between the Dutch and the Indians that he was finally enabled to sail for home.

A conquering hero, or a great saint, could not have been received with greater honors by all classes in Europe than was this humble martyr of the Mohawk. The Pope called him a martyr of Christ, and Queen Anne of Austria said he was a living romance of wonder and heroism. His heart turned away from these honors and from the comforts of civilization to the rude life in the forest, and he longed to return to his chosen field of labor whither the vision of a martyr's crown lured him to toil.

After a few months' sojourn in France he again sailed for the New World, and was soon laboring among the Indians at Montreal. His long captivity among the Mohawks had enabled him to learn their language well, and when Governor Montmagny had concluded a treaty of peace with these people, he selected Father Jogues as an

[1] The Dutch States General, at the request of the Queen Regent of France, had given orders to secure the release of Father Jogues.

ambassador to ratify the terms in the land of the Iroquois. He was received with honor in the land where he had been a slave, because he came as the ambassador of a powerful people. His mission was not merely for peace, but he wished to prepare the way for the preaching of the Gospel; so he brought the sacred vessels and vestments for the altar, and he left them where they would be convenient for his ministry when he returned as the ambassador of Christ.[1]

He had a presentiment that he would never return from his third journey to the land of the Mohawks; and before setting out he wrote to a friend in France: "*Ibo et non redibo.*"—"I go, but I will not return."

The superstitious Mohawks imagined that he left some evil spirit in the box in which he had enclosed the articles for the altar, or that he brought some evil okki to spread pestilence and death throughout the land for the injuries they had inflicted on him during his captivity; so they cast the box into the river, and they only awaited a favorable opportunity to treat him in the same manner, or to knock out his brains with a hatchet. The prospect of a most cruel death did not deter this holy man from his mission, but these Indian tortures were like the Siren songs that lured him to death. He did not desire any greater reward for his labor than death in the service o his Master.

The Mohawks had been the greatest scourge of the Church, and the greatest terror of the French; what greater good, then, could any one do than to bring these savages into the Church? He might not succeed, he might even lose his life in the attempt, but failure would

[1] Father Jogues did some missionary work on this visit, in hearing the confessions of some captives, and baptizing children, or those who were ill. At Saratoga he met Teresa, the saintly Huron, who was overjoyed with his presence.

not injure the cause, and his life was in the hands of God.

With John de LaLande, a young Frenchman, and some Hurons, Father Jogues started at the end of September for his new Mission of the Martyrs among the Mohawks. The Hurons had not proceeded far on the journey when fear of their old enemies, or presentiment of impending evil, conquered their courage and all but one abandoned the party to its fate. A great change had come over the spirit of the Mohawks since the embassy of Father Jogues. Their corn crop was a partial failure, and a pestilential disease had ravaged their homes. According to their theories, these misfortunes were caused by the evil spirits sent into their land by their enemies. They resolved, therefore, to renew the war against the French, the Hurons, and the Algonquins; and war parties had already set out against the French whilst Father Jogues was on the way to announce the gospel of peace to these people. One of these parties met Father Jogues near Lake George,[1] and they immediately bound him, and led him prisoner to the town in which he had spent so many dreary months of captivity. They consoled him by saying they would soon put him to death; and although they tore the flesh from his arms and devoured it, to see if it were the flesh of a Manitou,[2] yet they said his torments would be of short duration.

There was a difference of opinion in the village in regard to the fate of the prisoners. The Wolf clan strenuously fought for the preservation of their lives, whilst the Bear clan was resolved to put them to death. The decision was referred to the council at Tionnontoguen, but

[1] Father Jogues was the first to give this lake a name, and he called it the Lake of the Blessed Sacrament, because he discovered it on the feast of Corpus Christi. It retained this name for more than a hundred years, until an English sycophant changed it to George, in honor of his king.   [2] Martin, Life of Jogues.

members of the Bear clan had sealed their fate before the delegates could return. On the evening of October 18th, some members of the Bear clan invited Father Jogues to a banquet at one of their cabins. He went willingly, as he wished to gain their good graces to prepare the way for the introduction of Christianity. As he was crossing the threshold of the cabin to which he was invited, a blow from the tomahawk of a treacherous member of the Bear clan felled him to the earth, and his head was cut off and placed upon a palisade over the town, as a warning of the hostile spirit against the French existing among these savage foes.[1]

Those who knew Father Jogues well looked upon him as a saint in his life, and he was surely a martyr in his death.

After more than two centuries an interest has been awakened in the sufferings and labors of these early Christian heroes, in introducing Christianity and civilization among the savage nations of the Iroquois League. A shrine has recently been erected over the place where Father Jogues met his death, and every year thousands of daintily clad feet tread the ground once hallowed by the rough moccasined feet of the Jesuit saint, and they kneel in prayer at the tomb of him who was first to bear the tidings of Faith to the Indians of the Mohawk valley.

[1] Father Jogues was most probably adopted into the Wolf clan during the period of his captivity among the Mohawks; and when he came as ambassador to the nation he gave a present to the Wolf clan, requesting them to keep their fires lit for the French, and to entertain them in their homes. The Wolf clan, therefore, pleaded for his life. Kaotsaeton, the great chief, also cast his influence in favor of the Jesuit's life, but the Bear clan had already solved the difficulty, before the council had time to decide.

CHAPTER XXV.

MISSION OF THE PRESENTATION.

FATHER PIQUET FOUNDS A MISSION FOR IROQUOIS—ENGLISH OPPOSITION—MISSION HOUSE BURNED BY MOHAWKS—PIQUET'S MISSIONARY CRUISE—FRENCH FORT AT OGDENSBURG AN ENCROACHMENT UPON ENGLISH RIGHTS—WAR INCIDENTS—FRENCH FORTS FALL—PIQUET RETIRES—RETURNS TO FRANCE.

THE Rev. Francis Piquet, a Sulpitian, was stationed at Two Mountains in 1740, and in 1745 he accompanied the warriors of his flock in their attack on Fort Edward. During this period he came in friendly contact with many of the warriors of the Iroquois cantons, who led him to believe that they were favorably disposed toward Christianity. After some correspondence with the Governor, and with Jonquiere, who was then at Niagara, Father Piquet started in September, 1748, to select a site near Fort Frontenac for his new mission.

He selected a beautiful location on the banks of the Oswegatchie, where its waters flow into the St. Lawrence, and here, on the site of the present city of Ogdensburg, he built his little palisaded fort, and erected the chapel which he called LaPresentation, in honor of the patronal feast of the Sulpitians.[1]

The harbor would afford shelter to many canoes, or even larger vessels, in rough weather; the lands were fertile, the timber good and abundant, and the place was

[1] Shea, "The Catholic Church in Colonial Days."

favorably situated for a fort and trading post as well as for a mission. When the chapel was ready, Father Piquet visited the Iroquois nations to invite those favorably disposed towards Christianity to come to dwell in this new home. Many were preparing to respond to his call, but the English[1] incited the Mohawks to destroy the new mission, as they saw in it an obstacle to their trade and a menace to their power. A band of warriors descended upon the defenseless fort in October, 1749, and applied the torch to the chapel and the palisades.

The zealous missionary was not discouraged by his loss, but immediately made preparations to rebuild his chapel. A detachment of soldiers was sent from Fort Frontenac to protect the place from further incursions of hostile Indians; work was begun on the new fort and chapel,[2] and provisions and ammunition were sent by the Governor for the warriors, who would come to dwell in the new mission. In July, 1747, when all was in readiness at the new mission, Father Piquet made a cruise around Lake Ontario, in one of the king's ships, as far as Fort Niagara, to invite the scattered Iroquois to come and dwell at LaPresentation. He visited the Senecas, and brought a number of them to the fort at Niagara, where he said mass for them in the chapel. Then he cruised along the south shore of the lake to the Genesee River, whence he visited more of the Iroquois towns. The English were apprised of his scheme, and they sent quantities of liquor among the Indians to incite them to acts of hostility against the French, and to prevent the

[1] Paris Documents.

[2] The cornerstone of this chapel was found some years ago, and now occupies an honorable place in the chief building of the city of Ogdensburg. There is a Latin inscription on the stone which in English means, "In the name of Almighty God, † Francis Piquet began this edifice in 1749."

Iroquois from leaving their homes. Many of the Iroquois, however, followed the Father to the new mission on the St. Lawrence. The mission began with about thirty Iroquois, but in two years the number increased to three thousand; and the place gave indications of being the most prosperous community of Christians in the New World.

Father Piquet obtained from the Governor a strip of land along the banks of the river, upon which he erected a saw mill where his Indians could prepare lumber for the markets; and he also taught them the art of husbandry and the customs of civilized life. In May, 1752, a notable event occurred at the Presentation. The Indian neophytes had manifested such an excellent spirit and had learned the teachings of Christianity so well that Bishop Du-Breuil de Pontbriand, of Quebec, resolved to visit this portion of his flock and administer the sacrament of Confirmation. He, accordingly, came in May with many officers and priests, and administered the sacrament for the first time in the State of New York.[1]

The English viewed with alarm the ascendency of French influence over the Indians of the State of New York, and they openly urged the Iroquois to extinguish the fires of the new settlement at Oswegatchie. The officers of the English government most strenuously urged the chiefs to restrain their people from leaving their homes to dwell at the missions of the French. Many of the Iroquois themselves grieved over the loss of so many young warriors from their nation, as their departure would imperil the prestige of their famous league, and would eventually involve the ruin of their race. Hendrick, the great Mohawk chief and orator, appealed to

[1] Shea, "The Catholic Church in Colonial Days."

his brethren at a council with the English, in September, 1753, to keep the weeds from the trails between Onondaga and the English forts. He also reminded them of the traditions of their race, which foretold the fading of their glory when the fires went out at Onondaga.

A call was issued, early in 1754, to the different English colonies to send representatives to a congress at Albany to discuss plans for union among themselves, and to adopt means of defense against the encroachments of the French, and the hostilities of their Indian foes. This congress proclaimed that all the country between Lake Champlain, Lake Ontario, and Lake Erie, belonged to the Iroquois, and was, by the treaty of Utrecht, placed under the protection of the crown of Great Britain. The delegates also looked upon the mission of the Presentation as an encroachment upon British soil, and they condemned the practise of leading the Iroquois from their own homes to dwell at this mission of the French. The Iroquois were shrewd enough to penetrate the false guise of friendship, under which the French and English diplomats addressed them. They understood that each of these nations was seeking to deprive them of their lands, and that some day they would be forced by those powers to abandon their country and the homes of their race. Oswegatchie was the nearest place for them to go to learn to pray and to have their children baptized; but if the English insisted, their young warriors would extinguish the fires lit by the French on the banks of their pleasant river.

The English had a fort and a trading post at Oswego, and the struggle for a monopoly of the Indian fur trade led to many conflicts between the English and French; and in this strife the young warriors of the Presentation made frequent raids upon the British traders coming up the Mohawk and Black Rivers on the way to Oswego. Such conflicts could only lead to war, and each nation was merely awaiting a favorable opportunity to descend upon the strongholds of the other. The French had made an expedition into Ohio to reduce the Miamis to subjection, and had taken possession of the country in the name of their king. Oswego had fallen before a force of French and their Indian allies; and these numerous hostile acts paved the way for a fearful clash of arms.

In the war of 1754 the young men from LaPresentation destroyed many of the forts along the English frontier, and they also destroyed the English fleet on Lake Ontario, in their little bark canoes.

Father Piquet took an active part in the wars between England and France, and he encouraged his young warriors to fight bravely for France in the struggle for supremacy between these two powers. He was very useful to DeQuesne, the French commander, on account of his knowledge of the country and his influence with the Iroquois. His service to France rendered him more odious to the English, who only awaited a favorable opportunity to destroy his mission.

Early in the summer of 1759 the French forts along the lakes fell by the prowess of English arms; and in September of the same year the dominion of the French in Canada was overthrown by the fall of Quebec.

Father Piquet did not feel secure from the English at LaPresentation, so he abandoned the site in 1759 and retired with his Indian flock to the Grand Isle aux Galope, where he built a chapel.

General Amherst, the commander of the English forces, would have rejoiced to secure the services of

Father Piquet for the English crown, but his heart was attached to France,[1] and when he could no longer serve his country, or minister to his faithful flock, he fled up the lakes with a band of his young men till he was beyond the reach of British power. He proceeded to New Orleans and, after a short sojourn, returned to his native land. Without a shepherd his flock wandered away through the forest in search of a new home, and many of them went to St. Regis where, under the guidance of Father Gordon, they founded a new and prosperous mission.

[1] DeQuesne says of him: "He has equally served religion and the State, with incredible success, during nearly thirty years."

CHAPTER XXVI.

THE REDUCTIONS.

HURON SETTLEMENT AT LORETTE – PRARIE DE LA MADELEINE–NEW HOME FOR IROQUOIS CATHOLICS–FIRST SETTLERS–CHAPEL BUILT–SCHOOL STARTED–VISIT OF BISHOP LAVAL–CHANGES OF LOCATION–MODEL CHRISTIAN COMMUNITY–FAMOUS PASTORS–BELL FOR THE CHURCH–BELL CAPTURED BY BRITISH–INDIANS LAMENT THE LOSS–TO THE RESCUE–RECAPTURED–REJOICING–THE SAINTLY MOHAWK–CAYUGA SETTLEMENT–SULPITIAN MISSIONS–RECOLLECTS–ST. REGIS COLONY–CHURCH AND SCHOOLS–MOHAWKS FIGHT WITH THE BRITISH IN THE REVOLUTION–ONEIDAS FRIENDLY TO AMERICANS–ONEIDAS IN THE WEST–RECENT CONVERTS–EXPEDITION AGAINST ONONDAGAS–SULLIVAN'S EXPEDITION–REMNANT OF THE RACE.

WHEN the Iroquois devasted the Huron country in 1649 and 1650, massacred the missioners, and burned the chapels, the Fathers who escaped death fled with many of the faithful Huron Christians to Quebec, where a Catholic Indian colony was formed at Lorette under the protection of the French. When some of the Iroquois became Christians and found that they could not worship God in peace in their own land, but were subject to annoyance and persecution from their friends and relatives, on account of their faith, they willingly embraced the opportunity of migrating to a Catholic settlement, and dwelling at Lorette among their former foes.[1]

[1] Shea, "History of Catholic Missions among the Indians of the United States."

A HOME FOR CATHOLIC IROQUOIS.

There was a beautiful level tract of land opposite Montreal, called La Prarie, owned by the Abbe de La Madeleine, who transferred it to the Jesuits for ecclesiastical purposes. Here the Jesuits began a residence in 1669, as a home for the sick or aged missionaries, and as a place of retreat for the members of the order.[1] Father Raffeix was here at this time, and, knowing from experience the difficulties the Iroquois converts encountered in their own land in the practice of their religion, he conceived the idea of making this a home for Catholic Iroquois. The French Governor encouraged the project; as it would increase his fighting force in war, and would withdraw these brave warriors from the influence and dominion of the English. At this time there was at Quebec a pious and intelligent Erie convert, Catherine Ganneaktena, the wife of an Iroquois chief, and, as she had been the hostess of Bruyas at Oneida, she was well instructed in her religion; so the Fathers selected her as the foundress of the first Iroquois reduction, which was named after St. Francis Xavier.

In 1670 about twenty families had settled on this site, and a government was formed according to the customs of the Iroquois nations. According to the first laws established in the mission no one could become a member of the community unless he renounced three things: belief in dreams, changing wives, and drunkenness; and any one offending against any of these laws was to be expelled.[2]

At the request of Governor de Courcelles, Father Fremin was recalled from the Seneca country to take charge of this new church; and he left shortly after for

[1] This property is still owned by the Jesuits, and was the subject of recent national dispute.   [2] Shea, p. 305.

France to obtain assistance for his new Indian community and for a new chapel. The early settlers were principally Oneidas and Mohawks, who followed in the footsteps of chiefs of their respective nations. The wife of Kryn, the great Mohawk chief, became a Christian and went to dwell at the new mission on the St. Lawrence, as her life was not safe in her Mohawk home; and Kryn, part in anger and part in sorrow, wandered away through the forest until he came to the new community, where he was so charmed with the peaceful, happy life of the people that he begged to be admitted as a member and instructed in the Christian faith. He afterwards returned to the Mohawk country, and led back to the St. Lawrence a little band of forty faithful Christians, who joyfully embraced the opportunity to escape from the Pagan vices and persecutions of their race. The Oneida chief, husband of Catherine Ganneaktena, also brought many of his countrymen to this new mission, and the community increased with the advent of members from many different tribes and nations. They built a little chapel, where all heard mass every morning with the singing of hymns and the recital of prayers; and again at evening, when the day was drawing to its close, they gathered around the altar to return thanks to God for the blessings of the day, and to seek His protection for the night. On Sundays they had more elaborate ceremonies in the services of their little chapel, and the solemn music of the high mass was sweetly sung by a choir of Indian youths and maidens. A school was started for the boys; but the Indians had not yet learned to appreciate the advantages of civilized education and the knowledge of books. The fathers wished to see their boys learn to trap the beaver, to hunt the bear and the deer, and to draw the finny tribe from their watery homes; as it was by these arts that they provided for all the necessities of Indian life. They had no desire to adopt the business laws and usages of their civilized white neighbors, nor to imitate their social forms; so they could reap no benefit from the school, as hunting and fishing were sufficient to provide for all the wants of their humble homes.

Bishop Laval visited the mission in 1675, and administered the sacrament of confirmation to one hundred well-instructed Indians. The Indians lined the bank of the river, and as the Bishop landed from his canoe he was received with a formal speech; and at different stages of his journey to the chapel he was obliged to halt, whilst some chief delivered an address of welcome in the name of his nation. The Bishop remained here several days, and he was delighted with the piety and fervor, and the thorough Christian spirit manifested by these semi-civilized children of the forest. The locality was not healthful; and when the chiefs saw so many members of their little flock languishing with the fever they decided to select a new habitation; so they removed in 1676 about two miles further up the river to a site which the Iroquois called, "Kateritsitkaiatal", which means the place where Catherine Tegakouita was buried.[1] They moved shortly after to Sault St. Louis, or St. Francis Xavier Sault, as some called it, and which was known to the Indians as Caughnawaga, or the Rapids. Here the little bark chapel was replaced in 1678 by a stone church sixty feet long; which, however, was poorly constructed, as it was demolished in 1683 by a great hurricane.

They moved again, about 1689, a little nearer to the

[1] There is a cross there to mark the place where Catherine was accustomed to come to pray. Burtin.

Rapids, and they remained here about twenty years when they chose the site of their present location opposite Lachine. They had evidently determined to establish a permanent home at Caughnawaga, and they erected one of the handsomest church buildings in Canada, as a memorial of their attachment to the Faith. Here they lived a life of most extraordinary devotion. "In no place in the New World," says Charlevoix, "did I behold such piety as in the Indian Christian community at the Rapids." M. St. Valier, the pastor of the church in 1688, says: "The lives of all are very extraordinary, and the village would be taken for a monastery."[1] The labors of many zealous priests contributed to the fervor and the piety displayed in this mission. Father Chollenec came in 1675 to assist Father Fremin, and he left to posterity an account of the remarkable virtues of Catherine Tegakouita. Father Bruyas also came here to continue his labors among the Christians he had instructed in their own country, on the Mohawk or at Oneida. Father Garnier and Father James de Lamberville knew the language well, and when they were driven from their missions they came to this other little Iroquois nation, where they were joyfully welcomed by many of their old friends. Father Lafitau labored here for some years, and gathered material for his important work on the customs of the Huron-Iroquois nations. The last Jesuit to labor amongst them was the Rev. Joseph Huguet, who was there as their pastor when the order to which he belonged, and which had effected so much good among the Indians, was suppressed.[2]

[1] Charlevoix Letters, p. 343.

[2] Letter of Rev. J. V. Burtin, O. M. I., April 2, 1895. Rev. Joseph Marcoux spent thirty-five years amongst them, and wrote a grammar and a dictionary of their language. The Rev. J. V. Burtin, O. M. I., who had charge of the mission from 1864 to 1892, is now engaged in collecting material for a history of the congregation.

THE PURCHASE OF A BELL.

The site was most beautiful and picturesque, and where the land jutted far into the river they built another church[1] which could be readily seen by the voyagers on the St. Lawrence. There was a belfry in the church, and a bell in those times was much needed to warn the people of the time for services in the church and to call them to morning and evening prayer; so the pastor advised them to set aside some of their valuable furs that he might purchase a bell in France. The simple-minded Indians understood that a church bell was some sweet voiced spiritual being, whose presence was necessary for the welfare of the parish, and its office was to warn them of their duty, and to invite them to pray. The furs were soon ready, and the bell was bought and shipped from Havre in the Grand Monarque, which, however, was captured by a British war vessel, and was sold with its contents at one of the ports of Massachusetts. The inhabitants of Deerfield bought the bell for their little church, but during the war the Indians of Caughnawaga raided the town, captured the bell, and hung it up in their own little church, where it still tolls the tidings of joy or sounds the knell of death.

To the simple Indian mind the bell was a mysterious spiritual monitor, who was to dwell in the belfry, and whose duties in the parish were only second in importance to those of the priest. They felt keenly, therefore, the loss of the intended inhabitant of the belfry. When they beheld the vacant tower they bemoaned the lot of the bell, and they longed for an opportunity to rescue it from captivity and place it in its home. In imagination they could hear its voice, sweeter than the songs of the bobolink or the blackbird, more thrilling than the

[1] The church was built in 1721 near an old fort, which was called Fort St. Louis.

notes of the tsiskoko[1] ringing out over the waters and resounding through the forests at early dawn and again at evening with the sweet notes of the *Angelus*. They longed to hear its dulcet tones floating through the air, adding its sweet melody to the harmony of Sunday and calling them to the little church to worship the Master of Life.

Councils were held to discuss the best means for rescuing the captive bell, and prayers were offered to God for guidance in this important affair. The solution of the problem came when the Marquis de Vaudreuil resolved to send an expedition against the British colonies of Massachusetts. They did not need to be urged to join the expedition against the town of Deerfield, but they immediately raised the war-cry and prepared for the fray. The inclement season did not restrain their ardor, for they left their homes in the depths of winter to join the army of M. de Rouville, at Fort Chambly.

The Indians followed silently in the wake of the French soldiers, and glided noiselessly on their snow shoes through the frost-laden forests in the direction of Lake Champlain. This was an unusual and a very severe season for war, yet the Indians moved rapidly without a murmur, seemingly indifferent to the intense cold or the deep snow. The French were hardy soldiers, but they did not manifest the endurance or cheerfulness of their Indian friends. Some very important matter must surely have given them this determination, and led them from home and family at this season of the year.

They had only the furs of the deer and bear to protect them from snow and cold, but they were not sufficient to shield them from the storm or renew the strength

[1] The thrush.

of their wearied limbs in restful repose. The holy cause, however, of their mission supplied warmth to their limbs, and gave elasticity to their step, and in an incredibly short time they reached the little village of Deerfield. Here they made an attack on the town, and captured the bell.

The Indians would not seek rest until they had paid their respect to the mysterious bell; so a soldier was sent to ring the bell to comply with their desire. The sweet sound amid the scene of carnage, and in the stillness of the forest, was as wonderful to the simple minds of the Indians, as was the voice of the angel announcing the birth of the Saviour to the shepherds of Judea.

The bell was taken from the belfry and, placed upon a strong pole, was borne in triumph upon the shoulders of four Indians through the forest towards their distant home. It was too heavy to be carried conveniently in this manner, so they buried it in the forest, near the banks of Lake Champlain, to await a more favorable season for its transportation.

When spring returned, and the ground was hard and dry, and free from snow, the chief organized a party and selected some zealous braves, who, with the assistance of a yoke of oxen, would bring the bell from its tomb in the forest to its new home in the belfry of their little church.

The bell was carefully bedecked with fragrant wild flowers, wreaths and garlands were placed upon the heads of the oxen and upon the pole from which their precious treasure hung; and they proceeded joyfully on their way to Caughnawaga.

At the village all had heard of the wonderful qualities of the bell—the marvelous sweetness of its voice, and the power of its tone—and all anxiously awaited its advent as they would for the arrival of some great chief.

In the twilight of an early summer evening, whilst the women and children were discussing the qualities of the sweet-voiced dweller of the belfry, a strange and pleasing sound was heard faintly floating through the forest. Stronger and more clear the sound grew, until they knew it was the welcome and expected guest. They received the bell with great rejoicing, and placed it in the belfry where it still tolls the hours, and its sweet sound floats over the waters calling the Indians to prayer.

In 1677 an humble maiden, Catherine Tegakouita, came to this community from her home at Gandaougue, on the Mohawk River; and, although of simple appearance, yet she was destined to become one of the most famous of her race, and she showed by her life that the Indian was capable of attaining as high a degree of perfection as the greatest saints of the Church. Her tomb became a shrine to which thousands from many nations came to pray for the intercession of the holy Mohawk virgin. The little bark chapel was the home in which she spent, in prayer, all the hours she could spare from the drudgery of an Indian woman's life. She never married, as she considered the state of virginity more holy; but she labored like other Indian women of her condition for the support of the family of her relatives, with whom she lived. She died here in 1680 in the odor of sanctity, and her tomb immediately became a shrine of devotion for the pilgrims of New France. She may yet be enrolled among the number of the saints, as her canonization has been solicited from the Holy See by the Fathers of the third Plenary Council of Baltimore.[1]

[1] Shea, p. 309.

THE NEW MISSION. 251

The Cayugas were continually at war with the powerful Andastes, who dwelt southward of the Iroquois region; and in 1665 some of them, becoming weary of this perpetual strife, decided to emigrate to a more secure region where they would not be molested by these troublesome neighbors; so they selected a site on Quinte Bay near the present Kingston, Canada. When they heard about the chapel that was erected in their old home, and about the beautiful truths taught by the "Black Gowns," they sent a delegation to Montreal to ask for priests to come to instruct them.[1] Bishop Laval invited the Sulpitians to take charge of this new mission; and the Rev. Fathers Fenelon[2] and Trouve were selected to labor in this new colony. They reached the Bay of Quinte in October, 1668, and began the same routine of labors that the Jesuits fulfilled among the Iroquois.

One of the wealthy members of the "Society of Montreal" made a handsome donation of money to build the little church, and the Governor granted land and certain commercial privileges to the new community. Although the Indians received the Fathers joyfully and listened to their teaching willingly, yet they did not become Christians in large numbers, and it was principally the sick or the dying that were admitted to the sacraments of the Church.

There was another little settlement of Iroquois at

[1] Faillon, p. 191.

[2] There has been considerable discussion in regard to the identity of this Fenelon. Hennepin incidentally calls him "The present Archbishop of Cambray;' and many have been led to believe that the great Fenelon actually labored on the Canadian mission, because Hennepin was good authority as he labored on the same mission himself, at a subsequent period. The Fenelon referred to was an elder brother of the great Archbishop, who labored for many years on the Canadian mission. Fenelon the Archbishop and author, was only seventeen years of age when his elder brother was ordained, and although he also desired to labor among the Indians of the New World, yet his health was not rugged enough for the climate and life.

Gandoseteragon, near the present site of Toronto, and these people also asked Father Fenelon to come to teach them the truths of Christianity; so he visited this place, leaving the newly-arrived missioner, Father Urse, to continue his labors at Quinte. Fathers de Circé and Marriot, Sulpitians, also labored for a time in these missions along the northern shore of the lake:[1] but as all these were temporary towns, established probably for convenience in hunting or fishing, or for purposes of trade, no permanent good could be effected among the inhabitants; so the Fathers induced many of the better disposed to retire with them, in 1676, to the Island of Montreal, where they started a new Indian Christian community. In 1701 this mission was removed to another site, near the Sault au Recollet. In 1720 it was again transferred to the shores of the lake of Two Mountains, a short distance from the place it occupies to-day. In 1732 it was established at its present location; but many of the inhabitants have emigrated to the Muskoka region, and the remaining few have united with their white neighbors in the French-Canadian parish.

Count Frontenac, Governor of New France, started a large fort at Quinte Bay in 1673, and he invited the Iroquois to meet him, in order to gain their confidence and their trade. He advised them to become Christians, but at the same time he allowed his traders to sell them liquor without limit, and his soldiers to scandalize them by their bad lives; so that the poor Indians were demoralized, and were not disposed to believe in the truths taught by the missioners.

La Salle went to France in 1674, bearing some very

[1] Greenhalgh says some of these villages were thirty miles inland, but he is so unreliable in regard to distance that a person does not feel safe in accepting his statements.

highly commendatory letters from Governor Frontenac to the French court, and with these, and through influential friends in France, he obtained from the King a grant of the unfinished Fort Frontenac and considerable land adjoining, on condition that he would rĕimburse the government for what it had already expended on the fort, would garrison it with at least twenty men for two years, and would build a church there within five years.

The Recollets or Franciscans were the earliest missioners among the Iroquois-Huron nations, and in 1669 the King of France wrote to the provincial of the order, at Paris, to request him to send some members of the order back to their old missions among the Indians of Canada.

Frontenac was not favorable to the Jesuits, neither was he pleased with the Sulpitians; so when the Recollets came to Canada, La Salle, to please his master, immediately secured them for his proposed church at Quinte Bay, and for the neighboring Indian missions. It was here that Father Hennepin, with the other Fathers of the same order, labored zealously for two years, but without much success, many of the Iroquois returning to their old homes near Lake Tiehero, or in the valley of the Genesee, and others going to the Iroquois settlements near Montreal; so when La Salle started on his famous expedition to the West the mission was practically abandoned.

Proximity to the French towns, and especially to the military and trading posts, was not conducive to the moral welfare of the Indians; so in 1760 the Rev. Anthony Gordon led a colony of Catholic Indians from Caughnawaga up the St. Lawrence River to a beautiful site at the northeast extremity of the present State of New York, where a new village was started and named in honor of St. Regis.

THE IROQUOIS AND THE JESUITS.

Here, on the banks of the two rivers, they built their little log chapel, with a partition at one end for the home of the priest; and here they erected their own cabins, and they gave the name Akwisasane[1] to one of the most beautiful spots on the St. Lawrence River.

The little log chapel was burned some two years after its erection and the first records of the church were destroyed, but since that time they have been preserved with scrupulous fidelity, showing a long list of souls of this faithful flock.

An Indian legend assigns a different origin to St. Regis. It relates the capture of two white children in the town of Groton, Mass., shortly after the settlement of Caughnawaga, who were carried off by the Indians, and grew to manhood with all the customs and habits of Indian life. They took Indian girls for wives, and became prominent in the councils of their adopted nations, but as their minds were not thoroughly Indian, differences of opinion arose in the tribe, which finally compelled them to emigrate with their families to some distant location. They selected the site on the St. Lawrence which was afterwards christened St. Regis.

The locality was most beautiful and picturesque; and the contented settlers soon built another church, with a little cupola and a place for a bell.

Father Gordon's health failed in 1775, and he went back to Caughnawaga, where he died two years later. The little mission was then deprived of a resident priest for some years, although priests came occasionally from other places to minister to the spiritual wants of the people. The Rev. Roderick McDonnell came in 1785, and built the present stone church, with its gallery for strangers and its beautifully decorated altar.

[1] The place where the partridge drums. Hough.

The Indians present an inspiring sight as, squatted on the floor, they follow in respectful silence the priest in the different parts of the mass, or listen reverentially to the explanation of the Gospel in the Mohawk tongue. Father McDonnell died in 1806, and was buried under the choir where the Indian singers often chant the requiems for their departed benefactors and friends. The little Indian church has had its regular resident priest ever since; and for many years it has had its school, where the children are taught to read and write, and where they learn the rudiments of English and the principles of their religion. The Catholic Indian population[1] of St. Regis numbers 1,128 souls, and there are four schools for the children and youth; but these are not always well attended as the Indians have not even yet learned to appreciate the benefits derived from education.

Three, and sometimes four priests were kept busy attending to the spiritual wants of the faithful Iroquois at Caughnawaga. They held conferences every day; and the Indians were well instructed in their religious duties. One of their own race, Joseph Rontagonka, instructed them in music, and Catholic hymns were translated into the Iroquois tongue, and were sung in the church during the celebration of mass. They abandoned all the Pagan rites and festivals, and to-day they only celebrate the planting and the harvest feasts.

During the Revolution many of them took up arms under Atiatonharonkwen[2] and fought alongside their old friends, the French, for the independence of the infant colonies.

[1] Canadian Report Indian Affairs, 1893.
[2] Atiatonharonkwen, better known as Col. Louis, received his commission from Gen. Washington, and with the Indians from Caughnawaga, St. Regis, and Oneida, did gallant work during the war. He was educated by one of the Jesuits from Caughnawaga.

They have now generally adopted the peaceful pursuits of their white neighbors, and they till the soil and engage in light traffic, whilst their children attend the Catholic schools, where they receive an education and are instructed in their religion.

The Mohawks remained along the banks of the river which still bears their name until the time of the Revolution. The white settlers had been gradually encroaching upon their domain; yet the Mohawks reserved valuable lands[1] along the banks of the river, and they might still be dwelling near their ancient site had they not fought with the British against the Colonies in the war for independence. In 1771 they had three villages in the valley: one at Schoharie, one at Fort Hunter, and one at Canajoharie; and they continued to reside here until British agents induced them to take the war path against the Colonies, and large numbers left their homes never more to return.

The Iroquois had borne the brunt of many battles in the preceding war with the French, and when the Colonies resolved to cast off the yoke of Great Britain the leaders on either side sought alliance with the fierce warriors of the league. The Americans endeavored to secure the neutrality of the Iroquois; but with war all around them, and with so many inducements to lead them into the fight, they could not long remain at peace. They had agreed to remain neutral; but the Johnsons[2] had wonderful influence over the Mohawks, and British agents offered arms, provisions, clothing, and money, to secure the aid of these formidable fighters. The Ameri-

[1] By the treaty of 1678 the Mohawks retained the northern part of the State.
[2] These were Col. Guy, and Sir John Johnson, whose father, Sir William Johnson, died just before the Revolution. The Johnsons had many large possessions at Johnstown, N. Y., where Sir William lived in barbaric splendor with Brant's sister.

cans were too poor to pay their own soldiers, and they could not, like the British, offer great inducements to the Indians to aid their cause; so the Iroquois were gradually drawn into the fray, and they cast their lot with what they believed to be the stronger power. There was no unanimity, however, at the councils of the Five Nations on the subject of the war; so each nation was free to follow its own counsels, and whilst the others fought with the British the Oneidas either remained neutral or proffered their services to the Americans as scouts or guides.

The Mohawks, under Brant, followed Johnson to Oswego; they spread desolation and ruin through many settlements, and when the Americans triumphed they sought an asylum in Canada under the aegis of the British flag.

The Oneidas long retained their love for the Black Robes and their teachings; and at various times after the close of the missions Jesuits surreptitiously dwelt among them. In 1771 they had two villages, and about 600 souls; and many of these were Christians, "Being instructed partly by French Jesuits."[1]

The advancing tide of immigration was gradually forcing the remaining Iroquois farther westward; and in 1815 the United States Government gave the Oneidas a large tract of land at Green Bay, Wisconsin, in exchange for part of their lands in the State of New York. Many Oneidas soon after removed to their western home, but some few still remained near the ancient rock until the last vestige of the nation disappeared from the state, and the reservation was closed.[2]

The Oneidas still flourish at Green Bay; and of late years many have manifested a desire to embrace Chris-

[1] "Memorial" of Rev. C. Inglis in 1771. [2] It was closed in 1890.

tianity as it was taught to their forefathers by the Jesuits more than two hundred years ago. The first convert, Stephan Cornelius, was baptized there in 1884, by Father Lou at Greenville. Five years later some children were baptized by the Franciscan Fathers at Keshena,[1] and the next year several adults were received into the Church by Bishop Katzer. The rapidly increasing number of converts suggested the necessity of a church for the Catholic Oneidas, where they might assemble on Sundays to hear mass and listen to the word of God. Mr. Eli Skenendoah donated a parcel of land, and many white friends contributed towards the erection of a pretty little brick veneered church, which was dedicated, in 1891, to the service of God.[2] The Rev. J. A. Selbach looks after the spiritual interests of this little flock, and he has hopes of seeing a great number of the Oneidas enter the Church to follow the light first brought to their old homes by the ancient Black Robes.

The Onondagas dwelt at different places around the valley which bears their name until the Revolution, when they were driven from their homes by a detachment of American soldiers, who were sent in 1779 to punish them for the part they had taken in attacks upon several defenceless settlements. The Onondagas fled westward, and settled down on the banks of Buffalo Creek, where they were soon joined by their brothers from the Seneca and Cayuga nations. Some united with the Senecas; others later returned to the site of their ancient town, and there they still dwell amid the scenes of their departed glory. They have clung to their old customs and Pagan belief, and have only adopted some of the dress and some of the vices of civilization.

[1] There is a fine Indian industrial school at Keshena under the management of the Franciscans. [2] Letter of J. A. Selbach, March 18, 1895.

SULLIVAN'S EXPEDITION.

The Cayugas had three villages a short distance from the eastern shore of their lake until General Sullivan routed them from their homes. The Iroquois had visited some of the settlements with all the horrors of Indian warfare; and as soon as the American army got a respite from the struggle an expedition was fitted out to punish them. General Sullivan, with a large force, approached the Cayuga territory, from the south, in the summer of 1779, burned their homes, devastated their fields, and forced the nation to fly westward to seek a new home. Some fled to Canada, like the Mohawks, others joined their brethren at Buffalo Creek, and they gradually lost their identity and were absorbed by the more numerous and more powerful Senecas.

After routing the Cayugas General Sullivan advanced on the towns of the Senecas. There was a village at Geneva, and one at Canandaigua;[1] there was a very large town at Cuylerville, on the west side of the river; there was another large town on the Genesee opposite Avon; and there were some smaller hamlets scattered through the valley. All these towns were destroyed by the American soldiers, and their inhabitants fled westward to join the Onondagas and Cayugas at Buffalo Creek; and here they dwelt for many years until the advancing tide of immigration forced them to seek new homes at Cold Springs, Pa., at Tonawanda, on the Cattaraugus, or the Allegany reservations.

The Iroquois[2] in New York are still governed by their traditional laws; they still raise up their chiefs; they have their dances and their festivals as of yore; and they

---

[1] This was also the name of the Indian village.
[2] The Tuscaroras came from North Carolina in 1712, and were admitted as the sixth nation of the league. They settled near the Oneidas, and afterwards removed to the reservation near Lewiston.

still cling to Pagan practices that were condemned by the Jesuits two hundred years ago.[1] They are to-day but a picturesque remnant of departed glory, and but a memory of the most powerful confederacy that ever existed among the North American Indians.

[1] Protestantism did not make much impression on them. In 1845 out of a total population of 3,760 but 350 were reported as Christians. Schoolcraft.

CHAPTER XXVII.
THE MISSIONERS.

THE MISSIONARY SPIRIT—RELIGIOUS ORDERS—MISSIONARY LIFE—TRAVEL TO THE MISSION FIELDS—LIFE ON THE INDIAN MISSIONS—MISSIONERS SCIENTIFIC EXPLORERS AND DISCOVERERS—MISSIONERS FIRST HISTORIANS—JESUIT RELATIONS MOST AUTHENTIC SOURCE OF EARLY HISTORY—JESUITS PIONEERS AMONG THE IROQUOIS—MARTYRDOM—MISSIONER'S REWARD—BLOOD OF MARTYRS THE SEED OF CHRISTIANS—VIRTUES OF THE MISSIONER.

CHRIST commissioned the Apostles to preach the Gospel to every creature, and in obedience to this command they visited many strange lands, bringing the light of faith to the nations "sitting in the darkness and shadow of death." In every age the Church has sent forth her zealous and learned sons into foreign uncivilized lands, to proclaim the law of God, and to announce the good tidings of Redemption to men of every age and clime. Whole nations have been converted by one or two individuals, whilst, on the other hand, whole armies of Apostles have been slain before Christianity could obtain a foothold in some lands; yet there were always other soldiers of Christ ever ready to take the place of the fallen heroes, and to shed their blood for a martyr's crown.

St. Paul says: "Faith then cometh by hearing: and hearing by the word of Christ,"[1] and it was the thought suggested by these words that inspired many holy and

[1] Epistle to the Romans. Chap. xv.; 17.

learned men to leave home and friends to bring the faith of Christ to foreign lands. Many of the religious orders were established for the special purpose of supplying laborers for the mission fields of the world. These men believed that it would profit them nothing to gain the whole world if they lost their own soul, and the souls of savages were nearly as dear to them as their own, because, with divine charity, they loved their neighbor as themselves. The centre of learning in the Middle Ages was the monasteries, and from these institutions went forth the missionaries, as the heralds of civilization to barbarous shores.

Christ told the Apostles they would be persecuted even unto death by the world, and St. Paul appeals to his own sufferings as a proof of his sublime apostolate. The religious orders could appeal to the long list of their martyred sons as an evidence that they were doing the work of the Lord. The path of the missionary, in nearly every country, is a path of blood, and the history of the Church in these lands is a martyrology. The missions among the North American Indians supplied their full share of danger, and contained an unusual amount of suffering and privation. "That gloomy wilderness," says Parkman, "those hordes of savages, had nothing to tempt the ambitious, the proud, the grasping or the indolent. Obscure toil, solitude, privation, hardships, and death were the missionary's portion."[1] Far away from home and friends and from all civilized society, the life of the Indian missioner was indeed a life of solitude; and with nothing for food but the parched Indian corn or the tasteless sagamite, with a smoky, comfortless hut for a dwelling, it was a life of hardship and privation. Many

[1] The Jesuits in North America.

of these missioners were men of a delicate and sensitive nature, who had been well educated, and who might have enjoyed the ease and luxury of a comfortable fortune in France; but they preferred to labor for their brethren in the service of their Master. Many people wonder what enabled the noble Christian youth and the tender virgin to joyfully meet the martyr's fate under the Roman persecutors, because they could not understand the power and efficacy of grace. They called it a triumph of mind over matter, but it was a triumph of grace over nature.

The journey to the missions from Quebec consumed twenty or twenty-five days of incessant toil; in paddling the canoes against the current, dragging them over the shallow rapids, or carrying them on their shoulders over the portages. The bed of the missioners during this time was some protecting tree or sheltering rock, or in the inverted canoes to shield them from the rain. Their provisions were scant, because their baggage must be light. They suffered from heat during the day and from mosquitoes at night. They must sit in a rigid and immovable position, because the canoe is narrow and the least awkward motion would upset it. Each missioner had a *donné*, to assist in his labors, who was usually a student, or a young man seeking admission to the order, and this was the only civilized society to be found in the wilderness. They were obliged to live like the Indians, because this was the only manner of life their means and condition would afford. They dwelt in the same kind of dingy, smoky hut, they partook of the same insipid food, and they were sometimes half naked because their clothing had been worn to shreds. They arose at five o'clock and gave two hours to meditation, holy mass and to prayer; then at eight o'clock they opened their doors and began the day's labor among the Indians with instructions for all who would come. Then they went through the town to visit the sick, and they often met with insults and rebuffs; for these people thought they were magicians who wished to put them to death by some subtle science and send their souls captive to the heaven of the French. They gave another instruction in the afternoon to the children, and they managed to give some well-cooked soup or some plaything to their pupils to induce them to come again. They closed their doors at dusk, and spent the evening in reading their breviaries by the faint flicker of light from a pine knot, or the fitful glare of a hemlock log, in preparing a dictionary of the Iroquois language, or in translating their instructions into the Indian tongue for the next-day's lesson.

Often one missioner had charge of several towns, and then his life was a continual journey along the Indian trails to visit the converts, the catechumens, and the sick, so that no one would be deprived of instruction and the sacraments of the Church. This life of hardship and privation might terminate at any time in a martyr's death, accompanied by all the horrors of Indian torture.

Divine love, love of God and love of our neighbor, could alone have led these men from their pleasant homes in France into this life in the wilderness to labor for the salvation of these benighted human beings.

They not only labored for the enlightenment and salvation of the Indians, but they conferred benefits upon the human race by their important contributions to the knowledge of the history and geography of the world. They were the first[1] white men to enter many of the lakes and

[1] They were the first white men to visit Western New York, and the first to traverse many of its pleasant rivers and lakes. Brebeuf and Chaumonot were the first Europeans to visit Lake Erie and the River Niagara. Father LaMoyne was the first to travel along the borders of Lake Onondaga, and to discover the salt wells. Fathers Chaumonot and Dablon were the first to behold Lake Tiehero (Cayuga) and the pleasant valley of the Genesee.

rivers and distant lands of the New World. Whilst waiting at Quebec the call of their Divine Master, inviting them to some new field of labor, they would join some roving or trading band of Indians and accompany them to their far-distant homes. They were well versed in astronomy and mathematics; and they made maps of their journeys and described the locations and characteristics of their discoveries for the benefit of science, or for the guidance of the explorers who would follow in their footsteps. The names of some places, lakes and rivers, still remind us of the faith of the missionary discoverers, although their own individuality was concealed under the name of some saint.

As the news of new discoveries and of the wonders and beauties of the New World and its strange people reached the populous places of Europe, it created intense interest in the affairs of New France. There were very few people well educated in those days, and the missioners, as the most learned, naturally became the historians of the New World. The Jesuits began in 1635 to publish at Paris little pamphlets called "Relations,"[1] which contained a description of the country, of the manners and customs of the Indians, and accounts of their own labors on the mission. The "Relations" afterwards became famous as the source of much valuable information concerning the people and events of the time in which they were written. They are the most valuable of all works on Indian life and customs, because they were written by men who lived among the natives; who understood their language, and who knew their traditions.

[1] The late Dr. Hawley, of Auburn, translated, in a very faithful and creditable manner, so much of the "Relations" as pertained to the missions among the Senecas and the Cayugas. He also translated the accounts of missionary labors among the Mohawks, but this part was not published in book form, and the edition of "Seneca History" was limited to 250 copies.

They knew the Indians, moreover, before the latter had learned the habits of civilized men, and, consequently, before their lives and customs had been changed by association with Europeans. Later historians are obliged to get their information from the writings of the early missioners, or have recourse to second-hand and unreliable authority. Even the Indians of the present, or the past, generation are not such good authority regarding the history of their race as are the writings of the early missioners; because their history is merely oral, and must necessarily become hazy with the lapse of years, and truths that are transmitted by mere oral tradition will easily fade into fantastic myths.

The Fathers[1] recorded the important civil and political events of the times, as well as the religious history of their missions; and these works form the pioneer history of the New World. Father Jogues was the first to describe Lake George, which he named Lake of the Blessed Sacrament, and the route to the Mohawk country. Father Le Moyne discovered the salt wells of Syracuse, Onondaga Lake, the Oswego River, and a great portion of Central New York. Father Mesnard was the first to describe the beauties of the land of the Cayugas, and the charming lakes along whose shores these people dwelt. Father Chaumonot was the first white man to visit the homes of the Seneca nation, and to tell the world of the pleasant valley of the Genesee. Father Hennepin was the first to describe the marvelous beauty and power of the famed Falls of Niagara, that have since become the wonder of the world. The names of these modest missioners should have been associated with some of the lakes or rivers they discovered, or were the first to de-

[1] Jogues, Le Moyne, Carheil, Raffeix, Chaumonot.

scribe, but these men preferred to be dead to the world to live to Christ.

Death for their Divine Master, or martyrdom, was the highest reward to which the humble missioner aspired as a compensation for his sacrifices and labors.

"Greater love than this, no man hath, that a man should lay down his life for his friends."[1] Christ manifested his great love for mankind by dying on the cross to redeem and save men. What greater evidence, therefore, of love for God and man could any man give than to leave all the comforts and pleasures of life to labor among savage hordes, where a violent death would be most certain to terminate his career? Man's chief aim in life is to save his soul, and in what surer way can this be effected than by martyrdom for faith in the service of God? The greatest of all work is to coöperate with God for the salvation of souls.[2] Thus reasoned the missioner, and guided by these principles he left home and kindred, the association of educated and refined society, and the comforts of civilization, to bear the light of Faith to the nations sitting in the darkness of ignorance and the shadow of spiritual death. He penetrated vast forests, where the foot of white man had never before trod, and labored among people whose habits and customs were revolting to refined taste. Their food was insipid; their bed was the bare ground; their clothing was poor; their society was among savages, and they were in constant danger of death; so their only consolation lay in a sense of duty fulfilled for the benefit of men through the love of God.

To men who could not appreciate their motives the sacrifices of the missionaries seemed fanaticism, and their holy exaltation a species of spiritual frenzy.[3] Their devo-

[1] St. John, xiii; 34. [2] St. Gregory. [3] Parkman.

tion to their work, their holy lives, and their constant prayers brought them closer to God; and as they asked every morning for His grace and blessing, and returned Him thanks in their evening prayer, they felt that they were more immediately under the guidance of His care.

Father Jogues, frequently praying in the little chapel of St. Mary, among the Hurons, for a martyr's death could hear the voice of the Saviour, "Son, thy prayer is heard, thou shalt have what thou hast asked, take courage and be strong,"[1] and Brebeuf could see the great cross coming through the air from the Iroquois region; yet it is not improbable that thus the Master revealed their fate. They lived in the presence of death; but as death for their Master's cause would bring them nearer to God, they did not fear, but rather longed for the hour when their life would be glorified with a martyr's crown. Carheil, at Cayuga, was sadly meditating upon the loss of so many of these benighted Pagan souls, when the voice of a friendly Indian awakened him from his reverie to warn him of the determination of the young men to slay him during their drunken revelry. His sadness vanished, and his heart was light with the hope of immediate reward. Though no other prospect awaited him, yet he requested his superiors to permit him to remain in this desolate danger to the end.

Pierron among the Mohawks writes that he had used sweetness and force, threats and prayers, labors and tears, to establish here a little church to enlighten and convert these savages. There remained only a martyr's death to crown his work, which he desired with his whole heart.

When Millet sang some church psalms for the On-

[1] Harris, "History of the early Missions n Western Canada."

ondagas, and they requested him to sing the Christian death song, he consented by singing the missioner's soul song—his desire of death for their salvation.

The missioner must be meek and gentle as his Divine Lord to gain the esteem of the Indians; and he must be kind, for, although savage themselves, they appreciated deeds of kindness. He must be brave as a lion, for they could never respect a coward. He must be patient, for the work must necessarily be slow and tedious. Pierron said he would consider himself amply rewarded if he could save even one soul. The spirit of Christ in an eminent degree was necessary for any one who would lead the missioner's life, and who would do the missioner's work. He must be a man like St. Paul, who could exclaim "I live, but not I, it is Christ who lives in me."

The Indian missioners among the Iroquois were men endowed with virtues that have made them famous in the annals of the world, and their lives are to all men a shining light of heroic self-sacrifice and noble deeds.

APPENDIX.

IROQUOIS TRAILS.

THE Iroquois were indefatigable travelers, whether on the war path or the hunt; and journeys of thousands of miles offered but slight obstacles to their hardy forms. They traveled in their light bark canoes along the streams and the lakes, and they sped rapidly through the dense forests, in quest of scalps or game. They generally moved along in silence, in single file; and the most important trails were broad and well beaten by constant use. They were endowed by nature with the faculty of selecting the best and most direct route between distant points, and the trails stamped with their moccasined feet were approved by skilled engineers as the most feasible highways for travel through the state. They glided over the waters of their rivers and lakes in their light canoes; but they also had trails along the banks of the rivers and streams to vary the monotony of travel, or to waylay an unsuspecting foe. A great central trail passed through the state from east to west, beginning at the Hudson River, near Albany, and terminating on the banks of the Niagara. It ran along the old road north of the capital for a few miles, and then it branched off towards Schenectady, where it met the Mohawk River at an old fording place. It continued up both sides of the river,[1] past the Mohawk villages, to the Black River at Rome.

[1] The trails did not follow closely the bends of the rivers but took a more direct course.

APPENDIX. 271

The trails followed the water route up to the junction of the Black River and the Mohawk River, at the present site of Rome; here the main trail took a westward course into the beautiful land of the Oneidas. Another trail led northward from Rome, along the Black River, to the Oswegatchie and the St. Lawrence. There was a long portage in the water route from Rome to Wood Creek, which opened up communication with the lakes;[1] but the westward travel led through grand forests of lofty trees. The trail led to the homes of the Oneidas, at Oneida Castle; and then it entered the land of the Onondagas and guided the traveler to the capital of the league, south of Manlius. From the capital trails branched out in different directions towards the nations of the league or the land of stranger; for war, the hunt, or state affairs, kept the paths well beaten which centered in the town of the Onondagas. One trail ran northward past Ganentaa, on the shore of Onondaga Lake, thence northeast to the northern end of Lake Oneida, at Brewerton; and then it continued through the forests of the northern part of the state to Famine Bay.

The main trail proceeded westward through Auburn to the land of the Cayugas, when it ran southward to the chief town which was located about midway from either extremity of Lake Cayuga and about one mile back from the eastern shore. The trail then returned along the border of the lake to the outlet at Seneca River, and then it turned westward and followed this stream to Seneca Lake, at Geneva. From Geneva the trail passed on through Canandaigua[2] to the Seneca towns. From the

[1] Early emigrants followed this route, and transported their goods in large flat-bottomed boats.
[2] Canandaigua was the name of the Indian village, which was located near the site of the present pretty town.

Seneca towns there were trails to Lake Ontario, along either shore of Irondequoit Bay, and to the ridge below Rochester, whence a trail led along this elevation to the Niagara River. The principal trail crossed the Genesee near Avon, continued westward through Leroy and Batavia to Tonawanda Creek; and it followed along the banks of this creek to the present Indian reservation where it divided, and one part led to Lewiston, the other through Williamsville to Buffalo. The one entering Buffalo came along Main street to North street, where it again divided, and one branch went west to the Niagara, and the other led to Buffalo Creek, and then northward along the sandy beach to meet the other branch near the Ferry.

The route from the French posts on the St. Lawrence to the Mohawk towns was up the Sorel River to Lake Champlain, through Lake George, whence a trail passed direct to the Hudson River at Luzerne. Thence the trail followed the Secondaga to Northampton, and passed direct to the lower Mohawk town. Another route[1] followed the St. Lawrence to the mouth of the Oswegatchie at Ogdensburg, when it followed the banks of this latter river to Black Lake, and proceeded along the northern shore of the lake to Indian River. The trail continued along the banks of Indian River to the great bend near Evans Mills, when it crossed over to the Black River which it followed southward to Honnedaga when it crossed over to the banks of West Canada Creek, and it continued along this stream to its junction with the Mohawk River at Herkimer.

[1] This was the route traversed by Father Poncet when he returned rom his captivity among the Mohawks. Gen. Clark.

THE LEAGUE OF THE IROQUOIS.

The time of the formation of the league is involved in the mists which obscure all the remote events of Indian history, and it is probable that many moons passed before the work was complete. The league was formed long before the white man came to the land of the Iroquois, and it shows that the Indians were as plentifully endowed with the genius of statesmanship as their more civilized white brethren. The nations included in the league were undoubtedly of common origin,[1] and Indian tradition assigns the St. Lawrence River as the scene of their primitive home. The Indians were continually at war with neighboring nations, and the necessity of protecting themselves from the powerful tribes of the North suggested the union of forces, which resulted in the formation of a most wise and wonderful confederacy.

Indian tradition relates that Hiawatha was the founder of the league, but Hiawatha means the wise man, and this may be merely a personification of the virtue which they believed the author of the union to have possessed. Hiawatha, says Iroquois tradition, was the god Thoronhiawagon, who protected their race from the monsters which inhabited the St. Lawrence in the days of their exodus, and who finally married a woman of the Onondaga tribe, and taught the people the art of agriculture, hunting, and of war. The original group of families had dispersed through the land and had formed distinct nations, and so far had their interests become separated

[1] The Kahquahs, Eries, and Neuters, were probably of the same stock.

that at times they were at war with each other, and the great nations of the North and West might any day invade their lands and destroy their homes. Stray hunters brought word that the great tribes of the North were preparing for the war-path, and the old men hastened to Hiawatha for advice and guidance. He told them to call the wise men of the different nations to a council, and runners were sent out to summon the delegates to meet on the shores of Onondaga Lake. When the warriors and wise men had assembled, Hiawatha glided swiftly over the waters in his wonderful canoe to the council house. The warriors and wise men had discussed plans for the defence of their homes without reaching any conclusion, and all anxiously awaited the wise counsel of Hiawatha. Hiawatha advised union: "For if our warriors unite," he said, "we can conquer. We must have one voice, for many voices make confusion. We must have one fire, one pipe, and one war club."[1] Wise men were selected from each nation, and the supreme chief was chosen from the Onondagas, because these had been schooled in the wisdom of Hiawatha. Then Hiawatha gave them more wise counsels, entered his wonderful canoe, and disappeared in the clouds.

Morgan holds that the formation of the league was the work of time, and many councils were held before the confederacy was firmly established. Fifty[2] sachems were appointed to form the central council, and these possessed supreme authority over the nations of the league. All were equal and possessed joint authority but no territorial jurisdiction. The post, however, of honor was given to

[1] Elias Johnson. "History of the Six Nations."
[2] The Mohawks had nine sachems, the Oneidas nine, the Onondagas fourteen, the Cayugas ten, the Senecas eight; but the Senecas had the principal war chief.

To-do-da-ho,[1] an Onondaga sachem, and he was recognized as the official head of the league. Sachemships were hereditary, but the new sachem must be confirmed by a council of all the sachems of the league before he could exercise any authority.

The sachems of each nation constituted the council of that nation, and they wielded the same authority in their respective nations that the great council exerted over the league. They had no power to force their conclusions, and the effectiveness of the decisions depended upon the wisdom of their views. The Indian mind is averse to manifold laws, and he is not inclined to obey the mandates of others except when these commend themselves to him under the form of pleasure or profit to himself or honor to his race.

The league was held together by the ties of family life, and the different nations were merely inter-related families aspiring to the same end. The same clans ran through the league; and the Mohawk member of the Wolf clan was a brother of the Seneca Wolf, and so near was this relationship that no one was allowed to marry into his own clan. This principal made the league a great family, with identical interests, and established it upon lasting foundations.[2] The office of chief was not created by the founders of the league but naturally arose from the war customs of the people. Any warrior might form a war party by merely inviting others to join him in the war dance; and those who were most successful on these expeditions were gradually honored as leaders, and in time they became chiefs, with an influence and a following as great as that of the sachems.

[1] He was probably prominent in war, and Indian tradition apotheosized him.

[2] A short time ago the St. Regis Indians were received as brothers by the Senecas, after a separation of nearly 200 years. The political existence of the league ended in 1783, with the restoration of peace.

The women might also hold councils to discuss matters of public interest, and their conclusions often suggested arguments to the sachems at the great council of the league.

The structure of the league was admirably conceived, and its operation was free from many of the cumbersome features of the governments of civilized states. It was a popular form of government, which made the Iroquois the most famous and most powerful nation among the Indians of North America; and only the advancing hordes of white men could have broken the power of the league, which was feared from Hudson Bay to the Gulf of Mexico.

www.ingramcontent.com/pod-product-compliance
Lightning Source LLC
Chambersburg PA
CBHW032044230426
43672CB00009B/1463